What Goes Up

What Goes Up

*The Right and Wrongs
to the City*

Michael Sorkin

VERSO
London • New York

To the memory of Lebbeus Woods

First published by Verso 2018
© Michael Sorkin 2018

1 3 5 7 9 10 8 6 4 2

Verso
UK: 6 Meard Street, London W1F 0EG
US: 20 Jay Street, Suite 1010, Brooklyn, NY 11201
versobooks.com

Verso is the imprint of New Left Books

ISBN-13: 978-1-78663-515-0
ISBN-13: 978-1-78663-513-6 (UK EBK)
ISBN-13: 978-1-78663-514-3 (US EBK)

British Library Cataloguing in Publication Data
A catalogue record for this book is available from the British Library

Library of Congress Cataloging-in-Publication Data

Names: Sorkin, Michael, 1948- author.
Title: What goes up : the rights and wrongs of the city I Michael Sorkin.
Description: Brooklyn, NY : Verso, 2018. I Includes bibliographical
references.
Identifiers: LCCN 2017054469 I ISBN 9781786635150 (hardback) Subjects:
LCSH: Architecture—Human factors. I Architecture and society—New
York (State)—New York. 1 City planning—Social aspects—New York
(State)—New York. I New York (N.Y.)—Social conditions-21st century. I
New York (N.Y.)—Buildings, structures, etc. I MAC: SOCIAL SCIENCE
/ Sociology / Urban. I ARCHITECTURE / Urban & Land Use Planning. I
ARCHITECTURE / History / Contemporary (1945-).
Classification: LCC NA2542.4 £655 2018 1 DDC 720.9747—dc23 LC
record available at https://lccn.loc.gov/2017054469

Typeset in Sabon by MJ & N Gavan, Truro, Cornwall
Printed in the UK by CPI Mackays, UK

Contents

Introduction   1

New York, New York, New York

1. Jane's Spectacles   17
2. New York Triptych   21
3. A Dozen Urgent Suggestions for the Village   25
4. NYU's Tipping Point   35
5. Occupying Wall Street   39
6. The Sidewalks of New York   43
7. Learning the Hard Way   46
8. Sandy   49
9. Ada Louise Huxtable   52
10. Ground Zero Sum   55
11. Marshall Berman 1940–2013   62
12. The Fungibility of Air   65
13. Big MoMA's House   73
14. What's behind the Poor Door   79
15. Ups and Downs   88
16. Little Boxes   95
17. Business as Usual   102
18. Big and Bigger   108
19. Another City   113
20. Sow's Ears   121
21. Lost at Sea   124
22. Getting Together   132

23. The Cathedral at Ground Zero   140
24. A New New York, the Same Old Story   148
25. Manhattan Transfer   153
26. Preserving People   168

Elsewhere and Otherwise

27. Need to Know?   175
28. A Reminiscence of Hollin Hills   179
29. Back to the Burbs   185
30. Architecture without Capitalism   194
31. Informal Formality   200
32. The Trials of Rafi Segal   211
33. Krier ♥ Speer   220
34. Rumble in the Urban Jungle   229
35. Working Drawings   233
36. Cells Out!   238
37. Presidents and Libraries   246
38. Critical Measure   255
39. Two Hundred Fifty Things an Architect
     Should Know   277
40. Bull in China's Shop   285
41. Civilian Objects   294
42. Clear Light   301
43. The Architect as Worker   306
44. Travels with Zaha   316
45. Pinkwashing Zion Square   319
46. Burden of Gilt   323
47. Architecture against Trump   332
48. The City after the Autonomobile   336

In Memoriam   341
Acknowledgments   344
Chapter Credits   346
Index   349

Introduction

Credo

The moving finger writes: *Trump*. How bad can it be?

This surely ain't Berlin, 1933. The downtown lifestyle bubble shows no sign of bursting, and the stock market is soaring. We're slack-jawed at the buffoonery, but, having spent more than half a century undergoing saturation by television, the affair is easily assimilated as entertainment. From the Nielsen-rating perspective, the "all Trump, all the time" outcome of the election should please our sponsors.

The Donald's compulsive tweeting and daily hours watching "the shows" are a perfect, if risible, emblem of our culture of contracted attention span and celebrity shorthand. That his fortune has come from a merger of building and TV pretty much situates the public position of architecture nowadays. However, endless kvetching about the banality of *Trumpkultur* misses the mark. It takes a fairly exacting heuristic to distinguish the social or artistic meaning of the fulsomely gilded lavatory on Trump's jet from that of the gold paint slathered on the Prada Museum with Rem Koolhaas's tetchy ironies. All boils down to inflection and taste.

Which is to say, we're talking *personalities*. Trump, for worse, is a master of magnification in an age for which expressive subtlety is a formula for remaining unheard and unseen, a starchitect of the political. The man is *president of the United States*, and he did it via the brilliance of his self-commodification, the intensity—and the purity—of his brand: by becoming pure fetish. Trump is a master dialectician, amping up his assault on the "media"—which he describes, in his finest Stalin-wannabe style, as "the enemy of the people"—even as he remains their most beloved, codependent creature.

They can talk about nothing else. Even as Trump's agents shred the safety net, trash the environment, frog-march undocumented immigrants across the border, and bring on the police state, the back-scratching symbiosis is lock-tight; and Trump wins every round. The instant umbrage taken by the "progressive" media—which, when Trump attacked it, rose in near uniform defense of the integrity and patriotism of our beloved fucking CIA and the vast cohort of coup-plotters, assassins, torturers, and other apparatchiks of the deep state—truly marked a world turned upside down. Even now, the bien-pensant talking heads on MSNBC are *reassured* that, at least, *generals* are in charge at the White House.

In "Why I Write," a little essay from 1946, George Orwell declares that

> every line of serious work that I have written since 1936 has been written directly or indirectly, *against* totalitarianism and *for* democratic socialism, as I understand it. It seems to me nonsense, in a period like our own, to think that one can avoid writing of such subjects. Everyone writes of them in one guise or another. It is simply a question of which side one takes and what approach one follows. And the more one is conscious of one's political bias, the more chance one has of acting politically without sacrificing one's aesthetic and intellectual integrity.

In 1931, at an even more parlous moment, Siegfried Kracauer —in his "On the Writer"—described the duty of the journalist to "attack current conditions in a manner that will change them."

Could these credos be more succinct or germane? To be sure, matters are complicated by the translation—the guise-finding—involved in writing about architecture, a subject that always embodies both an aesthetic vector—with a (relative) autonomy that (*pace* functionalism) can have a very loose fit with building's other purposes—and an eternally complex mode of production and distribution. For me, the problem of an apt critical register is further confused by my parallel design practice, which, I've always hoped, also sometimes strikes a blow against totalitarianism and for democratic socialism, and challenges the reifications of class and power that architecture embeds. This is hard to argue cleanly—my studio works for state agencies in China, for developers (only "enlightened" ones, of course!): people and organizations with enough money for building. But the provision and organization of shelter always asks where to draw the line, with a complexity and contingency that seldom arises in criticism practiced in our liberal democracies, where "free speech" is assimilated as safety valve rather than risk. Our Dear Leader *thrives* on assault, the conduit of column inches and air time and the quantum of clicks.

The idea of a critical *architecture*, full stop, is nearly impossible because of an entrapping web of externalities that generates either a category of production—"paper architecture"—that relies on its own self-externalization, or immersion in a class of building (for disaster relief, refugees, the very poor, or with truly radical forms of sustainability) that demands Ghandian levels of commitment and self-sacrifice. To be sure, there's an emergent class of architects that practices a difference-splitting tithe: the Pritzker Prize is lately enamored of a few who spend most of the week on the high end and periodically jet—business class—to an earthquake or tsunami site to make some marginal, if highly publicized, contribution. The critic must distinguish conscience from cover story.

We, too, via community work, theoretical projects, and visionary propaganda for equity and the environment, search for a happy, useful mean and consider the incremental infusion and progressive extension of conventional artistic, social, and environmental practices (especially in the urbanism we attempt in China, the crucible of city futures) to be critical in creating a context for our larger practice and as vital research for applications *on the ground*. We don't shy from the pursuit of small victories: once departing the realm of theory, negotiation must ensue. The struggle is to find a productive outcome, whether via self-criticism, *détournement,* holding feet to the fire, cajolery, or just through making the case clearly.

Critical *writing,* on the other hand, is constrained only by correctness of argument, succinctness of expression, and access to a public. Nevertheless, it's eternally constrained by the inescapably secondary nature of its own effects: you can't write a building. In this sense, writing, teaching (one-on-one design instruction is surely the most personalized and intimate form of criticism), activism, and advocacy are complementary, even compensatory, for the weak critical valence of most building. As a result, my *formal* practice has itself long been divided in two in an effort to make it critically more precise. On one side sits Michael Sorkin Studio, focused on "commercial" projects, and on the other is our NGO—Terreform—that does voluntary, generally clientless, work as a "friend of the court," seeking to broaden the critical discourse and to raise expectations via a propaganda of the possible. It also conducts research, organizes collaborations, and now publishes books under the UR (Urban Research) imprint.

I'm now at a point where *only* such a complicated, hybrid practice is possible, even though its mixed registers of representation, program, and patronage sometimes feel incompatible, if not contradictory: this is the condition of architecture. As a critic, I'm drawn to both the liminal and the central sites of spatial production but admit to a growing ambivalence about covering—just from a position a little further to the left—what other perfectly solid critics cover. It's the Trump thing again: lambasting the bloated Hollywood blockbuster from *our* position also affirms its importance. And, like those jet-setting architects who pop in on the refugee camp for a few days, the compensatory coverage of the little independent film or the outsider art that appears from time to time is a wan substitute for the rage that's really required.

In putting this collection (my fourth) together (that is, choosing what *not* to include), the local focus of the majority of the pieces written in the last half dozen years was no big surprise. The reasons are hardly obscure. I live and work in New York City and revel in its saturations. The period covered in this book also corresponds with a major lifestyle change for me, a move from a crappy walk-up apartment in a miserably maintained tenement (albeit in the heart of Greenwich Village) to pretty posh digs in Tribeca. Forgive me: two senior members of the professoriat pooling their resources for three decades can, in today's blessed America of cheap mortgages, aspire to the suburbs of the 1 percent.

The move wasn't physically far: I've lived and worked in downtown Manhattan for decades, and my concerns and sensibilities have been steeped, and filtered through, the particulars of this place. Like that legendary moment when new-to-New-York Jane Jacobs "discovered" the Village on emerging from an unfamiliar subway station and found urbanist Kismet, I've spent forty years in an environment that wonderfully condenses an enormous variety of desirable urban qualities, both social and morphological. Its spaces and habits have, over the years, been contested at every scale in struggles with adversaries ranging from the next-door neighbor to the landlord to the municipality to the rapaciousness of development and its overventilated spawn, gentrification. Being here has served to deepen my experience and focus both my architectural and critical production. It has also offered countless lessons in how to live *somewhere* and in what it means to be *at home*.

In the neighborhoods where I live, work, and pass every day, New York's key urban questions ramify with inflected particularity. Ground Zero is just a few blocks from where we live and, as it nears build-out, shows little lapse in its capacity to generate a capacious field of metaphor, far exceeding the particulars of its architecture. Nearby Zuccotti Park, erstwhile home of Occupy, retains a wispy aura of rebuke, standing—albeit mutely—for the freedom of speech and assembly increasingly under stress, not just from our autocrat president but from the regimes of surveillance and privatization that define and drastically compromise the very idea of public space. The demolition of the funky old building on the corner, home to the last surviving bodega for miles, speaks its own volumes.

The breathless pace of change down here beseeches the question of equity. Cities are distribution engines, organizing space, bodies, and power, but we've lost any real compact for collective integration and security; there's really nothing else to write about in New York, from a critical-spatial perspective. It would be hypocritical to denounce the pleasures of artisanal cookery, the liveliness of street life in prospering Brooklyn, the increasing congeniality of our town to bikes, or even the rapidly growing number of buildings around the city designed by architects with authentic artistic aspirations. But too much celebration is an affront when so many are being forced out and the housing question remains so unanswered. While fatted Gotham may be a limp avatar for the toxic squalor of Lagos or Mumbai, the extremities—and proximities—of our own income gaps cry too for justice. The question for each of us is to what degree our own comfort distorts our view and our authority, and what to do about it. Sometimes the answer, buttressed by Orwell and Kracauer and Jacobs, is to write another article.

A key question: How to process and respond to the more and more desperate quality of attempts by our well-meaning municipality to maintain "affordability," even as the means at its disposal—direct construction, rent regulations, occupant subsidies—are continuously reduced in favor of deal making and developer welfare (the lineaments of trickle-down)? How to counter with the neoliberal ethos that shuns both restorative redistribution and a capacious idea of the common good? Virtually every government intervention in the built environment is now obliged to find indirect forms of finance—a "public-private partnership" in which the negotiation must yield a positive outcome for the developer in exchange for some delineable—if often illusory—public benefit: fractional inclusion of housing at below-market rates, adjacent park space, or simply development where the market claims it can't make it on its own.

I'm far from the first to note the displacement of public sector physical planning by a devolution to zoning, to guidelines rather than actions. This legal regime takes many forms. A "monetarist" version manages the supply of buildable air throughout the city. The "preservationist" mode identifies the neighborhood *genius loci* as a matter of physical fabric, ignoring the real ecologies of place that neighborhoods nurture, and helps our local communities more and more become brands, rather than cultures. A neighborhood is a place of mix—a social and spatial condenser—and the task of neighborhood planning and organizing is to manage, finesse, and defend the stability of its variety. But this demands some set of principles that allows both the building of a culture at once distinctive and democratic, and the means of assessing the basis of its completeness. If one were to stipulate, for example, that a harmonious neighborhood should provide everyone with the critical elements of daily life—work, commerce, recreation, education, environmental management—within walking distance of home, the implications would be both immediate and deep.

To begin, the array of uses—and architectures—required by such neighborhoods must be rich. Most crucially, a neighborhood in which the barista, the boiler maker, and the banker are all able to walk to work will be radically integrated in income, lifestyle, and—by inevitable extension—race and ethnicity. While this might seem "impractically" idealistic, no urbanist can operate without convincing ideas about what constitutes a *good city*. To me, it's certainly a city that fights against totalitarianism and for democratic socialism, and the struggle demands both a clear articulation of a politics of general welfare and a generous, tractable, and sustainable vision of its spaces.

In a democratic environment, this flows from the "right to the city," a deeply consequential idea, now even incorporated in the constitutions of Brazil and Ecuador. Articulations of this "right" by Henri Lefebvre, David Harvey, and others throughout this volume should suggest not simply the urgency of reading the city for rights—including the right to imagine a city that fulfills desires firm and historic as well as others as yet unimagined—but of a style of participation grounded in both need and consent.

Although she's lately subjected to bilious critique by representatives of a more managerially inflected urbanism, Jane Jacobs remains a model of the theoretically informed community-based activist as well as of the highly constrained, reactive style of community participation in planning that's indigenous—and indispensable—here.

This Janus—planning as a centralized, bureaucratic discipline versus planning as something that rises from the streets—could be productive dialogically, but power tends to be very unevenly apportioned with the result that authentic and equitable collaboration is rare. If any popular M.O.—even movement—has grown in the past decade, it's the idea of a spontaneous, "DIY" urbanism that cobbles together a multitude of small interventions to tip a town, without awaiting the sanction of the authorities. This "spontaneous" style is the outcome of renewed attention to localism and caps historic practices of community organizing and participatory planning, which grow from—as with Jacobs—a spirit of resistance to the Man's designs. It's also an outcome of the widespread experience of urban abandonment and dysfunction (for which Detroit has surely been the poster child for many years, even if its resuscitation as sparse *sylvania* may be an overly sweet reversion to a fantasy too constrained and marginal).

In my own neighborhood, organizing has been shaped and motivated by the tools at our disposal and by the issues that unifyingly vex us in the here and now. Much of this revolves around "preservation," which, if understood capaciously and not just architecturally, shorthands the larger question of what actually constitutes a good neighborhood and, by extension, of how to find consensus about who and what have the right to remain. Often (perhaps always) such rights can only be realized in conditions of the permanently provisional—in a warm welcome to newcomers, in the kind of activated marginality that sees waves of immigrants alight, transform, and move on from places like the Lower East Side. This mobility is the hothouse of planning's teleology, and, despite the one-dimensional worship of the dynamics of perpetual change, it must also incorporate ideas about end states, climax, and fixity.

Our neighborhood battles are largely over this issue of stability: over a new generation of towers that dramatically alter familiar scales, views, and ensembles; over the defense of neighbors in "unlandmarked" rent-regulated buildings subject to demolition; over the loss of local businesses to gentrification pressures; over the protection and expansion of our limited public space; and over a somewhat vague—and nostalgic—notion of character and "authenticity" in a neighborhood that has undergone repeated transitions over a life of more than two centuries. Who's to say when—and if—we climaxed? Who's to say that the idea has any validity in a city that has always thrived on its own continuous rebuilding? Sometimes destruction is not creative, but merely destructive. Some things, though, have gotta go.

The Trump perplex is not likely to add nuance to this discussion, but it will surely supply bite. The question is, *quo vadis?* Must criticism of building devolve now on an ever-deeper connoisseurship of crisis? Is a focus on "quality" and connoisseurship co-optation, or mistake? Is it possible to write about Frank Gehry when Aleppo or Dadaab loom, and the Antarctic calves bergs the size of Delaware? Increasingly, liberal-minded critics and institutions adopt a rotational strategy: this week an urgent address to the environmental fight-back, next week a righteous practice focused on the poor or the dispossessed, and the following a formal critique of some celebrity excellence or excrescence. Not a completely irrational approach to a twisting waterfront, but surely challenging for production as sporadic—and delimited by venue—as mine.

For the past seventeen years, I've directed the Graduate Program in Urban Design at the City College of New York—the legendary CCNY, erstwhile "Harvard of the working class." (We prefer to think of Harvard as the CCNY of the ruling class.) The college is part of a much larger institution—the City University of New York—which serves more than a *quarter of a million* students. It is underfunded, disorganized, a frequent political football, and occasionally a titanic bureaucratic pain in the ass. But it's great in the way New York is great. We kvell over the peppy messages from the president's office letting us know that more languages are spoken on our campus than any other on the planet. Graduation day is always incredibly moving, with thousands of immigrant parents celebrating the first in the family to receive a college degree. And lately, we've been actively instructed by our humane administration about which rooms—design studios, our offices—can be used to offer sanctuary to our undocumented students when Trump's Gestapo tries to take them away.

That this is still a true portrait of New York City is why I love it, can't leave it, must defend it. Its hospitality to striving and difference is surely under siege—by the real estate industry, by the apes in power, by seemingly ineradicable racism, by NIMBYism, by the winnowing of diversity's meaning to a census of ethnic cuisines. But still, there it is around every corner, the bulwark of our everyday and the motor of a hybridity that sets a benchmark for the world. In the course of a trip from my apartment to my studio, I buy a *Times* from a Bangladeshi guy who keeps me au courant on cricket and whom I advise on college choices for his bright daughter, take a taxi driven by a Sikh, get my iced coffee from a pizzeria run by Herzegovinans, greet the Nigerian at the front desk, and walk into my office, populated by colleagues from China, Japan, Venezuela, Los Angeles, the Philippines, Michigan, Holland (via Thailand), India, Great Britain, and (for the summer), Cuba.

We work very well together here.

Envoy: What the Hell Gives?

I take the elevator to and from my studio on the fifteenth floor and I am almost always the only person not connected—*cathected*—to a device. Same on the subway where I find myself the lone folder and creaser of a newspaper. Dystopian thoughts about mind control or the singularity. The vast neural network that is fast forming a planetary single mind, every intrusive, exhorting cookie looping me in. Or are they just listening to Beyoncé or afraid to break contact with mama? Only disconnect!

Not to overwork Victor Hugo's enervated bromide, but this *could* kill that. Architecture was never really at risk from the printing press, if the ecclesiastical messaging system was surely shaken. But the tide of the virtual, the disembodied, the cyborgian, the whole appliance store of sentimental humanist paranoia, is begging a hell of a lot of questions for space. That inside every squalid hutment in Dharavi glows a tiny screen is revolutionary—and risks forestalling the revolution forever. Mark Zuckerberg is orders of magnitude more dangerous than Trump: Facebook is a surveillance machine with 2 billion souls under scrutiny, a wet dream beyond any of the NSA's and with a lot more to sell.

Is privacy kaput? Democracy—like all forms of governance—is a system of adjudicating the line between public and private. At the moment (and every other), I am tied to the digital umbilicus, writing this piece, looking at apartment listings on Zillow, watching TV. The latter is showing the news, and the local channel has surveillance video from a couple of the day's crimes. The miscreants caught in the unblinking CCTV eye seem unaware of its gaze, as if their schooling in the panoptics of the peeping state hasn't been quite adequate—who are these dopes? As observation ratchets up by degrees, camouflage becomes, if not exactly redundant, certainly casual. The ubiquity of this sensorium—and the whole flamingly obtrusive apparatus of the "smart" city—has the effect of making Trumps of us all: it doesn't matter what you do or say as long as it appears on Instagram! Or is it that we don't—needn't—put so much trust in the algorithm that's meant to recognize our faces or to vet our e-mails for the giveaway word (or phrase) that fingers us for ejection, a casual stick-up, incarceration, assassination, or simply a deluge of ads? Grafted to our bits of technology, have we become too easily persuaded that the hum overhead is the drone from Amazon speeding on its way an organic peach from Whole Foods, rather than the General Atomics Reaper about to unleash a righteous Hellfire through the window of the boudoir?

This is the world in which architecture operates. I've got a good friend—a famous architect—who is designing a US embassy, and it's now impossible to visit his office without signing in and showing ID. One floor is totally off-limits to civilians, requiring extreme vetting, passes, iris scans, the whole nine yards. As I've heard from other colleagues with similar commissions, designers are even required to provide spaces in their architectural drawings that remain blank, to be furtively kitted out by nameless design spooks at the Agency. You've gotta love the national security state for its capacity to spin out metaphors, and that embassy certainly fixes the agenda for criticism with demented flair, defining no-go zones and invisibilities, infusing the project with space politics, and foisting stupefying confusions about the valence of design. It's a special form of stealth, added to the inherent stealthiness of an unconstructed design, unpacked from its paper wrappings by the critic's ability to read, and now, to hack.

It will surely be a bracing era between this collection and the next, and Trump will be the least of it. On the one hand, the consequences of climate change—rising water, mass migration, violent storms, starvation, resource wars—will impact the form and life of cities decisively and unpredictably: already, available technologies and social systems of planetary sustainability are vastly more mature than the political desire to implement them. Other disruptions will be more saturated with intent, if with likewise unpredictable consequences. The impending arrival of autonomous vehicles will radically reconfigure urban morphology, recasting the current character of that most fundamental armature of urbanity: the street. And, the takeoff of virtual reality has the capacity to transform both spatial and social relations and to advance the surrogacy of simulacra to places unimagined. VR the world? I was wired up for the experience for the first time recently and, prompted to walk a digital plank between towers up high in virtual space, *could not do it*. The vertigo was real. And the smell of fear.

Which returns us to criticism and that Orwellian imperative. As ever, the balance between revolver and velvet, mayhem and hope, not only maps the terrain of critical intervention but continues the dialectical task of producing the principles that inform its vision and methods. Trump (and the constellation of fellow fascists rising alarmingly across the globe) will be a highly useful idiot as both agent and foil. Care, however, must be taken with how we attend to the worst of *their* agenda, the border walls and prisons, the labor camps, the slums, the concrete manifestations of inequality so formalized in places like New York. Criticism incapable of celebration and estranged from manifold styles of connoisseurship—of corroborative precision—is empty. The worst outcome may be that the creeps keep us from smelling—and planting—the roses.

New York, New York, New York

1

Jane's Spectacles

Jane Jacobs saw the city through corrective lenses. In her case, these were held in cat's-eye frames. The contrast with the canonical glasses of her conceptual nemesis, Le Corbusier, is clear. His were rationalist spectacles, circular and dour, and emblematically male. Jane's were not simply more cheerful, more feminized, more biological than mathematical in their inspiration; they were more timely in their fashionability. And so it was with her view of the city: her gaze took in both the feral and the cooperative, a way of looking that saw urbanity not in the reduction of its order to the regularity of clockwork but in its vivid spontaneity and expansive, ever-transforming difference.

We all wear cat's-eye glasses now. Too many, though, wear them to be seen rather than to see. One of the most succinctly trivial news items during the debate about the design of Ground Zero was a squib in the *Times* about the eyewear of the architects who were up for the job. All were studied and expensive (and included at least one pair of the Corb/Philip/Pei-wannabe classics), parcel of starchitecture's most elemental displacement: the idea that the style and celebrity of the author are more than certification enough for the architecture to come.

Jane Jacobs's celebrity was more substantial, not the result of whom she knew or how she looked but of what she did and how she thought. Like any great activist, her reputation shaded into notoriety and was voluminous enough to encompass many versions of her persona, from the economic thinker of depth, originality, and elegance, to the woman ready to climb on the table to be heard or to snatch a stenographer's notes to redirect a bureaucracy's remorselessness, to the door-to-door organizer of neighborhood will. Her stomping ground was the White Horse Tavern (just down the block from her legendary Hudson Street pad), not the Four Seasons or Century Club, with their refined rituals of exclusion. Jane preferred a spot where crowds gathered cheek by jowl, got sauced, and poured out onto the sidewalk.

Such sociability was and is a primary transaction of the way of seeing so expansively elaborated by Jane Jacobs. She was acutely sensitive to the membranes and thresholds—both visible and invisible—that structure the gradations from private to public, from the interior to the extroverted life. These shadings—in their richness and specificity—characterize the vitality of the city. Part of Jacobs's greatness as an urbanist is her simultaneously fearless and measured powers of extrapolation. She had a unique ability to move from the particularities of the local interaction of incident and morphology to the larger patterns of urban life, as well as the capacity to see the way in which the economies of life and exchange are embedded in what can only be inadequately described as "lifestyle."

I am continuously impressed by both the scalability and the translatability of Jacobs's fundamental insights about urban form and have long used her specs to see cities more clearly. For many years, I've lived and worked within the ambit of Jacobs's Greenwich Village and, in both its excellences and deficits, the place remains a wonderful laboratory for urban observation. Like Jacobs, I've been accused of myopia, the criticism being that the Village is simply too exceptional, that the rising price of admission is exclusionary, and that there are insuperable issues in translating the virtues of a thickly developed and historical set of ecologies to the tasks of building the new. As the planet adds a million people to the urban population every week, it is both impossible and dangerous simply to expand existing cities, creating the urbanism of megacities, slums, and sprawl without end. Calling Jane's analysis irrelevant to this project is a strange critique, one that purges aspiration and memory from the necessary pursuit of the new.

Here is where Jacobs is especially vital, and it is crucial that her message be received in its authentic context. Jacobs is plagued by misappropriation and reductionism. While the prosody of her urban proposition—the short blocks, the multiple uses, the mix of building types and ages—is timelessly relevant, there is always a risk that formalization (as in the monochrome, mock-urban suburbs that often claim her imprimatur) will rob Jacobs's vision of its social core, of its politics: her message is not reducible to form. In seeing the city both as artifact and as habitat, Jane Jacobs was not simply offering a riposte to the sterile, disciplinary order of modernist planning; she was anticipating a refreshed urbanity, capable of merging the social, environmental, and constructed environments into a single discourse. This is at the core of her innovation and the center of relevance today.

Henri Lefebvre, another great urbanist and rough contemporary of Jacobs, shared many of her principles, if expressing them in a somewhat different theoretical register. His argument for a shared "right to the city" is crucial to their common reading of the urban. Lefebvre understood this right in the simple, instrumental sense, as a defense of the public realm and a critique of the city of compounded discrimination and stratification. But, more importantly, he insisted that this right must include the empowerment of citizens to work toward the city of their own dreams and fantasies, the right to a multiplicity, the right to a city in which contention is permanent and negotiation unending.

For Jacobs, the negotiation was not simply cultural but economic, and this came to be more and more at the center of her work. Jacobs was ahead of the curve both in her command of the intricate, balletic ecology of urban economies and in her insistence on the relationship between the physical city, exchange of every variety, and the defense and expansion of individual liberty. She argued that in economic systems—as in natural ones—diversity founds resilience, and she examined and exalted cities as diversity's most secure habitat. Her arguments for import substitution as a driver of urban development (indeed, as foundational for cities) brought the question home to both the personal and the political. It was not simply economies that were expanding but choices, potentials, and freedoms.

The lenses in those glasses were polyfocals and allowed Jacobs to see the city with unrivaled richness and nuance, and the ballet she saw was complex and rich with the beauties of everyday transaction. But it is a dance in which the choreographic role is ceded to every individual. Rejecting the "ballet mechanique" of modernism as an autocratic dance like the maniacal, dehumanizing North Korean "mass games" (as well as the more elegant but equally prescriptive constraints of *Giselle*), she saw the decisive beauty and democracy in the ineffable yet concrete intercourse of the conventional and the creative. She recognized that the city can only be the crucible of dreams if it offers a stimulating home to every dreamer.

So much to see through those cat's-eye frames!

(2010)

2

New York Triptych

For over twenty-five years I lived in an apartment with a wonderful view of the Empire State Building. It was our icon, *our* skyscraper, and we knew the weather from clouds scudding by, the holidays from the colorful semiotics of its illuminated top—green on Saint Patrick's, lavender for Gay Pride—and, always, that we were in the middle of New York. After a recent move, however, there's a new shaft in our lives: Frank Gehry's seventy-six-story apartment house on Spruce Street, the tallest residential structure in the city and Gehry's first tower. This building too has many intoxications: its sculpted, shimmery stainless steel skin catches the light in moments of startling beauty. Its facades—comprised of the eccentric scales that have long been a favorite of Gehry's—billow, ripple, and crease in a composition that is authentically vertical, not simply the laying up of horizontals. And as a figure on the skyline, it presents itself with supple variety when glimpsed from both near and far. But no urban building is ever simply about, in Le Corbusier's phrase, "the magnificent play of forms under light."

In 1836, A. W. Pugin, the English architect at the wellspring of the Gothic Revival and one of the designers of the Houses of Parliament, self-published a polemical little book called *Contrasts,* an argument for the superiority of the Gothic over the

neoclassicism of the day and an assault on the formal and social
depravity of the industrial city. Perhaps the most famous image
in the book is one showing the contrast between a "Catholic
Town in 1440," with its picturesque city wall and skyline of
graceful church spires and "The Same Town in 1840" in which
the skyline is dominated not by steeples but by factory chimneys
and, in the foreground, modernity's direst expression, a panop-
tic prison. Architectural partisanship aside, Pugin was making
an argument about the legibility of social and cultural values in
the form of the city.

The Empire State was for decades the tallest bar in the graph
of real estate values that is the Manhattan skyline. But it was
more than a monument to quantity. Along with other buildings
of the great Deco efflorescence—most notably its dance partner
the Chrysler Building—it signified both the high-water mark of
a style immensely indigenous to New York but also its collapse
in the great depression, after which buildings were very different. It was the emblem of a capitalism that demanded buildings
in which many different firms of many different sizes were
housed together. And, it was the preeminent symbol of what the
Manhattan economy does so uniquely: turn the sky into land.

Frank Gehry's beautiful tower also reconfigures the image of
the city indelibly. It joins two great neighbors—the Woolworth
Building and the Brooklyn Bridge (themselves part of the endgame of the Gothic Revival set off by Pugin) to form a startling
urban triptych. This ensemble is ode to the technical and expressive possibilities—and the ambivalences—of modernity, a lyrical
coda to a project begun in the nineteenth century. They embody
three great functions of the modern city: mass movement, corporate bureaucracy, and large-scale multiple dwelling. And they
depend on technical innovations—steel frame, long-span sus-
pension, elevator, telecommunication—that have been gestating
for two hundred years.

The Spruce Street tower's meaning cannot escape one other
comparison: its relation to the drama being played out at
Atlantic Yards in Brooklyn. That enormous complex, originally
designed by Gehry for the same client, Bruce Ratner, has been
vexed from the get-go, tarred as too large, too narcissistic, too

burdensome on stressed services, and too uneven in distributing its benefits. As the project headed south under pressure from the bubble-burst of the market, Gehry was laid off the job and his scheme—which, had it been built, would have been the most dramatic re-weighting of the skyline in a century—appeared lost. Ratner has now (although it may simply be a negotiating ploy with the construction unions) announced his intention to build a first housing tower on the site (another record setter for height) out of factory-prefabricated modules. The building appears the anti-Gehry. Uniform and repetitive instead of variegated and singular. Generic rather than bespoke. Austere rather than flamboyant. Ugly rather than beautiful. "Affordable" rather than luxurious.

Which throws the meaning of both buildings back onto hoary modernist tropes. The dream of factory-made housing, which had its sorry endgame in the dreary panel-buildings of the Eastern Bloc, was a product both of a romance of industrial production associated with revolutionary egalitarianism, and of the modern movement's goal of linking architecture with justice and social progress. This rapidly deteriorated into a two-tier system in which a universalist austerity devolved into the segregated, penal architecture of so much of our public housing, built in clear antithesis to our official aspirational domestic pattern: the suburbs. For some time, though, apartment buildings in New York, for poorer *and* for richer, participated in the same deracinated system of signification. The hundreds of white, red, and buff brick apartments at the core of our middle-class stock—from Stuyvesant Town to LeFrak City to the doorman ghetto of the Upper East Side—look not so different from the tens of thousands of units built by the Housing Authority.

Nowadays, though, architectural branding is far more than calling a fancy building the Cornichon or the Grey Poupon. It isn't enough for Ratner's building to be taller than Trump's (boys *will* be boys); it must be more striking, more beautiful, more *artistic*. Not that there's anything wrong with that! The stillborn design of so many apartment towers contoured by inches to the functionalist specs of real estate consultants (something not entirely escaped by the smallish, low-ceilinged apartments of

Spruce Street) has been increasingly overtaken by the corroboration of luxury by a starchitect's signature. Interestingly, there seems to be some anxiety on Ratner and Gehry's part about *apparent* sumptuary excess, and the argument is bruited that Spruce Street's extraordinary expression cost no more than the conventional version. Which means that better design for better people is not an *economic* choice.

New York Times columnist Charles Blow recently offered familiar alarums that New York is being pushed "ever closer to becoming a dim, stilted wasteland of the wealthy from edge to edge." I share his fear. As the media increasingly focuses on architecture as expression, it slights its meaning as effect. Frank Gehry's beautiful building is hardly the tipping point in the class struggle. But, like any other building, its meanings far exceed its form.

(2011)

3

A Dozen Urgent Suggestions for the Village

1. Greenfill One Lane of Every Street

As we all know, this neighborhood is one of the poorest in green space in the city. If our streets are often bowery, our parks and playgrounds, however lovely, are too few, too small, and too far between. Where can we find more public space? I've always thought the answer was straightforward: our streets occupy far and away the largest area in municipal ownership around here, and this territory is not being put to its highest and best use. Does anyone actually think that dedicating a fifteen-foot-wide swath of street for the storage of a dozen private vehicles is the best thing we can do with each and every curb lane? Not me!

Let us switch one lane of every street in the Village from the automotive to the public realm. Here are some benefits we might realize: enlarging the space for pedestrians; adding innumerable trees to reduce temperatures and sequester carbon; providing for bike riding and storage; housing small play and social spaces; nurturing community beds and gardens; capturing

---

This piece was derived from a talk at an event organized by the Eighth Street business improvement district.

stormwater; providing a logical place for managing waste and recycling; making us the greenest neighborhood in town.

2. Recover Sixth Avenue

Not to slight Seventh, but Sixth Avenue is not simply the spine of the business improvement district (BID) but a particularly bleak and wrongly scaled part of the Village. I'm thinking in particular of the stretch from Eighth Street to Fourth Street and not simply of the too-wide street but of the fact that there's a cathedral's worth of space below grade. West Fourth Street is one of the busiest—and grottiest—stations in the subway system and it limply awaits its turn for what passes for renovation by the Metropolitan Transportation Authority. Instead of the paradigm of a slightly cleaner version of a public toilet, this is the site to launch an adventure that simultaneously brings light, air, and greenery deep into the station and that reconfigures the street above.

The possibilities are enormous. The mezzanine level of the station is easily the largest single *room* in the Village. Why aren't we dancing there, bowling there, gardening there? And, the potential effect of capturing additional sidewalk space above is especially evident and compelling. We all know how it feels when, due to an anomaly in our urban geometry, the Sixth Avenue sidewalks dramatically enlarge between Bleecker and Houston. These wide sidewalks—scaled to the proportions of a Paris trottoir—support one of the happiest collusions of outdoor cafés and restaurants in all New York. Not only is there room for rows of tables; there's plenty of sidewalk left for strolling and plenty of buffer from the traffic. Let's establish this condition all the way to Fourteenth Street!

3. Build a Tiny Trolley for Eighth Street

We are currently blessed by miraculously enlightened leadership at the Department of Transportation and with it the recognition that an effective movement system for New York depends on a richly mixed transport culture, with walkers in the alpha mode and public systems in the beta. This means that innovation must be both forward-looking (bus rapid transit, light-rail, airport access, soaring intermodal stations) and back (wide sidewalks, bicycles, and ... trolley cars). Time to restore a few of the routes that once laced the town, and what better place to resume than Eighth Street. I'd imagine a line going from Tompkins Square Park across St. Mark's Place, Eighth Street, Greenwich Avenue, ending in the Meat Market. The scale of these vehicles would be small, like the cable cars of San Francisco or—even better—the trams of Lisbon. How delightful! What a ride! What a convenience! What an *attraction*!

4. Curb the Appetites of NYU

We are, of course, grateful to King Juan Carlos and to the university for the use of these premises and we must recognize with gratitude the intertwining of the fates of the Village and of New York University at virtually every level. We are not simply joined in our struggles to retain our neighborhood as one of the world's defining Bohemias but as a factory for Bohemians. This means finessing the mix of our people and uses to keep a vibrant balance, defending the possibility of a marginal culture against the predations of both gentrification and big education. It means rent control. It means limits on development.

NYU's current proposals to cram buildings into the Washington Square Village and Silver Towers sites are simply too much space for the place. I recognize that there are limits to the idea of disaggregation if NYU is to maintain a walkable sense of its own community, but it must moderate its model of infinite growth ... today the Village, tomorrow Abu Dhabi and Shanghai, next week *die ganze Welt*. Caught between the traditional American campus model and the more distributed European paradigm, NYU wants a campus in the Village too badly. The good news is that the university already recognizes the need to distribute itself in ways that have both positive impacts for the university and its neighborhoods. Putting engineering in Brooklyn or biotech up by the hospitals suggest logical synergies. Cramming dorms too large into the East Village or high-rise hotels on Bleecker Street goes too far.

This suggests that the university expansion focus both on other parts of town and, locally, on already-existing bulk (can it acquire no property on Broadway, fill none of the existing gaps there?) and on what we might call "interesting" sites. Of these, the broader neighborhood offers none more spectacular than the fraught Pier 40, potentially one of the greatest academic locations on the planet. But that's not the only big possibility.

5. St. Vincent's Mews

Another well-known "interesting" site in the neighborhood is the enormous parcel occupied by the corpse of our much-missed St. Vincent's hospital. I don't know where the project stands at the moment but do know that luxury housing cannot remain the default for every tasty parcel downtown. Let's remember that the current disposition of the site is a remnant of a failed negotiation that was meant to produce a new hospital but did not. My suggestion here is a double one that draws on the established character of the site in both scale and use. Already and historically institutional, there is no more logical location in the village for *some* academic use. The cultural and technical infrastructure already has this capacity. The scale is established by both precedent and context. And the location could not be more convenient. As with all planning, though, the key is in the mix. *Some* academic use implies some others as well.

This pivotal site also represents an opportunity that would allow the recovery of another disappearing aspect of the village. One of the key formal principals advanced by Jane Jacobs, our beloved patron saint, was the importance of offering choice to pedestrians. For her, this meant not simply a variety of scales, ages, and uses in neighborhood architecture but the literal opportunity to elect to make a turn every 150 feet or so, to experience the city as a labyrinth of opportunity. The St. Vincent's block is enormously long and the fact of a single owner occupying the majority of it with a single use suggests the opportunity to reduce the scale of the block by creating at least one connection between Eleventh and Twelfth Streets in the middle of it. This should be mapped and irrevocable and purely pedestrian. And should lead to others.

6. Let My People Cross

Many of us remember the long history leading from the working waterfront, to the fall of the Miller Highway, through the Westway battles, and culminating in the wide "boulevard" and immaculately done Hudson River Park of today. Inter alia, these struggles were over how we were to move, and how we were to invest in the systems we chose. Although the utter stupidity of the Westway Interstate was rebuked, and although the principal of trading in highway money for mass transit funding was established, it's one of the weird outcomes of what has been built that it is entirely bereft of public transportation. No tram glides down the highway. No ferry wends its way up- and downriver. Even the bike path is already overstressed, and don't get me started on how long it's often necessary to walk to find a place to cross over to the park.

Actually, I'm already started. The small suggestion is to increase the number of crossings, to add traffic lights, to connect the park far more intimately to the city. The big suggestion is to finally add public transportation to the coastal mix. I want two lanes for a tram line. I want water buses to ply the Hudson. I want a couple of crosstown lines (like that Eighth Street trolley) to make their way to riverside inter-modes where travelers will conveniently find their way from the clanging delights of the new network of trams to tooting ferries that will sail us all around town.

7. Green Every Roof

Here's another slam dunk. Global warming is a fact of life as is the inadequacy our antique combined sewer system. Green roofing can have an enormous impact on both at reasonable cost and mighty benefit. It insulates buildings. It curbs carbon. It provides habitat. It soaks up rainwater. It can provide agriculture, recreation, ornament. And employment. This is a point that obviously extends well beyond the Village: recreating the roof-scape of New York offers a tremendous opportunity to provide training and work for what will only become a more and more vital area of our urban economy and ecology.

Allow me to dilate a little more on who might do this work. We are a nation that is engaged in one of the most egregious campaigns of mass incarceration in history. Colleagues at Columbia and the Open Society Foundation have identified a series of so-called "million dollar blocks" in which so many residents are in jail that a million dollars or more are being spent "on" each. Although the Village is not exactly full of such blocks, the statistic suggests that we need to think creatively about ways in which this investment can be literally brought home. Here's the idea: instead of simply spending the equivalent of a Harvard education to keep prisoners in the slammer, train them in green skills, the skills that will not simply give them economic opportunities but allow them to make constructive contributions to the broader community.

A green roof can be legislated like other aspects of our building laws designed—over many years—to continuously improve the health, safety, and amenity of the environment. Why don't we have them already?

8. Freight Management

If my proposals focus in large measure on movement and circulation, it's because this is a preeminent function of the public city. Cities are juxtaposition engines, instruments for bringing people and things together. The nature of access is not simply a matter of convenience; it's a question of democracy itself. If the city does not continually unfold new possibilities—including the possibility for accidental meetings and encounters with those we would not otherwise meet—it fails.

There are, however, some kinds of encounters that we expect to be more structured and disciplined. One of these is the delivery of goods and services, including the thousands of tons of stuff that comes into the city and is distributed around it every day. Much of the clotting and danger of our streets is the product of an unmanaged system for the movement of materials. Here, there's an important distinction to be made between big stuff and small stuff. Nobody would want to interfere with the postal worker walking their appointed rounds nor with the possibility that a bicycle delivery from Sammy's will lose a minute getting that moo shu pork to the front door. On the other hand, the mile-long truck from McDonald's disgorging its fat-saturated slime, the grinding of the commercial garbage carter at the crack of dawn, and the sundry road-blocking deliveries by gas-belching trucks of all sizes and descriptions around the clock are unnecessary nightmares.

Solving this problem is a question of scheduling and technology. Issues of schedule—restricting deliveries to fixed hours—are simple matters of legal action. The technical innovation must come via a system of depots (Pier 40 is again an obvious choice and might be served directly from the Holland Tunnel or—even better—by barge). At such a depot, large loads might be broken down and placed on special electric (or bicycle) urban delivery vehicles, scaled to the size and character of our streets. This might be a mandate for the city as a whole (and why not insist on local manufacture of the special vehicles as well!), or, as I'm about to suggest, it could come as a more local initiative, perhaps with our BID leading the way by testing this on Eighth Street!

9. Declare the Village a Zero-Emissions Zone

I'm a believer in what might be called the semi-autonomy of neighborhoods and think it's important—one of the ongoing tasks of citizenship—that the limits and possibilities in the relationships of the different scales of collectivity in the city are supplely harmonized. It's one of the imbalances of the way we plan in the city that local efforts, in general, do not have enough force. Our 197-A community plans, for example, are strictly advisory, and we get what we want down here—when we get it—because we have acquired the habits of raised voices and excel at the techniques of organizing ourselves. But too much of this is resistance and we are too often in a reactive, not an imaginative, role.

The idea of a business improvement district—with which I do have some serious issues around questions of equity—is a kind of secession model, the creation of an independent confederacy to redress the perceived failures of the central government. This is a model that might extend, however, to the way we think about our neighborhoods, an expression of our right to be more progressive, more autonomous, more organized, than other neighborhoods that, for *whatever* reason, aren't ready or able to take leaps forward. This does not relieve us of our duties to the general welfare but does assert our rights to work together on behalf of our local interests.

Here's one secessionist proposal: let's clear our air by declaring the Village a zero-emissions zone. This would have two principal focuses: buildings and vehicles. For buildings we might begin by outlawing oil-fired boilers and move to the requirement for rapidly achieving complete carbon neutrality. There are few technical obstacles here, and these changes should not be pitched to owner altruism but to long-term economic benefits both to building operation and to the value of the neighborhood and its quality of life. Vehicles also present no technical problems, although organization would be an issue and might take a little time. The key obstacles would revolve around the noncompliance with local restrictions by vehicles coming from the outside. This might require a dedicated passage or two for nonconforming through traffic and a series of opportunities to switch to bikes and our prowling zero-emissions cabs, trams, rickshaws, and other environmentally advanced means of circulation.

This is not an absurd vision but an inevitable one. Even now we make our tentative steps—providing bike lanes, mandating that every new cab be of a single type (not remotely innovative enough, alas), widening the occasional sidewalk—toward taking back our streets. But this is not a tentative town. Time for us huddled masses to truly breathe free

10. Go Slow

Let me carry on with this secessionist theme just a bit. The future of the urban street lies in its transformation from the model of a high-speed, single-mode traffic conduit to a far more modally mixed, slower-moving, accessible, and safe kind of place. There are a few preconditions for this—including a dramatic reduction in the number of large vehicles—but the most fundamental is that traffic move slowly. Those new zero-emissions vehicles we'll soon have should have their top speed capped at around twelve to fifteen miles per hour (which is, parenthetically, around the average speed for Manhattan traffic). If this should happen, our streets will assume a very different character. Walkers, bikers, wheelchair riders, and other vehicles could cross and move almost at will. In many places, traffic signals would become needless. The distinction between street and sidewalk would start to erode. Our public space would become a whirl of conviviality and convenience.

11. Defend the Book and Other Special Uses

If you walk down Sixth Avenue, you'll find the scene of a bracing example of the relationship of private and public enterprise and of the way in which certain rights reproduce themselves in the city. I refer to the collection of booksellers who line the east side of the street in the two blocks from Eighth Street to Washington Place. Protected by the first amendment but regulated by a set of municipal requirements focused on access to adjacent buildings, these merchants may not have titles to suit every need but they do provide a service that the "normal" market is increasingly unable to provide. As our bookshops are continuously replaced by either chains or online services, something absolutely central to the character of our community is being lost. And, part of the way in which we assert not simply our sense of autonomy but a sense of our own neighborhood particularity is to defend the uses and people that make us special.

So, two suggestions. First, no need for these guys to sell from such crappy and unattractive folding tables. Let's institutionalize bookstalls with something at least as charming as those lockable cases you find along the Seine. Second, let's refine our zoning to, at a minimum, grandfather every existing bookstore as a use forever fixed. And, while we're at it, we probably need to include tattoo parlors and sex shops.

12. Keep the Bars Open Even Later

Otherwise, why bother with the rest of it. Of course, we'll keep our voices down when we spill onto the street and try not to smoke.

(2011)

4

NYU's Tipping Point

Urban universities inscribe themselves in place according to two patterns. One is the campus, the state of exception, the morphological anomaly in the fabric of the urban everyday. Our local classic is Columbia—that ordered enclave—a place where the territoriality is unmistakable: walled, homogeneous, exclusive, deliberate, *architectural*.

The other paradigm is more typically European and distributes facilities in disaggregated fashion within the accommodating texture of the city-as-it-is. The Left Bank of Paris, massively inflected culturally by its dazzling institutional concentration, is the classic example. The genius of that environment, however, is a product—at least in part—of the way in which academic facilities are placed, by their sporadic architectural presence, their fundamentally recessive tectonic relationship to the vibrant and variegated city in which they sit. (Ironically, several of the Left Bank *grandes écoles* are being moved by the French government to a huge, vapidly designed campus in the suburb of Saclay, in what is, inter alia, a real estate deal to simultaneously capture prime property in the city center and urbanize and revalue the periphery.)

New York University has rapidly moved from a nice instance of this pattern of inscription—and its relatively congenial relationship to the fine-grained community which houses it—to what more and more resembles an autonomous campus. I won't comment on the logic of the NYU administration's ambitions to become a global mega-university save to say that the mega-scale of construction this fantasy predicts has an entirely different formal and political relationship to the sandy and despotic wastes of the Abu Dhabi desert than the physically, historically, and discursively rich terrain of the Village.

This push to imbalance the delicate—and in so many ways flourishing—niche NYU occupies in the ecology of the neighborhood devolves, from the perspective of the constructed environment, on three issues: scale, concentration, and quality. And NYU's planners persist in ratcheting up the magnitude of error in each. Buildings get bigger and bigger. Design quality tends to the abysmal, almost never rising above the mediocre. And—like the creation of "facts on the ground" by the settlements on the West Bank—the colonizing insinuation of this construction in thicker and thicker concentrations works to squeeze out the delicately finessed mix of uses and people that lies at the core of great urban neighborhoods.

I don't dispute the NYU administration's assertion that its space is relatively scarce compared to that enjoyed by its "peer" institutions, nor that there are huge benefits—wonderful social and intellectual synergies—arising from the multiplication of face-to-face encounters in an academic community that shares a walkable environment. Of course! But these arguments are falsely, deceptively, deployed. There's a willful myopia in the assertion that more bulk near Washington Square helps either of these concerns as the claims are reverse engineered onto the argument that, no matter the formal conclusion, massive growth must be the predicate. The peer-footage argument neglects, of course, that a great neighborhood is the extension of a campus by other means, that a café can be as valuable as a classroom. One isn't surprised that Princeton, Yale, or Cornell, situated in their nothing-else-to-do contexts, calculate their needed turf on the basis of having to build the infrastructure for all of everyday life themselves.

The argument from propinquity is likewise blinded by a dumb

notion of the complete elasticity of social spaces. Agreeing that the atmosphere is already great, the NYU plan risks creating its own "tragedy of the commons" by overloading an environment that is already at the point of evanescence under the pressures of gentrification and the accelerating annihilation of commercial and residential diversity. As Jane Jacobs would surely remind us, from her perch overlooking this folly, the distortions of a dominating single use and the obliteration of the social, economic, and physical tractability of urban neighborhoods are a formula for doom. And, looking at the fact that *virtually every faculty member to whom the question has been put* has voted to oppose this expansion would seem to suggest, at the very least, that there's high anxiety that a fine university will become a factory, a University of Phoenix, a marketing machine rather than a temple of inquiry.

From a purely planning perspective, NYU is also at a tipping point and risks what has historically made it great *as an urbanism*. Make no mistake, NYU has the truly stunning advantage of occupying easily the best possible site for a university in the United States, the most historic and well-textured bohemia in our greatest city. Drunk with the reflexive idea that universities must occupy campuses, NYU has already arrogated Washington Square—now predominantly surrounded by its own, too-often thuggish, structures—as its quad. And now, it seeks to densify the blocks down to Houston to amplify this. One recognizes the familiar defensiveness posing as righteousness in the faux responsibility of PR arguments from property as propriety: this is *already* our land, therefore any building is at once our unassailable right *and* not a threat beyond its edges. A very familiar line, indeed, and one that has had a particularly vigorous workout at Atlantic Yards (not to mention Columbia) where a similar, "it won't affect you because we're just doing it over here on our site," claim was rolled out by the developers. And the riposte is the same: you are going to compromise and over-tax our infrastructure, distort our demographics, drive prices up, and remake the scale and character of the place forever.

In Brooklyn, the disputed site was a rail yard, a terrible barrier and a blight crying out for some address. Might have made a nice park, a lower density, neighborhood-stitching, development, perhaps even a great university campus! But NYU's administration wants to build on blocks that are almost completely fine, indeed superb in many ways. Absent the imperative of expansion, what is their highest and best use? Approached from the perspective of simply making them better, one might certainly have thought about replacing the hideous Coles gym with something more street-sensitive, porous, elegant, and aptly scaled. The supermarket is unlovely, if harmless and familiar, and some lapidary replacement on that corner might improve things, although, given the superb quality of Silver Towers, the site offers serious architectural challenges. The one-story taxpayers along La Guardia actually work well but might be remade to recuperate the possibility of a great through-block park. But that's it. Beyond these limited interventions, it's all shoehorning and will only make these blocks—and this neighborhood—worse.

Message to President John Sexton: size isn't everything. Those big buildings are a bad idea.

(2012)

5

Occupying Wall Street

The choice of Zuccotti Park for the occupation of Wall Street was a canny one. Compact dimensions assured that the threshold for a critical mass was tractably scaled. The location in the belly of the beast was apposite for a spectacle of equality encamped on the field of insane privilege. The selection of a site across the street from Ground Zero, rapidly being developed as a zone of constricted speech and wanton surveillance, made a crucial point about free assembly. And, the anomaly of the park's strange, if increasingly typical, public-private "partnership" was paradoxically enabling. Zuccotti was legally in a state of exception from the time, place, and manner restrictions usual in municipal parks, which permitted it to be occupied around the clock.

As has been widely observed, the spatial organization of the occupation was itself a model of urbanism, balancing communal and individual desires under a regime of extreme neighborliness. The encampment was zoned with its alimentary, educational, sanitary, consultative, recreational, and media districts, its avenues of passage, its sleeping and resting areas. It confronted issues of citizenship and crime, evolved styles of cooperation and cohabitation that were singular and precise, and devised fresh forms of communication and governance. The nature of its bounding membrane and its relations to a friendly and hostile periphery were subject to both spontaneity and institutionalization.

And the occupation powerfully evoked another form of urbanism: the "informal" settlements that are home to more than a quarter of the world's population and the most extreme manifestation of inequality at urban scale. The encampment at Zuccotti Park reproduced, if in theatrical and ephemeral style, many qualities of these despairing but often intensely organized places, illustrating struggles focused on property and legality, lack of essential services, impossible levels of overcrowding, the need for local economic organization based on scarcity of jobs and resources, tense relations with the authorities, and a gamut of the social and physical architectures of threatening impermanence.

Whatever their broader agendas and affinities—and notwithstanding the critique of the fluid specifics of their political demands—it is clear that the occupations of 2011—and the movements of the Arab Spring, the Indignados, and others that inspired it—were part of a long history, not simply of remonstrances at urban scale, but of events enabled by the special political character of urban space. The idea that a social manifestation might not simply take place in a city but actually *create* one is an originary vector for the mass gathering, and there is a special power that flows from occupying the city as we know it with another city—the city as we'd like it to be. This practice has a history of millennia, revealed in festival days, the ordered response to epidemics, as well as in the evanescent redistributions of power and privilege of political uprisings. All hail the Paris Commune!

Although the idea of utopia is in too many ways discredited, the spirit of Occupy lies precisely in the creation of intentional communities. My own earliest experience of occupation was based on the reinhabitation of buildings and the conversion of their purpose. I spent many weeks during the sixties hunkered down in various academic administration buildings (and, later, squatting abandoned houses) in the name of opposition to then-current styles of warfare and rapacity. The medium was crucial and the power of the action sprang both from the expropriation and invention, from the demonstration both of strength and of alternative styles of cooperation. Strategically temporary communities do tend to be infused with special meanings. Whether in the form of a military bivouac in the field, the Bonus Army or Resurrection City on the National Mall, refugee camps around the world that follow disasters, Burning Man, or Woodstock, these ephemeral assemblies are particularly purposive—demonstrative—and force both inhabitants and observers to think about communities that do not embrace business as usual. Whether consecrated for pleasure, survival, or protest, they share an idea of scale, and one can distinguish these virtual urbanities from smaller communalisms that simply elaborate the familial.

This combination of occupation and proposition also undergirds what has come to be the salient theoretical underpinning of these urban actions, the idea of the "right to the city," articulated by Henri Lefebvre in 1967 but embedded in the work of community organizers, communards, and revolutionaries for more than a century before. Lefebvre understood the concept both as an assertion of a series of conventional rights—of assembly, or access, of movement—but also—and crucially—as the right to imagine the kind of city that might emerge in full consonance with fresh-born desire. The Occupy movement—and all its contemporary predicates—springs from this double valence and asserts, by its present-ness in urban spaces programmed for relaxation rather than insubordination and by the inventive and equitable models of community they practice there, that the possibility of another kind of city—another kind of society—is immanent in their gathering.

The emergence of fresh styles of assembly and communication (public microphones and pizzas delivered on credit cards from supporters on the other side of the globe) reinforces the idea of the occupation as both an act of protest and a cooperative effort of imagination. The dismissal of the movement for the "incoherence" of its demands misses the point and the power of the occupation. Of course, there is an overarching demand for equity, a claim against the crazy, widening income gaps of the developed world, a more general cry for justice. But the main force of the movement springs from its defense of desire, its claims that a good city must emerge that right now exceeds anyone's capacity to completely imagine it. To propose some exacting singularity, some "pragmatic" tinkering at the margins, would be to sap the real power of the movement's message: justice is the certainty, but a social poetics constantly contested and renewed must define the real city and its practices. Provocation is not enough: the *system* must change.

(2012)

6

The Sidewalks of New York

1. The Streets belong to the people!
2. So do the Sidewalks.
3. A minimum of 50 percent of the Street space of New York City shall be taken out of the realm of high-speed and mechanical locomotion and assigned the status of Sidewalk.
4. This minimum shall apply on a Block-by-Block basis.
5. The entirety of a given Street may be transferred to the status of Sidewalk with the consent of 75 percent of the membership of the Block Committee.
6. A Block Committee shall be comprised of all of those of voting age whose primary workplace or residence is accessed from a given Block.
7. All New York City Sidewalks, including these additions, shall revert to ownership by the City of New York, which shall assume primary responsibility for their maintenance. Notwithstanding this obligation, the right to control the disposition of uses on each Block shall be shared by the Block Committee and the City of New York, subject to the overriding general Rights of Passage and Assembly.
8. A Block shall be understood to be the space from corner to corner defined by a single Street, not a square block, and shall encompass the Sidewalks on both sides of the Street.

Each square block shall be understood as including portions of four different Blocks.

9. Block Corners, the junctions of Blocks, shall be assigned to one of the impinging Blocks such that each Block shall control two out of the four Corners it engages.

10. Such assignment shall be random.

11. The consolidation of Blocks for purposes of the administration by the Block Committees of elements of the blocks that exceed that space of a single Block shall be permitted as long as the consolidation is of Blocks that are contiguous.

12. In no case may this consolidation be permitted to exceed four contiguous Blocks.

13. All uses on the Sidewalk shall be public or accessible to the public.

14. Neither the Right of Passage along the Block nor the Right of Assembly within the Block shall be fundamentally infringed or impaired.

15. No Assigned Public Use (APU) shall impede walking or standing rest within the area of the designated minimum Territory of Passage (TOP).

16. The use of Sidewalks, other than for Passage or Assembly, including loitering and standing rest, shall be determined by Block Committees which may assign rights to their use other than for Public Passage or Assembly. Such subsidiary public rights shall be assigned on a rotating basis.

17. In no case may more than 5 percent of the area of any Block be occupied by a use that requires direct payment by the public to access its benefit.

18. Fees from the assignment of public rights shall profit the Block from which they are derived except in the case of High-Income Blocks.

19. A High-Income Block shall be understood to be a Block on which revenue from fees shall exceed by more than 50 percent the median fee collected from all Blocks, citywide.

20. Twenty-five percent of the revenues from High-Income Blocks shall be tithed to the Block Bank.

21. The Block Bank, the directors of which shall be composed of representatives from the Block Committees, shall make

Block Grants for improvements to Blocks that do not qualify as High-Income Blocks.

22. Permitted uses shall include sitting, the playing of games and miscellaneous other recreational activities, gardening and agriculture, the storage of bicycles, the capture of rainwater, the care of children, the management of waste, the planting of trees, public toilets, and the sale of books, journals, newspapers, and snacks.

23. The area of any Block necessary for access to the New York City Transit system, including both street-level and underground operations, shall be designated a *corpus seperatum* and its maintenance shall be the responsibility of the Transit Authority.

24. Uses of Sidewalks shall be classified as either Grandfather or Sunset uses.

25. Grandfather uses are to be permanent. Sunset uses are subject to annual review by Block Committees.

26. Grandfather uses shall include Minimum Passage and Street Trees.

27. Minimum Passage shall be a lateral dimension between ten feet and half the width of the expanded Sidewalk, whichever is greater, and shall be harmonized with the dimensions of contiguous Sidewalks. These dimensions shall be established by the Department of City Planning with the advice and consent of the Block Committees.

28. Street Trees shall be planted such that they shall, within five years of their planting, provide adequate shade over the full area of the Block during the months of summer.

29. The location and species of these trees shall be established by the Department of City Planning with the advice and consent of the Block Committees.

30. Sleeping on sidewalks shall only be permitted by permission of the Block Committees on application no less than one day in advance of bedtime.

(2012)

7

Learning the Hard Way

Almost two weeks after Hurricane Sandy struck New York, my wife and I got our heat and hot water back; electric power had returned a few days earlier. Our apartment in lower Manhattan relies on the Con Edison steam system, not a boiler, and the utility's slow repair process was the source of the lag between the restoration of power and the return of heat. In both cases, though, we had relied on a centralized technology, rather than a distributed one, begging fundamental questions about how we most usefully conceptualize and deploy necessary infrastructure. As we rebuild, we must be alert to the susceptibility of massive systems to massive failure.

Sandy's misery—and risk—was unevenly distributed. Of course, the greatest damage occurred in the lowest lying areas of the city, where homes were flooded and swept away. Up on the sixteenth floor of our apartment building, we were inconvenienced by having to travel uptown to shower and use the Internet, but this was hardly comparable to the real tragedies suffered by so many. And, because we live in a zone of privilege, the police were everywhere as was the upper-middle-class social safety net that offered provisions, mutual aid, and practical advice on finding a hotel room or cappuccino. The situation was very different in the city's public housing projects—where more than 400 buildings were affected and where, two weeks after the storm, over 15,000 housing units remained without heat, water, or power. The droll report in a recent edition of the *New York Times* about the Manhattan couple trying to decide whether to top up the toilet tank with white zinfandel or cabernet after the water ran out will surely strike few of those stuck in the projects as amusing.

It is completely clear to rational observers that the seas are rising, that the frequency and energy of storms is increasing, and that we're desperately unready. In many ways, New York was less prepared for Sandy than New Orleans was for Katrina. Although their system was inadequate and failed spectacularly, the pumps and levees were a long-standing acknowledgment of the real topographic and hydrological facts of a situation known to be parlous. While New York has been able to marshal far greater financial, material, and leadership resources, and has shown instances of remarkable resilience (the badly flooded subways came back amazingly fast), we have done virtually nothing to plan for the recontoured reality of climate change. Indeed, we are only slowly recognizing that it's a problem we've brought upon ourselves by the way we've built: an interesting map of lower Manhattan reveals the area of greatest danger is precisely the territory that was created by fill (beginning in the days of seventeenth-century New Amsterdam), further evidence of the substantially anthropogenic causes of the flood.

The problem can only be addressed by actions that offer both behavioral and physical solutions. Tunnels must be protected, barriers built, wetlands restored and constructed, combined sewers disentangled, attenuating shoals inscribed, pavement made porous, and generators, fuel supplies, and other critical equipment elevated or otherwise secured. The economics are clear: our failure to protect our lowlands will cost, just for Sandy, perhaps $50 billion, and the cost curve for repair has surely crossed that for protection. At NYU Langone Medical Center alone—which was forced to close when its generators failed, its below-ground MRI machines were destroyed, and many of the animals in its vivarium drowned—the damage is estimated at up to a billion dollars. We are now forced to think—as New

Orleans did—about environmental triage, about the necessary dialectic of protection and abandonment, a problem that far exceeds actuarial calculation.

This nexus locates the social dilemmas of environmental transformation. In New York City, we must ask whether working-class shore communities—such as the Rockaways in Queens and Midland Beach on Staten Island—have become our Lower Ninth Wards. How will we balance the claims of culture and community against the severity of the risk and the lifestyle economics of relatively low-density settlement on a fragile shore? It seems certain that we will protect, rather than abandon, the global assets of lower Manhattan. But an examination of the 600 miles of New York's coastline will surely demand serious, even radical, thinking about a broad range of protective tactics, from massive Dutch-style defenses to softer forms of naturalization to strategic withdrawal. These decisions will play out along lines that will not simply be technical but will focus the values that underlie the very idea of community, the meaning of mutuality.

Perhaps the most symbolically fraught damage caused by Sandy was the flooding of the 9/11 Memorial, the preeminent marker of the form of risk that has so dominated our thinking for the past decade. It's often remarked that generals always prepare to fight the last war, and it's time to recognize that we can no longer focus such disproportionate resources on yesterday's risks. Let us hope that the poisonous anti-government and anti-environmental politics of today do not prevent us from using our peace dividend to solve this urgent threat.

(2012)

8

Sandy

One of the unexpected outcomes of the staggering damage inflicted on the city by Hurricane Sandy has been a remarkably sanguine response from our public officials, a frank acknowledgement that the city must urgently fortify itself against rising seas and energetic storms. Surprising, too, is the broad consensus that this was a substantially anthropogenic disaster and that we risk repetition if we don't deal with questions both of defense and of habit: it's little disputed that we can no longer live how and where we have.

Technically, flood protection isn't exactly rocket science. The most difficult issues are distributive: matters of equity, of how we apportion risk and repair. As after Katrina, the discourse includes triage (whether to protect or evacuate those in harm's way), begging fundamental questions of the nature of habitability, and the right to it. But we are also in the midst of a broad epistemological shift—a re-understanding of our relationship to "natural" forces—recognizing that events like Sandy are a symptom of a climate change with a trajectory that could take centuries to reverse and that it's therefore myopic to engage event-based, local protective measures without a vigorous attack on the roots of the problem. Unless we radically reduce the number Buicks on the road, stop the inexorable rise in the combustion of coal, halt the global assault on our forests, and get the temperature down, we're fucked.

Given the failure of the international community to act decisively, we are obliged to make more concerted efforts at home, even if this risks discharging an ethical duty without much impact on the global environment. As building is the source of about 75 percent of greenhouse emissions in New York, architecture must lead, calling for radical changes in how we heat, cool, and light our structures, construct them, move between them, and in what we consume within them. Our progress is real but painfully slow. But, if we don't *also* make these changes, and simply focus on the flood, we wind up as so many Canutes, bashing away with our feeble swords at the relentlessly rising seas.

The current conversation is split between partisans of two approaches to flood mitigation: soft and hard. This division is both sentimentalized and politicized, in ways that are instructive but risk being unproductive. Most orthodox environmentalists take the light-lay on the land philosophical position that more "natural" forms of intervention are preferable to the machismo of massive constructions, of dams and dikes and giant barriers. Surely we do need ubiquitous proliferation of soft systems, even their eventual takeover. Pavements must become porous, bioswales should snake through town, roofs should become green, oyster beds and wetlands should be restored and extended, and flood zones should be abandoned. But, there are obvious limits on the ability of natural systems to offer protection. A standard rule of thumb for the capacity of coastal wetlands to mitigate storm surges is that a mile of wetland is required to attenuate a foot of ocean rise. A wetland extending twenty miles into the Atlantic and filling Long Island Sound is not entirely practical!

New York requires a canny combination of tactics of resistance and of acceptance. On the hard side, we must see the extensive construction of defenses along our coastlines and the growth of more amphibian forms of architecture, including the elevation of buildings and vital installations above flood level. We must also retrofit buildings for survivability via distributed forms of infrastructure—for waste remediation, energy generation, movement, freshwater supplies, and social contact—that will allow far greater resilience and much higher levels of local autonomy both during emergencies and in the normal conduct of civil life. We must disentangle our combined sewer system and protect our subways and tunnels.

And we will surely need some big, Dutch-style, moves. Although I'm still agnostic about the particulars of the massive flood barriers currently being proposed, I await the persuasions of evidence. Will a huge floodwall across the bight from New Jersey to Long Island actually protect the city from surges? What will be the consequences on either side of the thing from the displaced water? And, no barrier can protect us from permanently rising seas. But, we must act decisively and, although it will cost a fortune, questions of expense recede before what will surely be at least $100 billion worth of damage from Sandy, staggering numbers that make the critique of such massive interventions—from the perspective of proportionality—moot.

The need to think radically is clear. The climate scientist Klaus Jacob, observing the large territory on the high ground of Queens occupied by cemeteries, has suggested the logic of switching the dead and the living. It's a reasonable thought.

(2013)

9

Ada Louise Huxtable

Ada Louise Huxtable, the doyenne of American architectural criticism, died early this year at the age of ninety-one. She was the first full-time architectural critic at an American daily paper, setting the pattern and tone for a small legion of successors, and was central to establishing the relevance of architecture in the American mass media. Her writing was succinct and elegant, well attuned to the journalistic short form, and it truly embodied the style of the times, not to mention the *Times*.

In a fine piece of genre-bending media intertextuality, Huxtable is a key period reference in *Mad Men*, the hugely—and deservedly—popular television show about Madison Avenue in the sixties. This was the era in which Huxtable's sensibility found shape, and the acuity of the look and affect of the show cannily embodies the core context, if not the values, of Huxtable's taste and purpose. The sight of those advertising executives working to encompass their corrupt creativity along with the lifestyle and political changes of the era—feminism, civil rights, Vietnam, sex, drugs, rock and roll—as it devolves on the waxing and waning of lapels, the downward progress of side-burns, reefer in the office, and the whole mid-century modern look, somehow put me in mind of Ada Louise precisely for her having been the antithesis of such faddishness.

While Huxtable's work surely cannot be described as counter-cultural and she had little to write about the implications for architecture of the big planetary events that roiled the times, she did have a strong moral center and her eye was good, if narrowly focused. She was conscious that society was moving around her and found her vocation in trying to supply an anchor in the consensus of a great tradition, the stability of *quality*. Her prose was economical, cadenced, and laced with zingers, and she set a high standard of commitment in the tenacity of her affection for high modernist architecture (her tooth tended toward crispy-clean I. M. Pei, the better Bunshaft, the modernist Philip), in her powerful sense of the importance of the historical layering of the city, and her contempt for the vapidities of the culture of mass consumption. She did not suffer fools, and she surely understood much about the position of architecture at the nexus of money and an often-malfeasant governance. She was less concerned with popular forms of participation and betrayed little interest in the indecorous visual extravagances and experiments of a planet in rebellion, and youth culture pretty much passed her by. Nor was she particularly engaged with environmental issues.

Huxtable's last collection—published in 2008—is prefaced with an anecdote about a "distinguished French journalist" who asks, "Just what polemical position do you write from, Madame?" Treating this as a daft question reveals both Huxtable's position and her limitations. Her own formation as an art historian in the last days of old-time *Kunstwissenschaft* left her with predisposition to see the critic's role as an assessor of the *seriousness*—the correctness—of form. That she did not see this as a "polemical position" speaks both to a rapid shift in theory and criticism (much of it part of a great French emanation) that did not attract Huxtable, and to a certain conservatism in her understanding of the function of criticism at that present time.

Huxtable's outlook—its purview descending through her successors at the *Times* until a turn to greater social engagement by the most recent—involved an overidentification of architecture with architects. Looking back over her oeuvre, I was struck by its lack of real dialogue with that other great urban critic of the day—Jane Jacobs. In a sense, they'd complicitly divvied up the territory of critique, with Huxtable the guardian and connoisseur of form and Jacobs that of its effects. To be sure, Huxtable staunchly defended a certain kind of community value, especially the dignity of the traditional public realm and the visual character of the street: her special bane was bad institutional buildings, government pomposity, disorderly impositions on the spaces of collective memory.

It was as voice for what is now inadequately called "preservation" that she was at her strongest. She particularly loved the architecture of the Beaux Arts and was clarion for the protection of New York's important monuments, from Penn Station to Grand Central to the Custom House. Just a month before she died, she published a wonderful critique—as incisive as any she'd written—in defense of New York's great public library, a masterpiece by Carrère and Hastings that is on the verge of being trashed by its nominal custodians to install a limp Norman Foster–designed circulating library in the space now occupied by its remarkable, structural cage of stacks (the books, allegedly used too infrequently to remain in this valuable real estate, are to be decanted to New Jersey). It was Huxtable at her best: impassioned, learned, acute, rising powerfully in defense of an architecture of real value and real values.

(2013)

10

Ground Zero Sum

Many months before America's allegedly tallest building—the 1,776-foot One World Trade Center—was topped out in May, it had already asserted itself on the skyline, especially around my digs, half a dozen blocks away. The height of the building has been the object of some contention because 408 feet of it consists of a toothpick-like spire implanted on its flat top. The body empowered to adjudicate, the Council on Tall Buildings and Urban Habitat, has yet to reach a decision. This matter became controversial because the developer decided some months ago to forego, for reasons of cost, the fiberglass sheath with which the architect, David Childs, intended to protect the spire and visually establish it as fully part of the building. Childs was so indignant that he publicly criticized his client—a palpable nip at the feeding hand from the country's leading corporate architect. The ludicrous and jejune controversy has been joined, waggishly, in the architectural blogosphere by discussions of whether the natural expansion and contraction of the building as it heats and cools somehow queers the calculus. Because of constant thermal flux, might One World Trade Center not actually *be* 1,776 feet high *most of the time*?

Reconstruction at Ground Zero has been a delirium of quantification from the start. The prime number, of course, is the number of victims. But the human tragedy was rapidly over-shadowed by a real estate soap opera: yes, 3,000 people may have died, but *10 million* square feet of rentable space were destroyed! This quick reversion to business as usual was appalling, and I joined those opposed to any rebuilding on the site (including, among others, many families of victims and, improbably, Rudy Giuliani). There were plenty of other places in the city for office space, and none of the arguments I had heard adequately reckoned with the event's aura. Here was an opportunity for the spatial expression of democratic values, a generous place of free assembly rather than a real estate deal.

This opinion has only been reinforced as the first two replacement skyscrapers near completion, joining a third already built just north of the site and another across from it; a fifth is rising, the memorial is complete, and the PATH transit hub is emerging from the ground. In use and affect, the complex is a prime specimen of capitalist realism and its preferred forms of architecture and behavior. To judge these monolithic structures formally, the ratio of invention to bulk is an obvious criterion. Once you accept the minimalist premise, critique treads a narrow line. The three buildings now or nearly done are clad in identically proportioned mirror glazing (I omit the Goldman Sachs tower for the slight variation in its curtain wall). Like the NSA headquarters outside Washington, DC—a humongous, foreboding, mirrored glyph set in a parking lot—these buildings let us know that their business is none of ours. The two towers designed by Childs (Numbers One and Seven WTC) and the third by Fumihiko Maki (who is also just completing a miniature version uptown that looms over Cooper Union as a monument to that school's crisis of squandered opportunities) are almost completely generic, just shaped a bit. Cowed by rising to the symbolic occasion, the architects have produced buildings of neither originality nor weight. Instead, their structures seek, in fleeting reflections of sky and circumstance, to stealthily disappear. But, enormous, they cannot.

Whether or not One WTC prevails in the size stakes, it's certainly the tallest thing on our skyline and reestablishes the rhythm of Downtown and Midtown as twin high points on the

Manhattan mountain range. But it's mediocre: so little return in ideas for so much time and money. There's a tiny amount of styling for the envelope. An opportunity for serious environmental innovation, architecture's most urgent technical issue, is squandered: even in the venerable Empire State Building you can open the window. *Including* the larger site, there's no housing, no community space, no social or health services. The arts building—its scale reduced after the battle to exclude any institution that might, through the exercise of free expression, give offense—is taking forever to get going. And the twenty- to twenty-five-dollar fee floated as the price of admission to the 9/11 Museum is too rich, what with the hedge fund heroes in the surrounding offices stuffing their pockets with pelf as they look ungenerously down.

One WTC is a truncated obelisk, a circumcised Washington Monument at more than three times the size. Like the earlier shaft, its repertoire of details is very small, which is not necessarily a weakness. But, in expanding the shape of ancient obelisks or pyramids to the scale and uses required of skyscrapers, issues—and opportunities—do arise: this is not the solid stone and pure compression of Cleopatra's Needle! Childs's one big move is to shape the tower a bit by chamfering the square plan to produce elongated, vertical, triangular slices at the corners. Because of this geometry, facades must negotiate intersections that are not at right angles and are sloped. This produces a crisis in fenestration: the rectangular glazing panels must become irregular (on at least one edge) to butt with their neighbors.

Corners are one of architecture's most enduring and scintillating issues. Mies van der Rohe's Seagram Building, at 375 Park Avenue, is often cited for the perfection of its corner details, but one of its ugly secrets is the failure to resolve the "inside" corners in the back of the building with anything approaching the elegance of the "outside" corners of the main volume. At One WTC, the meeting of the irregular panes has been managed by covering the noisome joint with a tacky metal fascia. Given that prismatic purism is the one artistic leg left to stand on in such "minimalist" design (raising the question of just how big a minimalist work can actually be), an elegant solution was the least to be expected. In its place, the ornamental "piping" that outlines the corners (and meets at a klutzy three-way joint) simply thickens at the roof line, emitting a whiff of entablature.

Many have noted the remarkable similarity of the patriotic spire to a minaret, with its turreted top and muezzin's balconies. This towering symbol of the other, whose iconography all of this heroic skyscraping was meant to wipe away was weirdly foreshadowed in the weeks before its completion when a large fragment of one of the fatal aircraft was discovered in a narrow interstice between two buildings opposite the site of the now-abandoned Lower Manhattan Islamic Center. Blasé and paranoid, we enjoy our halal hot dogs from the vendors who ring the WTC site and seem undisturbed by the draconian surveillance that will turn the area into one of the most intensely scrutinized patches on the planet, a national vetting lab. Ringed by bollards and protected by "sally ports" (like a crusader castle), its defenders from various policing and public safety outfits claim these features will produce a pedestrian paradise. Big Brother as flaneur.

I was unwilling to visit the memorial for some time after it opened. One reason was that I wouldn't submit to the regime required to gain admission; another was that I feared being disappointed by architecture inadequate to the event. I finally went on an evening when neighborhood residents could dodge the advance-planning hassles. My misgivings were confirmed by the airport-style scrutiny at the threshold, but as I passed through the magnetometers, wound my way past construction fences and the ubiquitous cops, approached the two black canyons, and was drawn in by the sound of rushing water that masked the roar of the highway, I was more and more moved. The voids were signifying. The design was eloquent and the execution concise.

I'd expected the concept of the excavated footprints to be a too-familiar gesture. The voids have a strange ontological status, not actually having been *dug,* but constructed within the much-larger void of the excavated site. Numerous entries in the project competition—ultimately won and built by Michael Arad—were, as his, such intrusions into the earth. But Arad's has so much particularity and solved so many problems—the disposition of the victims' names, the shotgun marriage with a landscape architect, the uncontrolled architectural periphery, the clumsy intrusions of the museum entrance and mechanical stacks, the recalcitrance of the water to flow just so, the transition from day to night, the question of what a downward gaze would grasp—that the work impressed me as powerfully apt. The conclusive move, which makes the project, is the "excavation" of a smaller void in the floor of the big one. Looking over the edge, you see water roiling at the bottom of the great chasm and then spilling into the small square at its center, disappearing from view, impossible to see where, an incredibly moving evocation of loss.

Last summer, I slipped and suffered a fracture, which led to surgery and a long round of physical therapy. I was treated at a place on lower Broadway with windows that command an amazing view of the construction site, looking almost directly down on the oval hole that is to become the PATH station, designed by the renowned Spanish architect and engineer Santiago Calatrava. The vantage point made clear the effort, energy, and complexity of the labor—never mind the eventual nature of the results, which at the time remained energetically unclear. Gazing at this efficient determination, I understand the thrilled reaction of many at seeing the gigantic tower finally completed, the sense of recovery, another step toward the closure of that gaping hole.

I often pass by the station to watch the complex steelwork as it finally rises above the surface (a process that has suffered yet another delay—a year and half—blamed on Hurricane Sandy). But there is an issue with Calatrava's hub, and again it's about numbers. To serve 50,000 passengers a day, the station is being constructed at a cost of more than $3.8 billion, nearly double the initial estimate of $2 billion. Calatrava is purportedly among the richest architects on the planet, and questions about expense have dogged him in, among other places, Valencia, where his City of Arts and Sciences has been attacked by many (especially on the left) for his titanic fees, alleged to be around €100 million, and for the cost of the complex itself, somewhere north of a billion euros (a bargain by WTC standards!). There's a local website, calatravatelaclava.com ("Calatrava bleeds you dry"), dedicated to attacking the huge expenditure for a project that broke Spain can no longer afford.

This criticism fits PATH. A structure larger than Grand Central Station is being built to serve a ridership that's less than 8 percent of what passes through the terminal uptown—and one which does nothing to increase the capacity of the *system*. I can think of three fairly flimsy arguments in defense of this expense. The first is the potlatch theory, the ritual-cultural heft in willed extravagance, especially when it's ginned up on behalf of public space at a time when public budgets are tight. The second is the notion that the flamboyant station—which is all about value in *surplus*—can be paired with the austere monument to demonstrate our refusal to surrender our capacity for joy. The last is that Calatrava's building will redress the demolition of Penn Station, that soaring masterpiece of steel filigree and spatial generosity. Thin reeds.

So what of the building? I'm ready to like it! There has been an assault by a number of critics on Calatrava's style that deprecates his skeletal symmetries and the flamboyant, often biomorphic shapes that his bridges, airports, train stations, and cultural buildings have long embodied. To me, these are manna, and I have long found Calatrava's work beautiful and disciplined. It adheres to structural and aesthetic logics that give it a pedigree beyond exuberance (or extravagance). It is refined, elegant, even exciting. The charge that his work is too "representational" is silly. Architecture is elastic enough to accommodate fine work like Calatrava's bone structures inspired by *bone structures*, not to mention winged forms that find some affinity with *winged forms* (jet plane or bird). There is something a tad wack about the disappointment of observers over the elimination of the feature of the station's original design that had allowed the 150-foot-high steel wings on either side of the roof to open and close mechanically to let in light and air. The structure is now less avian and more closely resembles a stegosaurus, according to David Dunlap of the *New York Times*, an impression I share. I am not unhappy with this result, both because the stegosaurus was always my favorite dinosaur and because the operability of the roof plan was not that cool and, as with Calatrava's "operable" and bird-like addition to the Milwaukee Museum of Art, likely to be down for repairs most of the time.

Calatrava's train station is almost certain to be the only work of ambitious architecture at Ground Zero. I urge you to pass by the site frequently to watch the fast-forward cathedral kinesis of this creature being assembled. The completed building will affront the dour math that has dominated the rest of the site. Crowds heading to and from New Jersey, circulating turbulently through the space, will embody the unregulated mixing thwarted above ground, with its careful zoning for mourning and money. The PATH station will be unique in New York, perhaps marvelous. Whether it's worth 4 billion bucks in light of the larger scales of neglect of our infrastructure and public realm I will, however, leave to you to judge.

(2013)

11

Marshall Berman
1940–2013

In the summer of 1987, I went to Brazil for the first time to give a talk at a big conference in São Paolo. Although the local papers covered the event, their cultural pages were devoted to another—the book tour of Marshall Berman, there to launch the Portuguese translation of his masterpiece, *All That Is Solid Melts into Air: The Experience of Modernity*, first published in 1982. I remember being amazed and full of admiration at all the ink being devoted to a literary event by the mass media. Wherever people were reading newspapers—in cafés, on buses, on the street—there was Marshall's full-page face.

Marshall's great subject, not only in that book but also throughout the nearly fifty years he devoted to writing and to teaching at City College, was the production of modern people and the contexts and conditions that offer them the powers and possibilities for finding and distinguishing their private and public destinies. For Marshall, the primal scene for this self-development was always the city, and no one has been more loving or lucid in his depiction, criticism, and celebration of urbanity. The bright illumination where modernity dwells is not limited to the city's sidewalks or subways, its girders or grids, but can encompass all the tools of consciousness with which cities are both constructed and understood. As an observer, theorist, critic, and lover, Marshall's analytical ambit was indeed *grand*, embracing with equal incisiveness, originality, and nuance the Grand Concourse, Grand Central, the Grand Inquisitor, and Grand Narratives.

After the conference in Brazil, a few of us decided to visit that Mecca of modernity, Brasilia. As we stood at the front desk waiting to deposit our passports in the hotel safe, we noticed that Marshall's name preceded ours on the sign-in list. Sensing the ink was fresh, we turned and spotted him across the lobby and introduced ourselves. He was suffering one of modernity's characteristic inconveniences: the airline had lost his luggage. Fortunately, Marshall was able to overcome the sartorial challenge of being without a change of clothes—if anyone would look apt in a bed sheet toga, it was Marshall, the Socrates of Hamilton Heights, the Manhattan neighborhood where he taught for so long—and he shuffled off to the next leg of his victory lap.

Several months ago, I couldn't find my battered copy of *All That Is Solid Melts into Air* and ordered another. What arrived was a more recent edition, and it had a new preface that evoked, to my delight, the Brazilian trip. Brasilia had been Marshall's first stop, and he described the place as the antithesis of the kind of urban form and culture he held most dear. Marshall famously wrote about his transformative early discovery of the young Marx, conveying not simply the deep relevance of Marxian analysis for the city but its fundamental humanity and connection to an indispensably ethical happiness. He returned often to a phrase of Marx's that was also his own credo and goad: "The free development of each is the condition of the free development of all." In Brasilia, a dogmatic idea of order—the brutalism of concrete, glass, and vast windswept spaces—obliterates the kinds of intimacy and diversity that truly stimulate public engagement in a city. Marshall's trip became a conversation with Brasilia and the architect of many of its buildings, Oscar Niemeyer, in which Marshall argued, as he did so lucidly for so long, for a dialogic, not deterministic, vision of urban form and life, for a city of expansive opportunities and encounters.

Last month, I spent a day in Athens. Walking through the Plaka to a rooftop restaurant with a panoramic view of the Acropolis, I passed along a street lined on one side with alfresco diners and on the other with a public transit line. Beyond the tracks lay the remains of the agora. The section drawn through these three conditions—in both their cooperation and antagonism—was pure Marshall. Here were three visions of public interaction—ideal types of urban pleasure, mobility, and governance—that represented 2,500 years of work on the project of giving shape to urbanity and of producing the habits of citizenship that give it life.

Whenever we visit such places, we'll always have Marshall with us. We'll have his fascination and solidarity with the graffiti denouncing the interventions of the Troika in the contested politics of Greece. We'll feel his delight with the sounds of Hellenic hip-hop played in the street and long for him to trace its genealogical tributaries back to its source in the Bronx, where he was born and which always remained both his spiritual home and a barometer of the conditions of modern urban life. We'll know how the slow ambling of crowds of people from all over the world would have sparked his joy in the collusion of difference that only cities can induce. We'll wonder at how the rumbling train in its cutting might have sparked reflections on the ruinous trench dug through the Tremont neighborhood of his childhood to clear a path for a freeway. And we'll thrill in the way the proximity of the agora—the true locus classicus of so much he held dear—would have quickened his heart, recalled conversations with his ancient contemporaries Plato and Aristotle. In his remarkable writing, his wonderful teaching, and the sweet emanations of his great spirit, Marshall Berman led us all toward this dream of freedom for the city and for ourselves.

(2013)

12

The Fungibility of Air

Real estate is an extractive industry: it mines the air. Space is the essential raw material for building, and virtually every square foot of it in New York City has been exhausted. With the last of the city's green fields long since occupied, "growth" has become synonymous with density: to gain more ground, developers must appropriate more air.

Property, however, has historically only been measured in two dimensions, as a piece of the earth's surface, typically calculated in square feet or meters, acres or hectares, miles or kilometers. This seems straightforward, but the vertical dimensions of ownership confuse things. Consider the issue of access to what lies beneath, such as petroleum (where the possibility of lateral drilling remains contentious) and minerals (likewise). Matters are made more difficult by the presence of a variety of subterranean infrastructures, from sewers to subways. But the presumption has been that anything dug up or extracted within the perimeter of your property is yours.

The question of ownership of the space both below and above the surface was codified in the succinct medieval formulation, *Cuius est solum eius est usque ad coelom et ad infernos*: "Who owns the soil also owns up to heaven and down to hell." The principle remains an effective legal foundation for the determination of property's verticality to this day, but the simplicity of the concept has been undermined by transformations in technology and urban form. There is evidence to suggest that the originating conversation about air rights was prompted by the birth of aviation, first with the balloons passing overhead in late eighteenth-century Paris and later by the arrival of low-flying aircraft. Arguments about the height of the heavens have arisen from issues of trespass, of privacy, and of danger and nuisance.

The signal event in the creation of the modern concept of air rights was the construction, in 1915, of the Equitable Building in lower Manhattan. Rising 538 feet, it was the largest office building in the world when it opened, dwarfing its surroundings. (It is still a sturdy presence on Pine Street.) The Equitable cast an enormous shadow that prompted the city to draft its seminal zoning code of 1916, which imposed a system of setbacks from the curb for tall buildings so that sunlight could better reach the street. This, at a stroke, created a special value for air—for the void—that restricted the absolute capacity of a developer to occupy the space above the plane of ownership. The public right of access to sun and air were held superior to the uninfringed right to build *ad coelum*.

The regulation of building form specified by the 1916 zoning code was, in many ways, an extension of a decades-long struggle for tenement reform. That fight had prompted a series of changes in the city's building regulations, with sanitary systems, fenestration, and fire protection being progressively modified to provide natural light in every room, plumbing in every apartment, as well as at least two means of fire egress. By the end of the nineteenth century, government had asserted a purview over the form, use, and performance of buildings and spaces in the city that required the compliance of private interests and restrained their right to develop their properties without restriction.

The city's zoning regulations were extensively rewritten in 1961, largely to reflect the architectural fashion of the day. The changes introduced a new instrument—something called the "floor area ratio," or FAR—for measuring property rights and balancing them against the public interest, not simply in daylighting but in density. FAR is a widely used multiplier that specifies how much volume can be built on a given site. For example, on a hypothetical lot of 100 square meters with an FAR of two, a building with a total area of 200 square meters would be permitted. However, even with this change, zoning continued to stipulate a formula that sought to guarantee sunshine would reach the street and specified the uses permitted on a given site (indeed, the law saw a huge increase in the numbers of use and bulk categories). The most dramatic transformation to the skyline was the disruption of the celebrated "wedding cake" profile of tall buildings by new towers set behind plazas and rising without setbacks, a controversial break with the convention of uniformly aligned street walls.

The 1961 changes also opened up fresh speculative territory. One area involved air rights, which are formed in the difference between existing building and what zoning permits. FAR functions, in effect, as their gold standard, regulating the amount of air in circulation. It's a form of pure wealth, its exchange value floating free of actual utility. In another area of speculation, the city pursued a series of policies that commodified FAR in transactions of alleged public benefit. It was a crucial moment in the invention of the culture of the "public-private partnership" that has come to dominate planning in New York.

Two concepts underlie the monetization of FAR: bonus and transfer. With a bonus, the city grants the right to add bulk beyond the underlying zoning, and it is typically offered in exchange for some nominal public good. This swap has generally turned out to be a rum deal for the commonweal. Witness the scores of vapid mini-plazas and useless arcades in Manhattan, the work of developers seeking to outdo each other in their pursuit of maximum benefit for marginal improvement. Bonuses have also been given to prompt development in areas thought in need of stimulus. For example, the rehabilitation of Times Square and the west side of Midtown were induced by tactical up-zoning. The latest bonus gambit is so-called "inclusionary" zoning in which additional bulk is offered if the developer includes "affordable" housing as part of the project. As this bonus is strictly elective, it has produced only modest results. Mayor-elect Bill de Blasio has suggested that he will make such inclusion mandatory, which could be a crucial step in rebalancing the city's housing stock, if he can follow through.

A more promiscuous mode of trading in air is the transfer. The concept is that many lots are not built to capacity and that this surplus can be measured, sold, and reallocated to another lot. Historically, the distance over which this surplus value could be transferred has been largely limited to the block on which it originates. However, the Bloomberg administration has been open to far-greater fungibility of these rights, which were central to its increasingly desperate efforts to up-zone the seventy-three-block area around Grand Central Station. That would have effectively created an air bank into which the unbuilt and un-occupiable area above local landmarks (like Saint Bart's, Saint Patrick's, Central Synagogue, or Lever House) could be deposited and presumably sold at the market rate, driven by its inherent scarcity. The mayor withdrew the proposal in November when he realized that its defeat in city council was imminent but it is likely to reemerge in modified form.

Surely the most durable contribution made to planning during the Bloomberg years has been a massive rezoning of the city—over 140 separate actions affecting more than 40 percent of New York's total area. The rezoning, which has included both up- and down-zoning, has, in theory, been guided by the sensible belief that density is managed in relationship to accessibility and that growth should be concentrated around existing subway stops and neighborhood centers. Criticism of the policy has focused on its uneven effects. Down-zoning has occurred in wealthier, whiter neighborhoods (thus supporting property values dispro-portionately for the better-off), whereas up-zoning has mostly occurred in poor neighborhoods of color and on formerly indus-trial sites like the Queens and Brooklyn East River waterfronts. There, the city's promotion of a continuous edge of luxury high-rise construction will have a distorting and deleterious effect on the working-class and manufacturing neighborhoods that lie behind it, not simply threatening gentrification but walling off those neighborhoods from the river's amenity. The problem was foreseen by no less than Jane Jacobs, who wrote a strong cautionary letter to the mayor shortly before she died in 2006, urging him to desist from an "ugly and intractable mistake."

The Furman Center at New York University has done what seems to be the only substantial research on the net potential effects of the rezoning. In several reports it suggests that the final result is a substantial gain in the city's buildable volume, which, of course, was the primary motivation of the policy, part of the administration's effort to reconfigure the city to accept the additional million inhabitants it believes will arrive over the next decades. And by increasing the total volume of real property in the city, the Bloomberg administration has supported the industry with which it has the coziest ties and to which it owes the most fealty. There is also a trend among certain academics and public planning intellectuals—Edward Glaeser being the most prominent—to theorize density as planning's most important principle. The new school of close-packing argues, not without reason, that density induces sociability; that dense cities are more fundamentally sustainable; that by making room for more residents density increases tax revenue, allowing an increase in municipal services; and that the suburban alternative which has been our national model since World War II needs to be revamped.

Let us stipulate that all of this is so. The problem with the close-packers is that they tend to treat the idea of density as an absolute, leaving unexamined not so much what justifies density but what should limit it. At the end of the day, density's driver must be something other than the idea of maximizing economic return for those in a position to benefit from such development. It is true that certain values—historic patterns, landmarks, social ties, and other conditions that fall under the rubric of "context"—also form part of the equation, but I wonder if there are not more fundamental standards that might be invoked for establishing the value of urban air. To begin, the importance of sunlight and clean air in the prevention of asthma, depression, and other health problems remains salient. With this in mind, what might be the effects of tying buildable area absolutely to the availability of open and green space, a more capacious version of the motives behind zoning and housing reform? What if there were a formula by which the area of parkland became the gold standard for the production of bulk? At the moment, there is a multiplier of very roughly four or five in the relationship of habitable floor area and park acreage. New York remains one of the best-served cities in the nation for park space (and Bloomberg deserves kudos for his efforts to expand and enhance this), but no policy exists for linking built density with the corollary necessity for relief, save in the zoning legislation designed to guarantee that sunlight finds the street. By tying new density to new open space and by including a calculus of proximity, a more cogent vision of good city form might arise.

An abominable vision of the system gone wild is "Billionaire's row," a phalanx of Empire State–sized hyper-luxury high-rises going up on Fifty-Seventh Street. Some of these buildings will cast shadows *a mile long* onto Central Park on winter days, a pall created by the very limited environmental controls on the effects of air rights transfer, which mainly take the form of district preservation or "contextual" zoning that specifically limits building heights. The same conundrum is at the heart of legislation just signed by Governor Cuomo for the transfer of air rights from Hudson River Park (technically from the developable pier space within it) across the West Side Highway, where they will be sold to permit the construction of high-rise towers along the waterfront. The revenue would finance the completion and maintenance of the park, much as has been done with the new Brooklyn Bridge Park and with the High Line.

While there is nothing theoretically wrong with collecting public revenues from private uses—this is how the whole system works, after all—there are problems with the limits of the transfer and in the way in which it reinforces social stratification. The daisy chain of public amenity adding value to private holdings is simply too specific and too unregulated by any theory of the value underwriting the trade-off. The legislation dumps a strict regulatory regime for a bonus system and sidelines a progressive definition and enforcement of a set of public goods and rights for a system of exchange in which one public good is swapped for another. Some benefit (a plaza, affordable housing) is implicitly rated greater than some other (access to light and air, fewer demands on infrastructure, et cetera). But exactly whose ranking is this?

The only real baseline for it is profit. Creating FAR is the urban equivalent of printing money, and the Department of City Planning (which wags refer to as the "zoning store") functions as the Federal Reserve, manipulating supply. But these decisions risk being simply haphazard and opportunistic if they are not founded in a broad and firm set of formal principles and ambitions that arise from community desires, vivid imagination, a keen sense of what constitutes a good city, and an abiding struggle for real equity. The formal medium by which these conflicts should be resolved and a comprehensive vision of the public interest in the city advanced is a *plan*. As the urban planning professor and activist Tom Angotti, among others, has noted, our Planning Commission has never actually produced a plan (the last effort, in 1969, was never adopted), engaging instead in a particularly narrow, highly quantitative version of planning, wielding the power to zone as its principle instrument and an increase in both the amount and ease of development as its main motives.

The city's PlaNYC 2030, for all its excellent suggestions, was produced in 2007 with only minor input from the Department of City Planning and has never been vetted or approved according the process set out in the City Charter, giving it shaky legal standing. It was prepared by the Economic Development Corporation (which Angotti describes as "the mayor's proxy in negotiating deals with private developers") and based largely on the work of the management consultants McKinsey & Company. It is, thus, not the city's plan but Bloomberg's, and he's about to leave. Which brings us back to Bill de Blasio. Nobody seems to know whom de Blasio has consulted about planning nor, in any detail, his position on the future of the process. In the past he has supported controversial projects, including Atlantic Yards and the Williamsburg/Greenpoint redevelopment. But those who voted for him were surely moved by his commitment to using his powers of office to dramatically narrow our obscene income gap, and to reinforce the operation of governance as a means toward social justice instead of the trickle-down ethos of the Bloomberg era, so decisively rejected by voters. De Blasio has the opportunity to institutionalize the best elements of PlaNYC 2030 and to bring it into the community-empowering framework embodied in the 1989 charter revision. Planning must replace zoning, and community voices must speak louder than those of autocrats and plutocrats.

The celebrated motto of the Hanseatic League was *Stadtluft macht frei*—city air makes you free. It's time to free our air.

(2013)

13

Big MoMA's House

Schadenfreude ran deep at the Society for Ethical Culture in Manhattan last month when Glenn Lowry, the director of the Museum of Modern Art, and Elizabeth Diller, of Diller Scofidio + Renfro (DS+R), defended their recently announced plans for the museum's expansion. These plans have sparked controversy because they include razing the neighboring, now empty, Folk Art Museum building, designed by Tod Williams and Billie Tsien and purchased by MoMA in 2011. Vitriol from the local critical and architectural community has been raucous and ad hominem. The crowd at Ethical Culture was out for blood, wanted DS+R to be taken down a peg, to see them *shamed*. Why? To be sure, the quirky little building—it opened in 2001 just after 9/11—is worthy of defense. It is a beautiful and unusual work with the remnant scale of a row house street now being supersized, and built with the kind of artful detail so absent from the bland glass behemoths of the day. But more generally, that 650 people turned out on short notice to stand up for the structure speaks to the sense of disillusion about practices of architecture and development that flourished during the real estate–driven Bloomberg regime. And, being presented with a fait accompli—"We've made our decision," announced Lowry—only aggravated the crowd's sense of frustration with MoMA and DS+R.

Many of us feel especially proprietary about MoMA because it is a quintessential New York institution, and we closely identify with its joys and its betrayals. My own special memories are of college breaks during the sixties, trying to pick up Bennington girls in black turtlenecks and tights among the Matisses, and generations of visitors from the city and the world have been schooled in the cultures of modernity by its galleries, its café, its bookshop, its screening rooms, its garden. The sense—especially since the misbegotten shopping mall–style expansions of César Pelli and Yoshio Taniguchi in 1984 and 2004, respectively—is that the museum had sold out to a homogenizing commercialism, a feeling inflamed by this latest enlargement of its "campus," a weird and preening misnomer for a *row* of buildings.

The Folk Art Museum is perceived as a barricade, a point of resistance, not simply to a rampaging behemoth that has progressively made us feel less special as a public as we negotiate its airport-concourse crowds and Broadway prices, but to what is happening to the city more broadly. It's worth recalling that the three floors of the museum's primary expansion are to be housed in the base of a ridiculously tall mid-block tower for the hyper-rich. Clearly, the little building is seen as a last hedge against not only the foregone outrage directly next door, but also its acromegalic kith rising throughout the neighborhood, homes to absentee oligarchs swooning over their Damien Hirsts and Jeff Koons and other asset art. There's plenty of disquiet in the culture about the role the museum plays in all of this, as validator and coconspirator, and it's all spilling out.

In the mix, too, are feelings about the brutalization about to be visited on that dear old friend, the New York Public Library, which seeks to transform itself by eliminating from its central library on Forty-Second Street a crucial element of its architecture and function—its marvelous, structurally integral, book stacks. Of course, without the stacks, the books too will have to go, to make way for a more "democratic" concept of what it means to use a library. Although the Folk Art Museum is practically new, its demise is clearly associated with the specious imperatives of a faux-populist disrespect for revered traditions (the printed book, the quietude of scholarship, the rhythm of the variegated street wall, the art of craft) and with that more general anxiety that all that's solid is melting into air—or glass.

The problem on Fifty-Third Street is not just encroachment but a lack of respect for insubordination and difference, qualities that modern art has historically affirmed but which at MoMA have been weakened by its institutionalization. That MoMA has forsaken this mission and seems complicit in a greedy degenerate urban culture only stokes the rage. MoMA and its architects do try to argue for a restoration of some idea of edginess by claiming that a new generation of curators is aboard and ready to experiment. Indeed, the case for demolition is couched in terms of facilitation rather than constraint, but many perceive that the removal of the irritant—the sand grain that might have produced a pearl—in favor of the noncommittal—the installation of a retractable glass wall, an "art bay" and "grey space"—is an assault on the specificity of art itself. These new spaces represent avant-gardism at its most deracinated, and the idea of filling the ghosted outline of the razed and, in Liz Diller's word, "obdurate" little building with these rigorously vague spaces seems a gesture of melancholy resignation.

As several people pointed out at Ethical Culture, DS+R have done a meticulous, exacting job of proving a false premise. Once their client established that efficient circulation was the sine qua non of the expansion, the Folk Art Museum could only be perceived as an impediment rather than an asset. It isn't that the building couldn't have been saved but that there was, finally, no will to save it, no love. That would have required some imaginative delight in the stimulations of archaeology and exception, an interruption in the smooth horizontality of MoMA's vision of flow. DS+R are canny and skilled designers, and many of the intermediate renderings they presented showed fine strategies for incorporating the Folk Art building into the larger ensemble, filled with hints of a suggestive and productive merger. It was sad to see them forging on with attempts to thoroughly assimilate the found object into a set of routines that were simply anathema to it, finally obliterating it as if, having inexorably designed their way into a box, they genuinely had no way out.

Although DS+R and Williams and Tsien are generational contemporaries, steeped in modern art and experienced designers of spaces for it, they represent conflicting streams in architectural modernism. DS+R was an apt choice for MoMA because they are direct legatees of the Bauhaus tradition, with its aura of functionalist architecture, mass craft, and performance. Williams and Tsien, on the other hand, are more clearly linked to a branch that includes Frank Lloyd Wright, Louis Kahn, Carlo Scarpa, and, perhaps especially, Paul Rudolph—known for his brilliantly obdurate interiors—and other exponents of a thicker sense of materiality and of a specific style of complex orthogonality. Although their work is not demonstratively eccentric, their predilection for density and traditional construction contrasts with DS+R's penchant for transparency and ornamental technology.

At the evening session, Lowry, in response to a question about how he could trash a building when he'd never do the same to a painting, distinguished the character of architecture on the basis of its functionality, taking the issue of the Folk Art Museum's future out of the realm of "preservation" and placing it in the more tenuous category of "adaptive reuse." Could it be made into a good gallery, hallway, café, something *other* than it was designed for? Which means, of course, that the more precise the original design intentions, the more likely the demolition.

The question, clearly and honestly articulated by Liz Diller, thus devolved on how much of the building could be modified or removed before some essential singularity was snuffed. Her account reminded me of "The Birthmark," the story by Nathaniel Hawthorne. Gazing on his beloved, a scientist becomes obsessed by a birthmark he feels is her only flaw and wonders if it can be removed. She responds, "The mark has so often been called a charm that I was simple enough to imagine it might be so" but submits to her husband's desire. You know the story: he concocts many formulas and finally discovers one that excises the mark but, in so doing, kills her.

This death by transfiguration suggests another irony. Williams and Tsien are the designers of the new building for the Barnes Collection in Philadelphia, warmly greeted by virtually every critic who has trashed DS+R over the MoMA job. Although the original Barnes building was not torn down after the collection moved, there are legion who still fervently believe that the context it provided for the collection was continuous with the collection itself, that the symbiosis of art and domestic space was the genius of the place. By any ethical measure, this does not suggest that MoMA's demolition is some kind of karmic payback, but the parallel should prompt Lowry to think further about MoMA's own context, a neighborhood that it is helping to eviscerate by its refusal to value its neighbor's artistry.

Investigating the seam between art and architecture has long been the stuff of DS+R's practice. Their breakthrough work was the great "blur" on Lake Geneva—a "building" formed from mist, not simply a fantastic installation but one which strongly identified architecture with the immaterial and the performative. Their professional quest, in many ways, has been to retain that project's qualities of ineffability in more orthodox and concrete circumstances. The High Line (designed with James Corner) has been terrific because the project—an adaptive reuse long gestating in the minds of many—enjoyed such a singular and congenial armature, focusing such widespread desire, and because their additions to the old viaduct were a well-done combination of lapidary minimalism and fecund and ever-transforming plantings. Likewise, their renovations to Lincoln Center were inscribed on a strong but deficient template, becoming part of an enriched palimpsest that they cured of much of its inefficiency, imperial stodginess, and inconsistent detail.

DS+R also have a long history of exploring the political in their architecture and critique. In particular, they have worked in exhibitions, installations, texts, and buildings to raise questions about surveillance and privacy, mass culture and tourism, the body and its prosthetic extension, and the distorting seductions of vision. In MoMA's claims for the importance of its expansion, politics is invoked as a key motive but in a deeply diffuse and elusive way. The obsession with "access" merges too easily with the project's overriding emphasis on circulation. Art will be brought nearer to "the street" and people will be able to see it from the sidewalk. The cloistered garden will be periodically

77

opened to the public. All of this will be facilitated by flip-up glass that will vamp the fantasy of the "museum without walls."

Alas, this is a wan substitute for the genuinely political, which depends not on the generosity of private interests but on the creation and reinforcement of an authentically public realm and on real public participation in decisions that affect it. This dual dilemma was surely on the minds of those at Ethical Culture, and the disappointment at being invited to participate only after the fact was galling. Likewise, the question of preservation, and the fraught discourse of precisely what was to be preserved, was too easily dismissed—by belittling it, for example, as "facadism." Indeed, the argument for saving the Folk Art building is, for many, that it is a work of art, full stop. It's a good enough argument, but so is the idea that certain buildings—via their present-ness, familiarity, or eccentricity—are crucial parts of the city's fundamental physiognomy, a quality difficult to codify through the normal routines of artistic or historical judgment.

But these values are central to the city's sense of memory, respect—even compassion—and they must be fought out in a court without laws. Whatever the specific architectural merits of the Folk Art Museum, it is clear that its function on Fifty-Third Street is, in part, as a last bulwark of a Midtown in which mid-blocks were reserves of row houses, elaborately expressed and in happy contrast with the larger towers on the avenues. By demolishing the Folk Art Museum and snuffing its exceptionality, MoMA abets a money-mad engine in which nobody bats an eye at an eighty-story tower in the middle of the block, but no way can be found to save the lovely little treasure next door.

(2014)

14

What's behind
the Poor Door

Three and a half years ago, after over a quarter of a century in a rent-stabilized pad in the Village, we moved to a condo downtown. Conscientious sixties types that we are, there was some anxiety about landing in the climes of privilege (honey, property is *theft*) but we got over it fast. This was cemented shortly after our arrival, when we were called upon to weigh in on deliberations of the board about a pressing matter. When our building—formerly offices—was originally converted, it had three separate entrances. One was for commercial space on the lower floors, another for rental apartments in the middle, and a last for the condos at the top. The rentals had been fairly quickly converted to condos and the question we had to decide was whether the two lobbies should be combined into one, with its potential savings on staff and electricity and the possible production of new commercial space.

The downsides were that the wait for elevators would be fractionally longer and that the mail—which hitherto had been collected behind the front desk and delivered by hand—was to be placed in standard mailboxes. Of course, there were other non-spoken objections. The formerly rental condos were a bit smaller than the original batch and were, of course, *lower down*. A strong whiff of class and privilege was in the air, and our neighbors voiced concern about property values, if only under the guise of "reduced services" and "inconvenience." For our part, we were disturbed that after finally reaching real estate nirvana (decades in a ratty tenement in which even the rusty mailboxes were generally broken) our sumptuary delights (being actually *handed* the junk mail and *New York Review of Books*, a garbage room on *every floor*, riding an *elevator*!) were about to be snatched away. We voted "no" along with almost everyone else.

Cities are distribution engines and one of the qualities they assign is the place of class in space. While the distinction between the two entries to our building is exceedingly fine, even ridiculous, one of the by-products of the city's inclusionary zoning law is that a need to make this assignment has been bred in. The law—originated (in New York) under Bloomberg and now strongly endorsed by de Blasio—is an effort to produce affordable housing by offering developers subsidies in the form of additional bulk, a substantial tax break, and cheap financing, in exchange for the provision of this housing either within the project ("on-site") or elsewhere in the city ("off-site"). New York is only one of a number of cities—including Chicago, San Francisco, Boston, Denver, and San Diego—to use this strategy, although we currently deploy it to a far lesser degree than many places, offering the deal on a voluntary basis and only in "designated areas," including parts of the Upper West Side and the Williamsburg/Greenpoint waterfront. Projects making use of these incentives have tended to be large, and the affordable apartments have been mixed in with market units, in separate portions of buildings, even in separate buildings. Of course, separate buildings require separate doors and this has given rise to the "poor door."

There was a loud outcry this fall over a proposal by Extell for a tower at 40 Riverside Boulevard (currently under construction), a sorry-looking lump—with fabulous views—at the end of the long line of sorry looking lumps along Hudson built by Donald Trump below Seventy-Second Street. Like several buildings on the East River waterfront in Brooklyn—including the Toll Brothers Northside Piers—the building is divided into distinct affordable and market sections and each is to have its own entrance. The uproar was considerable, as the symbolism of the double doors was galling to what one might think of as the predominant sensibility of the good old UWS, and plenty of politicians, including Christine Quinn, piled on. Still, the question must be approached with a grain of salt, as this clarity of division has long been the medium of both official policy and the general expectation of culture, and nobody seems to offer a clear theory of either the value or the measure of such structured propinquity.

My own first years as a permanent resident in the city coincided with the build-out of the West Side Urban Renewal Area, first envisioned in 1955. This was the product, in part, of an infusion of federal funds and of an altogether different idea about the way in which difference was to be sorted. There was massive demolition of "substandard" housing and much new construction aimed primarily at middle-class residents (to counter the whispered fears of "white flight"). But there was some new public housing in the mix as well as the retention of large areas of existing New York City Housing Authority (NYCHA) projects, built not so long before as part of the Moses-era default of sweeping clearance and large complexes for the working poor. Setting aside familiar arguments about urban renewal, the results produced a mixture that retains a certain psychic influence over our paradigms of mix. Within a relatively small compass there was the wealth along the park, large complexes for both middle- and lower-income citizens, including scattered sites for buildings devoted to each. And in those days the number of units in the neighborhood under rent regulation remained high, further abetting diversity.

Some form of differential rent regulation is surely the most effective medium for assuring both affordability and mix in housing, although we do not have a successful formulation for harmonizing rent controls with appropriate incentives that would prompt construction by the private sector to accommodate these tenants and assure that they will not, in effect, be segregated. This has been the experience with the Section 8 vouchering program, often offered inadequately as redress for the demolition of existing public housing but tending to

reinforce existing patterns of segregation. We have no coherent national consensus about housing *as a right*, and the result
is that few politicians are willing to describe it as—at best—
anything more than a general good (like health, wealth, education, or sound nutrition). And reactionary Fox frothers continue
to pound anything that smacks of "entitlement" or redistribution (except upward) and to favor private sector solutions,
which nominal liberals have also taken up in their idealization
of "public-private partnerships" (read: corporate welfare).

If we concede that the market is not a system that has equality
as its first priority, then it's clear that we must interfere with it
in some way to produce equitable results. The idea of a distributive ethics in the city requires a distributive planning process
that embraces not simply use—its traditional interest—but
social access. The crunch comes when questions of the allocation of social goods are entertained in the realm of space. For
example, there has been an ongoing evolution in ideas about
the provision and location of "social" housing that has yielded
very different results at different times and in different places.
In Vienna (a particularly instructive example), fully 60 percent
of residents currently live in municipally built housing, which
is directed mainly toward the middle class. During its socialist
halcyon in the twenties and early thirties, the city built gorgeous housing for nearly a quarter of million members of the
working class: its legendary "Red Ring." In New York—from
the nineteenth century to the present day—we have been caught
in a debate that has as its shifting focus remediation in place,
the construction of large and concentrated new developments,
the scattering of new affordable housing, and the distribution
of subsidies via vouchers or rent regulations to allow existing
systems of housing production to be more welcoming and useful
to those with means that do not approach the demands of the
market rate.

But New Yorkers do seem to have far more tolerance for well-
motivated forms of "inequality" than might be expected. On the
one side, our huge income gap does not appear to be stirring
much insurrectionary rage. On the other, the better-off seem cool
with more quotidian forms of tolerance. I do not know of any

study that tracks the mental life of those who live in New York City buildings in which rent regulation induces wide disparities in charges paid for identical apartments (we occasionally got the rent bill in our tenement for a next-door neighbor who paid a quarter of what we did without suffering any ill effect). Nor do Americans more generally seem to be unable to deal with their banked rage at the other passengers in row 38 on United Airlines, each of whom is traveling at insanely varying fares. It does seem clear that such circumstances do not, in general, exceed our psychic capacities, and this suggests that we are able to abide as "normal" a certain miniaturization of distributive redress as a cure for larger inequalities as well as to tolerate the inequalities themselves. Indeed, in a city in which the richest census tract in America and the poorest are barely a mile apart, the lack of revolutionary discontent at this spectacle of inequality is both remarkable and symptomatic.

The bottom line in this discussion, seldom raised overtly, is that these are measures for *integration*—a word largely retired from our ethical and political vocabulary—and no policy can succeed until this value returns to the open. It's certainly striking that the discourse of mixing—of classes, ethnicities, races—always tends to be displaced, seldom honored explicitly as an objective for policy, reduced to more generic and less nuanced issues of "equity" or "fairness." But such matters must be central and up-front in any debate about our future as the growth of our income gap only accelerates. The statistics grimly accumulate. A paper from the International Monetary Fund—cited by Charles Blow—reported that the share of market income captured by the richest 10 percent grew from 30 percent in 1980 to 48 percent in 2012, and that the take of the wealthiest 0.1 percent quadrupled from 2.6 percent to 10.4 while poverty rates have failed to budge for years.

In New York, this disparity is exacerbated by a crisis in housing costs. A recently issued report by state comptroller Thomas DiNapoli found that half the renters in the state and more than a third of homeowners devote more than 30 percent of their income to housing, the federal threshold of affordability. As DiNapoli put it to the *Times*, "You've got households with less money and costs going up." Like the income gap, the percentage of those who cannot afford housing is rising dramatically, from 40.5 in 2000 to 50.6 in 2012 for renters and from 26.4 to 33.9 for owners. And the crisis is not simply limited to the city. DiNapoli found that while 57.6 percent of renters in the Bronx were paying more than they could afford, so were 54 percent of those in Green, Ulster, Rockland, and Orange Counties.

Given a general retreat from the idea of the public sector actually building housing, the idea of structuring inducements for private initiative is increasingly the only game in town. However, within this terrain there remains a lively discussion about the respective roles of the carrot and the stick. Under Bloomberg, it was all carrot, and compliance was entirely voluntary. As Councilman Brad Lander has documented in a 2013 report on the results of the program, the outcome of this policy has been unimpressive, although better in some locations (notably the Upper West Side) than others. The bottom line, though, is that a total of 2,769 affordable units (amounting to about 13 percent of total units developed in the designated areas during the period) have been produced in these years and that, obviously, if de Blasio is going to generate his promised 200,000 units over two terms, some other approach is necessary. This is particularly apparent given that rent-regulated units are disappearing fast, whether as the result of vacancy decontrol or the demolition of the buildings in which they sit. (Lander reports that the latter cost the city around 8,000 units between 2005 and 2012.)

The answer is to make inclusionary zoning both mandatory and general, a position advocated by Lander and, in the campaign, by DeBlasio as well as by other community organizations and politicians, including Manhattan Borough President Gale Brewer. Given that there seems no chance of any other municipal program yielding new affordable housing—nobody seems to be suggesting that the city simply build it as it once did—it may, along with the staunch defense of rent regulations and the rejuvenation of the New York City Housing Authority, be our best option. Moreover, making these rules mandatory and general would be the first big planning move—and first big real estate deal—of the de Blasio administration to offer a promising sign of commitment to making more energetic and equitable use of the program.

That deal was for the development of the mighty Domino Sugar factory and a surrounding twelve-acre site in Brooklyn. The project has been in play since the mid 2000s and planning has been controversial from the get-go. The initial moves came after Domino shut down operations in 2004 and sold its property to a developer, the Community Preservation Corporation, and two partners, for $55.8 million. CPC proposed a Rafael Viñoly–designed complex—part of the city's plan to line the east side of the East River with towers—to include 2,200 units of which 660 were to be affordable, distributed in a brace of thirty- to forty-story buildings. Criticism included sentimental protest over the reuse of the hulking industrial building (now landmarked), and fear of gentrification pressure on the neighborhoods nearby, of the strain on the benighted L train and other services by the new population, of the long shadows that the forty-story buildings were likely to cast inland, and of the likelihood that the waterfront park to be included would be a cut-off preserve. There was also a strong sense that giant buildings flanking the river might not be the most imaginative and productive use of the space, that Battery Park City is perhaps not the only paradigm for waterside development in the twenty-first century.

The project got its sign-off from the Planning Commission in 2010, but in 2012 the developer went bust and sold the land and rights for $185 million to Two Trees, the company owned by David and Jed Walentas (*père et fils*), who made their fortune gentrifying Dumbo. They brought in new architects—SHoP— who proposed more park space, a richer mix of uses, and a dramatically different architecture, featuring buildings much taller than Viñoly's, which, while homely, begin to look fairly good retrospectively. But the basic housing numbers remained the same—2,400 market and 660 "affordable" units—and de Blasio asked Two Trees back to the table for more. The good news is that there will be an additional forty affordable units, that there will be a greater proportion of larger apartments suitable for families, that the units will remain below market rate in perpetuity, and that there will be no poor door, with affordable and market apartments, according to SHoP, randomly mixed in each building.

Is this victory Pyrrhic? Certainly 700 affordable units are a good thing, particularly when the deal kicks up the percentage from the required 20 percent to close to 30 percent. It appears that there will be substantially more—and more nuanced—park space. The inclusion of more office space will help with on-site mix. But there remain many negatives. There have been suggestions that much of the affordable housing will be placed in the one building to go up on the inland side of Kent Avenue, and the actual strategy for mixing units is yet to be designed. The buildings themselves are *much* taller than the previous scheme, and the architecture—despite the disingenuous insistence that its arch-of-triumph morphologies will admit more light to the cowering low-rise streets behind—is dated, like something bought in a thrift shop in Rotterdam or Shanghai. And, speaking of which, it also represents the mayor's complete acquiescence to the Brooklyn-as-Pudong planning of his predecessor. Transportation will be a big problem. The Williamsburg Bridge will be unfortunately miniaturized by looming towers. And—most fundamentally—the survival of the character and ecology of Williamsburg itself will surely reach irrevocable compromise, as the borough is not simply walled off but overpopulated and deprived by risen values of the accommodating slack that made it so popular—and singular—in the first place.

As the de Blasio administration moves forward, I gain in confidence in its *quantitative* intentions vis-à-vis planning. But urban quality is more than a numbers game and I await some signal about the forms of life our streets and buildings and public spaces will support, some idea about *design*. Seven hundred units isn't just lipstick on the pig, but the old east bank of the East River—low-rise, working, funky, diverse—is probably gone forever. Too bad.

End Note

A student of mine, who happens to be from Morocco, visited Ground Zero the other day and was abashed to discover the graphic material on the walls and on printed brochures was offered in eight languages, none of them Arabic. She asked a docent about this and was told that these were simply the eight major languages of the world. Arabic, as it turns out, is actually the sixth most commonly spoken. No mosque, no Arabic, what next?

(2014)

15

Ups and Downs

I've been listening to New York City's deputy mayor Alicia Glen on the radio, explaining the de Blasio administration's recently announced program for affordable housing, and it's stirring to hear someone speaking with passion and intelligence about *progressive urbanism*. I've also been wading through a copy of the plan itself, and, while moved by its rhetoric and reach, I must admit that the more I read, the more dispersed and opaque it gets.

The good news is that the numbers are big, the plan embraces a wide variety of interventions, and affordability is being defined to embrace the truly poor. The mayor proposes to "build or preserve" 200,000 units (housing about half a million people) over the next ten years and touts the initiative as "the largest and most ambitious affordable housing program initiated by any city in this country in the history of the United States." This may be, but it's tragic and typical that the burden to produce economic housing for its citizens falls so heavily on the city. And, given that the financing is to be 75 percent private capital, there's a $41 billion question as to whether the menu of inducements in the plan will be sufficiently appetizing.

The largest and most ambitious affordable housing programs in the history of the United States were financed by Washington through the loan policies of the Federal Housing Administration (largely directed to suburban development, which was also stimulated by massive federal investment in highways and other infrastructure) and by the 1949 National Housing Act, which empowered local authorities to administer federal funds for low-income rental housing. Cities got the short end of the stick: the feds spent about fifteen times as much on the suburbs as they did on urban projects. The New York City Housing Authority—the most successful public housing authority in the country by almost any measure—was New York's agency for channeling this assistance, and it built over 180,000 units, most of which were constructed in the two decades following the war (during which Washington facilitated construction of more than 2 *million* units for defense workers around the country). To put the urgency behind this number in perspective, the Stuyvesant Town development on the East River had received 200,000 applications for 8,757 rental apartments by the time it was completed in 1949.

To yield its 200,000 units, the mayor proposes to preserve 120,000 and to build 80,000. But how many of these apartments will be truly and permanently affordable? The answers depend on two issues: for whom they will be affordable and how they will be institutionalized. The first calculation is based on a relationship between rents and Area Median Income (AMI), with affordable housing costs generally defined as less than 30 percent of income. This creates a structure of differential affordability that the city breaks out in five bands, ranging from "extremely low" to "middle" incomes. The crisis is acute at all levels: the city's own numbers suggest a dramatically widening gap between incomes and rents and a rise in households that are "severely rent-burdened": over 30 percent of New Yorkers pay *more* than 50 percent of their incomes for housing. There are close to a million renter households in the city with either very or extremely low incomes, but there are *fewer than half* that number of apartments affordable to them. And, we have at least 50,000 homeless.

Affordability is more than a simple issue of physical supply because the need for space is subject to far less variation than there is in income. Few suggest that a poor family of four should be housed in a quarter of the space inhabited by a middle-class family of the same size that earns four times as much, or that it be comparably inferior in construction. The only three tractable variables are the price of land (which is in short supply), the cost of construction, and the availability of subsidy. The first issue admits some flexibility, including the use of property in city ownership, a focus on development in neighborhoods with lower costs (such as East New York), and condemnation. The plan doesn't have much to say about architecture or building methods, just a wee tithe to the idea of encouraging sustainable construction to save on long-term costs, and some streamlining of the permitting process. Which leaves subsidy in one form or another.

Where will it come from? Not much from Washington or Albany. Federal funding—which accounts for 85 percent of the budget of the city's Department of Housing Preservation and Development (which de Blasio promises to double)—has fallen by half, the Section 8 voucher program (which subsidizes low-income rentals) continues to drop, and the plan projects only about 7 percent of its expenditures from the feds and the state, money that is often heavily constrained. Given a relative scarcity of funds for direct investment, the city's primary negotiable assets are air and taxes. The centerpiece of the initiative involves both: adding a mandatory version of the current voluntary inclusionary zoning bonus to the incentive repertoire and developing a "carefully crafted" approach to harmonize the offer of extra bulk with tax exemptions. These are deals that can oblige that affordability be permanent. So far, so good, but specifics are lacking. How widespread will the mandate be, can it be satisfied at remote locations, and will the development community on whom this all depends bite? Nor does the plan really make clear how existing affordability will be maintained. "Stemming the tide of rent deregulation" and "encouraging landlords in transitioning areas to restrict incomes and rent" are, without clear mechanisms, just bromides and, without a commitment to numbers, mere wishes.

And there's a huge elephant in the room, which is the possibility —indeed, probability—that, even with the complete success of this program, the *net* number of affordable housing units in the city will fall, and substantially. As units exit rent regulation, as market prices rise, and as more and more affordable stock is renovated or replaced, the city is experiencing a precipitous decline in low-cost apartments. According to a study by the Community Service Society, the average annual loss has been about 38,000 units, representing a 39 percent drop in apartments "affordable to a family with an income at 200 percent of the federal poverty line" during the Bloomberg era. In the last twenty years, the city has lost around a quarter of a million stabilized units alone. This number would mean—even were the mayor's plan a complete success—a net *loss* of 180,000 units over ten years.

Without money, the city must deal in its most primary resource: air space. "To become a more affordable city, we must become a denser city," insists Deputy Mayor Glen. Really? Although I tend to the Friedrich Engels position—"There is already a sufficient quantity of houses in the big cities to remedy immediately all real 'housing shortage' provided they are used judiciously"— I tire at the uninflected idea of density that has become such a staple of neoliberal urbanism. As the mayor's plan suggests, what's needed is something more than square feet. The objective of planning should be the creation and defense of good neighborhoods, rich and diverse in people and use, and managing density is just one piece of the puzzle. My real anxiety about this plan is that—as with the previous administration—the instruments are too blunt. Great places require incremental change, community participation, adequate investment, infrastructures of all kinds, and *design*. The fantasies of the Bloomberg administration were coldly quantitative: if we can just manage the floor area ratio, the rest will follow.

I worry about the yet-to-be-proven capacity of the administration to plan beautifully and sustainability, but I have high hopes. A good way to get this plan started would be to focus on city-owned land and to design exactingly. It also makes sense, as the Community Service Society suggests, to concentrate efforts on transitioning neighborhoods where the poor are at greatest risk of displacement. And, not to sound like a broken record, let's return to building housing *ourselves*. In 1950 alone,

NYCHA built an astonishing 35,000 units. Indeed, through-out the fifties, virtually 100 percent of subsidized housing was *public* housing. We've learned a lot since then about cities and their design, about *ghettos* and projects. Let's put it to use!

The Royal Institute of British Architects (RIBA) has just voted to call for the expulsion of the Israeli Association of United Architects from the International Union of Architects, which had, in 2005, condemned the participation of Israeli architects in settlement building and the failure of the IAUA to oppose it. My thoughts about this are unequivocally mixed. While I find Prime Minister Netanyahu odious, the Israeli occupation vile (undeniably apartheid), and the participation of any architect in any of this immoral, had I been a member of the RIBA, I would have voted for the motion. But there is always something disquieting about the sheer volume of condemnation of Israel by lock-stepping types from the creative classes. Likewise, I've always found boycotts of organizations (like Israeli universities) that give homes to strong voices of opposition to be tactically convoluted, and there's reason on both sides of the argument.

While all outrage is selective, there is still a reckoning to be done in the struggle against global injustice. It is insufficient to simply answer critics who wonder why the RIBA hasn't con-demned Syria, the Chinese occupation of Tibet, North Korean fascism, or supermax prisons in the United States with the riposte that it's irrelevant *to what we're talking about now.* ("This is not about China or anywhere else and I'm not talking about who is worse than who," responded Angela Brady, the former RIBA president who introduced the motions.) Likewise, the "if you're not part of the solution" argument doesn't really cut it, if isolated from our wider world of woe. Evil is not divis-ible in the act, only the motive. The RIBA resolution was canny enough to be specific in its framing, to attack the complicity of Israeli architects in the construction of the settlements and the wall, and for their collusion in a clear breach of international law. And, it is always uplifting to see professional organizations take progressive political and moral positions, which, to its credit, RIBA did by disengaging from South African institutions during the day. Nevertheless, if one were to compile a matrix of the official expressions of Western outrage by comparable bodies, the predilection for this particular evil is too clear not to demand some supplementary explanation, perhaps cultural, perhaps psychoanalytic.

Selective outrage is only gainsaid by a plenitude of protest, and I await the RIBA's next motion. Construction worker deaths in Qatar anyone? Indentured servitude in Dubai?

Glen Small is one of the dear eccentrics of American architecture, at once gifted and cantankerous. He's had something of a checkered career but was an early leader both in the movement for green building and in keeping the faith with the happy trippy-hippy hand-built morphologies of the sixties and seventies. Some years ago, he moved to Nicaragua and, during the mayoral administration of Herty Lewites in Managua, was awarded a number of commissions. The most visible, and delightful, was La Concha Acústica, a performance shell on the capital's lakeside Plaza de la Fe. It is Small's finest built work, with a fluidly rising form, like a cresting wave or flickering flame. Sturdily constructed in cast concrete, it formed the backdrop for many a civic celebration and was much loved.

It has just been torn down with tremendous difficulty, and its tenacity and resistance give the lie to the claims of the authorities that the demolition was ordered because the shell was structurally unsound, at risk of tumbling in the next big seismic event. The demolition appears to be the result of revanchist Sandinista politics. Herty, who built four structures by Small during his administration, had been an early partisan of the struggle against Somoza and was minister of tourism in the first Ortega government. He eventually fell out with him and became a major player in the oppositional Sandinista Renewal Movement (MRS) during the nineties but rejoined the Sandinista National Liberation Front in 1998 and was elected mayor in 2000. After another split, he went back to the MRS and ran for the presidency in 2006. He died of a massive heart attack four months before the election.

In a grieving exchange of letters among Glen's friends, one writer described the government as behaving like the Taliban. Yes.

Lampposts around my studio are festooned with banners from our local business improvement district, celebrating its success in branding our longtime in-between neighborhood as "Hudson Square," an interesting eponym as there's no such place, unless you count the smog-clotted entry to the Holland Tunnel, a delightful piazza for Hondas. To be sure, the business improvement district (nice people all) has been behind some valuable improvements, including tree planting and the installation of new street furniture. But the banner emblazoned with the slogan "Hudson Square Is Rising" soured my mood. I see no particular reason to be pleased with the sprouting of buildings twice the height of the current default (and every one of them hideous), and the impending arrival of many more. And I certainly see no reason to be happy about the rise that's likely to force me out of my old studio: the insane increase in rents down here. It's looking like it may be au revoir for us. Let the better-heeled enjoy their sandwiches from Pret a Manger.

There goes the neighborhood.

(2014)

16

Little Boxes

I was recently at a meeting filled with urbanists discussing housing affordability when a developer proposed that what the city needed was a revival of the single room occupancy (SRO) building, a type that originated as the boarding house but which ceased to be legal for construction in 1954. His thought was that these would not be the flophouses of old but more like post-college dorms, right down to the gang bathrooms—places of towel-snapping and bonhomie in which conviviality would substitute for space. This new class of very small apartments—micro-housing, as it's come to be called—has been much discussed of late; and the Bloomberg administration promoted such units as an important piece of the solution to our housing question.

Micro-housing has a long history and embodies a range of ideals and ambitions crucial to both the social and architectural practices of modernism: workers' housing, mass construction, prefabrication, egalitarianism, and more capacious ethical and artistic ideas about minimalism. The theory of "housing" is a relatively new one, emerging during the Industrial Revolution with the creation of a class that needed to be housed: the proletariat. In capital's unregulated heyday, workers' accommodations took the form of New York City tenements, Berlin *Mietkasernen*, and the English endlessness of tiny room-over-room row houses. As a movement to reform the unsanitary and overcrowded conditions of these places arose in the nineteenth century, it created a discourse that was simultaneously beneficent and disciplinary.

One outcome was the *Existenzminimum*—the minimum-living unit. This concept grew in response to a provision in the 1919 Weimar constitution calling for "a healthy dwelling" for all citizens, and architects with a sense of experiment and social solidarity responded. Walter Gropius, with typical noblesse, framed the question as one of "the basic minimum of space, air, light, and heat necessary to a man," who "from a biological standpoint needs improved conditions of ventilation and lighting and only a small quantity of living space, especially if this is organized in a technically correct manner." This reductive impetus, informed by modernism's stripped simplicity, produced a variety of housing experiments and projects built in the white-walled, asymptotic aesthetic of the "new objectivity."

The search for minima also drew on modernism's enthusiasm for technological elegance as well as its uncritical embrace of Taylorist "scientific" management, a double rationalization with efficiency as its touchstone. What better than a ship-shaped kitchen, precisely designed to put every appliance and cabinet within reach? This sense of technological enablement stands at the headwaters both of spatial and technical economy and of consumer extravagance. The legendary kitchen designed by Margarete Schütte-Lihotzky for Ernst May's New Frankfurt social housing project in 1926 (perhaps it is not a coincidence that the woman wound up doing the kitchen) is the predecessor of the bloated "labor saving" kitchens of our own suburban '50s: life is so much easier for the housewife!

But these two types are supported by completely opposite distributive ethics: there is a big difference between arriving at a minimum on the rise from deprivation and being circumscribed by it as a way of bounding personal entitlement. Much as American housing projects have looked to express, in their austerity, the limits beyond which the poor should not aspire, so the idea of a minimum existence oscillates between penitence and affirming, Shaker-esque simplicity.

As they developed theories about the "minimum dwelling," architects became increasingly interested in what Conrad Wachsmann—a German pioneer of architectural mass production —called "the dream of the factory-made house." Modernist architecture—especially its interwar mainstream—was enamored of the possibility of constructing buildings with the same logic and efficient organization that was rolling millions of cars off the assembly lines: Fordist architecture. (Though there were some who saw this prospect through the lens of the people's ownership of the means of production rather than capitalist optimization.) But despite this yearning, most modern architecture depended, and continues to depend, on traditional artisanship for its construction, posing a clear contradiction between aspiration and reality. Those crisp white buildings were achieved with a layer of stucco hand-applied over frames of poured concrete, and infilled with brick laid in the traditional manner. Technology tended to arrive in systems—electricity, central heating, elevators, mechanical ventilation—rather than in structures.

The desire to bring buildings under the discipline of the factory has taken three main directions. The first is the complete box, whether built as a single house (think mobile homes) or as a stackable element like Legos (think Moshe Safdie's Habitat 67), sometimes factory-finished down to the furniture. The second and far more pervasive is a system of partial structural prefabrication. Anyone who has visited the former Soviet Union or its dependencies will have seen the ubiquitousness of dreary-looking "panel" buildings—enormous houses of concrete cards, rapidly erected on-site. Finally, there is the prefabrication of specific, complex components—mainly bathrooms or kitchens—that can be quickly inserted, sometimes as a way of avoiding the use of unionized labor.

These types of industrialized urban housing have never taken hold in American cities, despite the vast deployment of mobile homes and the on-site assembly line practices that enabled the construction of replicate suburbs like Levittown. But now the buzz is back and a number of projects using factory technology are underway in New York City. The largest of these is

Atlantic Yards in Brooklyn, where construction is moving along on the world's tallest modular building, the first of fifteen. The developer, Bruce Ratner of Brooklyn's Barclays Center arena, estimates a 20 percent savings in construction costs over conventional methods. Will any of these savings be passed along to tenants, or will they merely enlarge the bottom line? And how much of the savings will result from lower-priced labor?— although unionized, the factory workers building the modules make about 25 percent less than the typical construction worker.

It's clear that something must be done about housing costs, and this is the aim of both modularization and the micro-unit. In early 2012, New York City launched a competition called adAPT NYC, which received thirty-three proposals for micro-housing from developer/architect teams; a pilot project designed by the winner, nArchitecture, will go up on Twenty-Seventh Street in Manhattan. I am particularly fond of a photo that appeared in the *New York Daily News* following the announcement of the competition. Mayor Bloomberg stands with then-directors of City Planning (Amanda Burden) and Housing Preservation and Development (Mathew Wambua, now in the mortgage business) in an outline of one of the tiny apartments drawn on the floor. It's a space that could hardly accommodate the wine cellars or wardrobes of Bloomberg or Burden, and the accompanying story cites an *Atlantic* article about the "health risks of small apartments"; such tight dwellings, the headlines tell us, might lead to "major psychological problems." My CUNY colleague Susan Saegert has suggested that these would shake out according to the demographics of the occupants: fun—even useful—for young singles fresh off the bus, otherwise obliged to cram in with roommates; but potentially nightmares for couples, a parent with a child, or older people, on whom the cramped conditions and lack of privacy would weigh heavily, perhaps even disastrously.

Saegert also points out another crucial consequence of the widespread construction of micro-units, which can be as small as 250 square feet—too small to actually hold a reasonable array of furnishings (the bed will have to be a Murphy) and would require a change in the city's zoning laws, which set a

400-square-foot minimum for dwelling units. Erected in large numbers, they are likely to raise the ground rent for *all* apartment buildings (by increasing return per square foot), which would force those who might have otherwise been able to afford a studio or one-bedroom to downsize. A recent report from NYU's Furman Center confirms this risk—in one micro-housing project in San Francisco, units will rent for almost 50 percent *more* per square foot than the city average for a studio apartment. According to Sara Shortt, executive director of the Housing Rights Committee of San Francisco, "It's disingenuous to say it creates affordable housing, it's just that you get significantly less space."

This new iteration of micro-housing reverses more than a century's effort to eliminate overcrowding and expand quality. Defenders of these initiatives may cite the pleasures of the dorm, but what underlies their arguments is the increasingly pervasive density absolutism—often masquerading as equivalent to urbanity—that afflicts a large segment of the planning establishment, for whom the answer to development is always more.

Housing types invent their ideal subjects and reify their status. In the *Atlantic* article, writer Jacoba Urist reminds us of the misalignment between New York City's 1.8 million one- and two-person households (around 33 percent of us are single) and our current housing stock, which includes only a million studio and one-bedroom apartments. The idea that there is a class of tenants who must ever trim their spaces to their demographic status is truly invidious, a return to the calculation central to the *Existenzminimum*, a designated minimum spatial entitlement that government is to regulate and facilitate. It's the same argument that insists that elderly folk in large apartments (particularly in NYC Housing Authority and rent-regulated units) are somehow cheating the rest of us, and that they'd obviously be better off in a smaller, more "manageable" place. Again, an *aspirational* minimum—a chicken in every pot—is one thing; an ongoing process of defining that minimum down to correct the "misalignment between the nature of the stock and the needs of renter households" (in the words of the Furman Center) betrays a lack of both imagination and compassion. Needs are not quite so easy to quantify, and some things are irreducible to numbers.

The city's proposed micro-apartments are the size of hotel rooms (and not suites!) and are similarly geared toward transience: starter apartments after which tenants, having paid off their massive college debts, will move on to fine co-ops. Advocates argue that the buildings that hold them will—like hotels—offer a range of amenities (a gym, a nice lobby, perhaps a shared kitchen) that will effectively supplement meager private spaces and induce a sense of communal contentment, though without the authentic communalism of ownership or a shared project beyond lifestyle. This may be true for some young singles—as it is for elderly people who are ready for smaller apartments—but there is no legislation to compel these amenities and no evidence to suggest that the real estate industry will work overtime to fill buildings with gyms and solaria when an exercise room could as easily be swapped out for another apartment or two. And the fantasy of easy mobility hardly reflects the experience of most New Yorkers and their difficulties in finding and hanging on to living space, particularly uncontrolled rentals.

There's a likely convergence between the design of micro-units and factory-built modules, and it's certainly possible that the type could take off if the legal door is opened. New York City's first true modular apartment building—"The Stack," erected in a mere nineteen days—opened recently in Inwood. It's a nice-looking building (designed by Peter Gluck), but the apartments are a more conventional mix of unit types, none micro. This is a promising development and should help diminish resistance to modular construction by those who know it only through its shabbiest and most unattractive examples. Isn't this a better idea than stuffing people into spaces that can only be inhabited by childless Zen masters and anal retentives? Shouldn't the city be a place where the investigation is of how to produce choice and not compulsion?

The grievous state of the environment demands that we should all dramatically reduce our ecological footprints, and building has a crucial role to play—the era of the McMansion must end. We must also recognize that we're living differently from our parents, that America's demographics are shifting dramatically to smaller households, and that there is a mismatch between supply and demand. It's crucial that we stop assuming the nuclear family (a shrinking minority) should be our paradigm and produce housing in a variety that fits our actual habits and needs. But, even diversity has its limits: these apartments are simply too small.

(2014)

17

Business as Usual

When does mixed use become mixed metaphor? At Ground Zero, from the moment the decision was made to rebuild as both a memorial and a vast office and commercial complex, the conflict between auras was on. The question has long been how closely mourning and profit can be squeezed.

Now that the museum and memorial are complete, buildings 1 and 4 are ready for occupancy, building 3 is back on the rise (thanks to yet another bailout for Larry Silverstein), and the Calatrava station is framed, it's possible to get a sense of the texture, proportion, distribution, and artistic register of the site. And, it's clear that the contest between dignity and banality has been resolved on the side of the latter, decisively and consistently.

I walked down to visit the museum a few days ago—I live in the neighborhood and have been in daily touch with the site for years—approaching along Greenwich Street, much touted by the planners as the eventual key to the reknitting of the site into the city and the grid, a healing suture for a wound that *preceded* the attack. For the moment, Greenwich is still blocked by the temporary PATH transit station and when it's demolished, the street will pass between the rear of the three skyscrapers fronting Church Street and Calatrava's porcupine on the east and the memorial plaza on the west. The entry to the site from the north will cross the little plaza—festooned with its pathetic Jeff Koons balloon dog (which will eternally trivialize the tone for arriving visitors)—in front of Number Seven WTC, and then between towers 1 and 2, both of which will be higher than the Empire State. Somewhere in this "gateway" space an art center may eventually rise if cash and a sufficiently non-controversial tenant can be raised.

Whether this stretch of street is freely open to vehicular traffic —it's likely that there will be security apparatus at either end— will make little actual difference to the pedestrian experience of crossing the site, and Greenwich's narrow macadam surface will not make much of a mark in an environment so overblown it will make its own weather. In fact, the one strong connective move that has been successfully included in the plan is the elimination of the podium on which the Trade Center used to sit, and its extension of the level of Church Street toward the river, resulting in thwarting walls on three sides of the site and undoing the severing of Greenwich. By simply following the slope of the ground plane, the site has now been made intrinsically crossable, and "streets" are not really necessary to this. The real function of the restoration of Greenwich is to demarcate the sacred and the profane. A key question remains the nature of the uses that will flank the plaza on the business side. Cafes and restaurants? Clothing stores? Souvenir shops?

This same sort of perilous segregating gradient will also occur in the project's vertical section. The main element in the idea of memorialization has been excavation, which applies both to the two sunken pools in the footprints of the original building and to the museum itself almost entirely underground, its main level *below* the bottoms of the memorial cavities. Elsewhere on the site there will be extensive underground commercial activity occupying the same strata as memorial and museum but with neutralizing seams to bulkhead the tragic from the cheerful. This segregation will likely be successful at least at the visual level but the meaning will persist.

One hears endlessly—like a mantra—about the success of the Vietnam Memorial in establishing a precedent for commemoration. It's incontrovertibly a fine work, although not necessarily one that establishes a formula for every subsequent memorial: a descent into the earth lined in black stone and a list of names hardly encompasses the full possibilities of creative memory. What's truly critical about the Vietnam Memorial, however, is that it honors those (Americans) who died in a bitter, failed, and divisive war; that its dignity had to be pared of any sense of celebration, of uplift. As we increasingly—and rightly—resist thinking of our wars as invariably just, our commemorations become more and more cautionary, admonitions of "never again." The grim landscape of the Holocaust Memorial in Berlin, the over-referential architecture of the Holocaust Museum in Washington, and the tombstone-surrogate chairs in Oklahoma City have become an abstracted default; but there's a need to question the nature of their presence in our cities; the point at which marking becomes a perverse celebration.

The memorial in Berlin occupies the heart of that city, addressing especially the criminals (and their descendants) who planned the act so nearby, an insistent alteration of the fabric of urban normality—interference. This quality of rupture, an evocation of horror via tectonic foreboding, is something almost completely lacking at Ground Zero, which seeks, in the end, *to fit in*. Although I found the memorial moving the first few times I visited, I now find it at once grandiose and bordering on anodyne. Part of the problem is the tenacious orthogonality of the planning, reinforced by the too-disciplined lines of landscaping, stripes of paving and grass with identical trees aligned with military precision. To be sure, there was some internal, largely arcane, conflict over the signifying power of geometry as the original "competition" took place in the waning days of deconstructivism, with its anxious fragmentation and dopey arguments about representing the instability of both knowledge and the world.

Poor Snøhetta. These good architects innocently bought into the skewed vibe as the authorized style (as all the other architects on the job tip-toed away), and their entry pavilion for the museum is a fraily built referent to a bygone sensibility, a squidge of irregularity in a field of right angles, although there are also a few mildly off-axis moves in the museum below, designed by Davis Brody Bond. Here—unlike at the modest Vietnam memorial—the descent is not a gradual and shallow one, but a long trip down flights of escalators to the level of the foundations of the original buildings. While the space is very big, with a certain pharaonic dignity and grandeur, and while the curators have obviously worked very hard and very sensitively to produce exhibitions that "tell the story" of 9/11, the whole draws the line too far over into aesthetic territory. Little feels truly raw, and the style of mediation—TV clips, interviews with Condi Rice, projections onto the walls that are ephemeral and dim—yields too much familiarity, dissipates too much emotion. Indeed, the exhibit that made the strongest impact was one without images of explosions and collapse, one without carefully curated "souvenirs" from the site: a simple room in which there were just portrait photographs of the dead, almost all captured at moments of happiness. A room filled not with *things* but with faces.

The design of the museum uses the same normalization strategies that take place above. Prominent throughout are elegantly mounted "sculptures" of twisted steel recovered from the Trade Towers' ruins that are selected and displayed with such refinement that they might as well be Anthony Caro's. In the context of the clean and ordinary architecture of the museum, they can only be read for their "artistic" appeal, not their horror—a cultural impression cemented by the twenty-seven-buck entry fee and the fact that the first list of names seen on entering is that of the corporate donors to the project. Even the vaunted slurry wall seems too-little heroic, too dissociated from the meaning of its original function, sandwiched between newly built simulacra that make it hard to know what's real and what's fake. And, the one truly galvanizing tectonic opportunity is blown. Much of the "useful" space of the museum—galleries, corridors, classrooms, bathrooms—lies under the great voids of the memorial. Although their walls in the museum interior appear legibly in a bland cladding of grey granite as they descend from above, the potentially extreme experience of walking *beneath* this monstrous and weighty framing of absence is completely lost. Once past a little overhang, you're just in a banal and ordinary anywhere without any sense of the subterranean.

As a piece of planning, the import and success of the project as a whole can be described with a certain autonomy, provisionally removed from the meaning of the site that derives from the horrific event. It isn't simply that disaster has been diminished by its repackaging as a tourist attraction but that the organizational parti—and its governing aesthetic—is so standard-issue that it has become little more than a basic site-planning exercise. The scheme doesn't rise above the parameters of big buildings around a plaza, because neither the buildings nor the plaza have any real aspirations to questioning or disquiet or originality or comfort, and because the quality of the design is so terribly and uniformly everyday. Too much of the signification of the place is simply tied up with the quantitative as if that were a suitable substitute for the emotive or the artistic. Who cares if that stupid building is the tallest in the city, the country, the world, the universe? Why should we?

I think there are particular displacements working in various surrogate roles for the invention of the meaning of the site. From the start, the governing powers had concluded that the only possible response to an enormous crime was an enormous—and enormously expensive—project, one that would replace all the *architecture* lost. Setting aside the thin film that this idea places over the desire of most of those empowered to make decisions to reap huge amounts of money, there was a kind of potlatch in the riposte, a compensatory extravagance: throw money at the problem. This reminds me of Reagan and Star Wars, of the idea that we could defeat our adversary by inducing it into an arms race to construct a system so fantastical and useless that bankruptcy was the only possible outcome.

What's been translated at Ground Zero is not so much the idea that we can best our asymmetrical foes with vastly expensive technology (ironically, we are failing at that because we are still too invested in this kind of antique bellicosity and the corporate welfare that sustains it), but rather an irresponsible militarization of our own extravagance. We are building a train shed for a commuter rail line that serves a mere 30,000 people a day for a price that may hit 5 billion dollars—the cost of two and half B-2 bombers! This scale of expense—including the equivalents of those endless thousand-dollar-toilet-seat rip-offs, the contractor-engorging cost overruns that are military par for the course—is a piece of the "bigness" syndrome that too much serves as guarantor for the project's relevance, even its excellence. If it cost that kind of money, it must be good!

At the end of the day, though, we will have the architecture and planning of an airport, police state modernism, and slick surfaces pared of originality and eccentricity, designed for the efficient movement of crowds—all overseen by a ubiquitous apparatus of surveillance and control, which becomes a validating part of the "experience." As a planning project, though, it will do one very important thing: eventually allowing pedestrian circulation to cross the site both east-west and north-south, scrutinized from every angle but largely unimpeded by physical barriers. But, a stretch of Church Street will become a glass canyon (prepare for very dark afternoons). And, one of the biggest and persistent problems with the site—the interruption of the pedestrian flow to the river by the highway-scaled West Street and the too-impermeable frontage of the World Financial Center on the opposite side—will remain. This is a good time to remember the proposal of the late great Fred Schwartz to recover West Street as part of the fabric downtown.

How much better this place would have been if it dared to exceed business as usual.

(2014)

18

Big and Bigger

On February 20, 2015, the front page of the real estate section of the *New York Times* featured two articles. One described the prefabricated construction of the city's first "micro-apartment" block, its teeny units ranging from 260 to 360 square feet. The second reported the fastidious mock-up in a Brooklyn warehouse of a single apartment, a prototype for the units in a hyper-luxe tower rising on West Fifty-Third Street in Manhattan. The faux flat—which could probably fit ten micro-units inside it—was estimated to cost a cool million and will be trashed after the finishes have been suitably agonized over. Here was the income gap made concrete, the tale of two cities, living large and living really, really small … I dream of Gini!

What gives? The rise of the dreadful, steroidal collection of towers near Central Park, with their absentee, tax-dodging, oligarch owners, their hundred-million-dollar price tags, their limp starchitect designs, their shadows over the park, their public subsidies, and their preening San Gimignano competition for the most vertiginous views, has launched a thousand critiques of the city's rampant up-bulking. How to write another? Let's go shopping! My beloved real estate agent made appointments at the sales offices for the Bob Stern–designed 30 Park Place—at 926 feet, now the tallest residential building downtown—and for 56 Leonard, the Herzog and de Meuron pile a few blocks north (and just a skosh shorter at 821 feet), the final (one hopes) member of the three gracelessnesses: the undistinguished (to put it mildly) apartment building at 105 Duane Street and John Carl Warnecke's windowless, A-bomb-proof phone-company fortress, which now conjoin to form the Great Wall of Tribeca.

The two condominium showrooms bear a strong resemblance to each other, beginning with the three small bottles of Pellegrino and three of Evian, lined up perfectly on the coffee tables in the cozy sales chambers awaiting arriving shoppers and setting up the basis for the pitch to come: branding. My head spins with the names of the high-end fixtures and fittings that festoon every room! These represent nothing about cooking or pooping but are avatars of *our crowd*: no way we'd let a Whirlpool anywhere near that Gaggenau!

The main brand, however, is architecture. Quotes emblazoned on the walls (at 30 Park Place, they come from the architect and developer; at 56 Leonard, from distinguished art and architecture critics), lush catalogs, and introductory films make clear that the lifestyle on offer is about much, much more than "chinchilla mink" marble countertops in the en suite bath. Although the 2008 promo video for 56 Leonard, depicting a rain of shards from heaven that amalgamate to form the building, offers some serious entertainment value, the best to be had is the more comedic 30 Park Place movie. My favorite scene shows "Bob" and "Larry" (the developer Larry Silverstein) kvelling in the back seat of the world's largest Mercedes about how a couple of boys from Brooklyn had crossed the river and gotten so frigging *de luxe*. My second favorite had the long-gone art studios of Mark Rothko, Jackson Pollack, and Jasper Johns popping out on a map of the neighborhood, followed by Bob's chipper declaration: "If you want to know about real estate, follow the artists!" But the most painfully hilarious moment in our visit was live action: the sales agent's anxious reassurance that—because it narrows toward the top—the Woolworth Building wouldn't really interfere with the East River views!

Thirty Park Place is a skinny limestone shaft that might be inoffensive elsewhere but here shamelessly diminishes Cass Gilbert's masterpiece next door (that one-time *world's* tallest is a mere 792 feet). The newcomer nonetheless claims roots in the genius loci. As Bob writes in the sales brochure, "We're reinventing a New York tradition. 30 Park Place will recall the towers of the 1920s and '30s with an intricacy of shape and a strong skyline silhouette. You'll get a first impression that's a knockout, and then as your eye travels over the surfaces, you'll begin to see a depth of detail." When I first saw the cladding being attached to the building, I actually thought it was under-detailed, that—given the proportion of void to solid on the flat facades—there was not enough plastic activity, the surfaces too inarticulate. But, as the building grows, more dopey doodads appear, a veritable breakout of architectural zits! Especially pustulous are the fat hood moldings (Stern's signature detail, indeed the one that launched his career when he stuck a squiggle above the door of the Lang House in 1974), glued on to signify the double-height joint between the hotel below and apartments—er, residences—above.

To learn something about how detail can emerge from and abet a larger concept, one need only look at a couple of other limestone buildings nearby from the period under reinvention. The first is the 1935 federal building and post office right across the street, designed by Cross and Cross in fulsome Works Progress Administration style. That building has a fine, if not exactly graceful, solidity with a wack decorative program, based on a merger of deco zigzag and stripped-down nationalist/classicist iconography. Stars and stripes and angular eagles—not to mention fasces!—surmount a beefy frieze of triglyphs and blank cartouched metopes, awaiting, one imagines, carved portraits of FDR (or Mussolini). The truly brilliant exemplar of the era—and one of the greatest skyscrapers ever—is Ralph Walker's fabulous Irving Trust Company Building of 1931, at the top of Wall Street. This is modeled with enormous subtlety—setting back without literal, squared-off, *setbacks*—and ascends from a base that houses a convulsive, mosaic-covered banking hall (the work of Hildreth Meière—none of Bob's retro Ralph Laurenesque décor here!) At the building's peak, Walker placed four great windows from which the plutocrats in charge could gaze upon the world they owned, puffing on their Havanas. No detail is superfluous, and everything flows from reinforcement and elaboration of the beautifully sculpted mass. This is how detail finds meaning—indigenously, not extraneously.

While one can still get a serviceable two-bedroom at 30 Park Place for 6 or 7 million, the cheapest thing left at the Herzog and de Meuron is a $17 million penthouse, and it's clear that these are where the architectural action will be. Their core conceptual idea is a Paul Rudolph–ish stacking of boxes, knit together at right angles such that *rooms* project into space, yielding a sense of flying. But this move is reserved for the top, the capital. Indeed, the building is traditionally tripartite and the main shaft (where 5-million-dollar bargain basement pads could have been had) looks heavily value-engineered: what's built so far is a blandness of exposed concrete slabs and a tacky-looking glass curtain wall. Here, the projecting spaces are not rooms but balconies. While these are staggered to produce something of the Lego conceit that appears up top and on a few lower floors, they have glass rails and so disappear into the slabs, leaving their rhythm legible only when you're close to the building and see the projections from below. And, given that the syncopation of the balconies is so regular, they don't always land in the most felicitous places. I'm not paying $17 million for a penthouse where the balcony ain't even in the living room!

These buildings are *vulgar*, lacking any sense of the civic. Vulgarity is not simply a matter of taste or artistic quality, but of excess and a flaunting of "civilized" norms. Both the Leonard Street and the Park Row buildings contribute to the rampant, selfish up-scaling of the city and use architecture as camouflage. But however fine the design, they're too damn big and too damn expensive, another driver of the flight of bodegas, diners, artists, rent-regulated hangers-on, and so many other ingredients of a neighborhood with a good if rapidly vanishing social and morphological mix. Rather than offering any solution, this new housing only *accelerates* our housing shortage. While we've debated the meaning and conscionability of the "poor door" that's been a by-product of efforts to achieve a measure of distributive justice via inclusionary zoning, 56 Leonard mocks it all: it will have its very own Anish Kapoor door! This is a form of excess that demands regulation.

Since the ancient Greeks, many societies have enacted "sumptuary" laws, circumscribing luxurious consumption. In general, these have been a means of fixing hierarchies from the top down, prohibiting the lower classes from the pleasures and display of the upper crust and calibrating the appearance of rank. In sixteenth-century France, only princes were permitted to eat turbot. In ancient Rome, purple could be worn only by the emperor and senators. The Massachusetts Bay Colony restricted fancy clothes to those earning more than 200 pounds sterling a year. And now we seem to be implicitly enacting a similar code. Brand name architecture has become the symbol of privilege and is reserved for high rollers and offshore creeps.

While few lament the passing of the era of generic white-glazed-brick, wedding-cake apartment houses from the 1950s and '60s, such buildings did have the distinction of being shaped by a clear idea of public benefit—light and air on the street, for one—and ranked the value of ensemble over today's narcissism of big differences. Back in the postwar years (back when we could speak of wars actually being over), there was an implicit consensus of the municipality and private developers that there would be great efforts to build for both the middle class (including returning veterans) and for the poor. The "projects" constructed by the New York City Housing Authority and enormous complexes like Stuyvesant Town or Parkchester were essentially indistinguishable as architectures. Say what you will about "towers in the park," but such developments were predicated on a form of egalitarianism, something quite different than towers looming over the park. While it's a mistake to think that this problematically uniform planning was ever the sine qua non of the good city, it did represent an idea about the shared one, about values in common, about convergence. We no longer mind the gap.

(2015)

19

Another City

I was part of a neighborhood committee that paid a visit to the New York City Landmark Preservation Commission to argue for the expansion of the Tribeca Historic Districts. To some, given the neighborhood's rampant fabulousness and its irreversible ascent into post-hipsterdom, this might seem like a vanity project of the 1 percent. Our argument, though, was not simply about the physical qualities of the place. The piece of the neighborhood we sought to have added to the district is home to its largest concentration of rent-regulated apartments, and we think that its inclusion would have the effect of preserving the long-term housing prospects of these neighbors. The commission should find a way to protect a historic social ecology that has symbiotically taken root in the neighborhood.

Our argument went nowhere, because the commission's focus is on architecture, not people. We knew that the case for integrating historic and community preservation would not be entirely clear, but so what? We wanted to emphasize that certain principles about housing should be sacrosanct. The most fundamental ones are enshrined in the Universal Declaration of Human Rights: protection against "arbitrary interference with ... privacy, family, [and] home" and "freedom of movement and residence within the borders of each state." The Declaration also stipulates an "adequate" standard of living, including housing and social services, participation in community cultural life, and a raft of other opportunities at the vital core of liberal democracy.

While Mayor Bill de Blasio's national "progressive agenda" includes nothing that will displeasure the near left, it is strangely mute on, among many things, a key component of his municipal ambitions: housing and the right to it. To be sure, getting more money into the hands of exploited workers and a little less into those of the plutocracy would redistribute wealth. Unarticulated in de Blasio's fourteen faultless points, however, is any idea about the redistribution of space, the primary raw material of wealth in the city. The mayor has come in for heavy criticism of a housing policy that not only relies primarily on subsidies to developers to induce trickle-down but also is likely to increase the physical gap between rich and poor. This worsening of the geography of privilege is evident not only in the spiraling prices in Williamsburg or Tribeca but in a policy that focuses on poor neighborhoods as the most logical locales for new housing for the poor. A case in point is the administration's choice of East New York as one of three pilot sites for its policy (the other two are Jerome Avenue and Flushing West). The neighborhood is already rife with speculation in anticipation of the city's intervention, and the risk is that rising land prices will inexorably define affordability upward—and out of reach of many of the people already living there.

Like his predecessors, de Blasio is caught in a dilemma about what it means to plan the city. His proposal, "Housing New York," has the revelatory subtitle "Zoning for Quality and Affordability." The replacement of planning by zoning is characteristic of the negotiation between public and private interests that's the stuff of any urban development policy. While there's general agreement that all cities must have some structures of constraint, drawing the line between the perks of property and propriety is never easy. In New York, this operates in both the realm of ownership (public, private, collective, institutional) and the "right" to transform property in terms of its use, size, performance, and appearance. The basis for both the operation and the progress of our system is that each of these constraints is subject to change—through negotiation, technological and social evolution, corruption, and reconceptualization. Paradigms shift and accidents will happen: one idea of the city succeeds another.

We are in the midst of such a shift, and it's visible all over town. The city is cluttered with construction projects, most of which rise dramatically above the default textures in which they are supposed to fit. Downtown, apartment buildings going up in SoHo are double and triple the height of their neighbors. "Hudson Square" is on building growth hormones, including many additions on top of existing structures. Below Canal Street, a clutch of super-tall towers dominates the skyline. Tribeca is going fast. According to research by my redoubtable neighbor and chair of the Tribeca Trust, Lynn Ellsworth, eight neighborhood buildings have been demolished in the past year, and at least twenty could become targets of the wrecking ball. These include the six along West Broadway just purchased by Cape Advisors for $50 million (at an astounding $1,000 per square foot), which *Crain's New York Business* speculates will require apartments selling at a minimum of $3,000 per foot (do the math!) to turn a profit. Ellsworth—the organizer of our trip to Landmark Preservation—estimates that the loss of all these buildings will eliminate at least 110 rent-stabilized apartments and about forty small businesses. Not gonna be any poor doors here!

While few tears need be shed for those lucky enough to freehold in this great spot, Tribeca's transformation could become far more general, both socially and architecturally. The place is a lab because it's full of primitive accumulators for whom a "good neighborhood" is understood primarily as one in which property values increase as quickly as possible, and "architecture" is seen as a price multiplier. This is the classic gentrification formula: the residual value of a neighborhood's historic "character" sanctions successor forms, creating, in the case of Tribeca, the spreading rash of monstrosities that loom over its low-rise fabric and arrogate its prestige. We're the happy rats who can't resist going back to the cocaine dispenser, and, because the price gyre is so fundamentally what the neighborhood has become, the war between the fiscal and physical is thrown into vivid relief.

What's happening in Tribeca is not simply a further "tipping" of the neighborhood. It represents a very particular—but strategically unspoken—assumption of the mayor's planners: the city works best by forced mobility, understood simply as a map of the circulation of capital, with the human consequences—including attachments to place—reduced to "externalities." One can scarcely pick up a copy of the *New York Times* without reading about the latest hot neighborhood transformed by its differential affordability: families priced out of Boerum Hill hightail it to more affordable locales like Jackson Heights. Assimilated to the B-school romance of "disruption"—celebrated as the central practice of canny CEOs—this destabilized state is not simply typical of New York City but of the country as a whole, as both housing and job security become increasingly tenuous, and Americans relocate ever more frequently over their working lives. How to finesse this? The overall recent trend is up.

The cruel economics of mobility also have an enervated aesthetic side. The city has too long been celebrated for the creativity of its destruction, the dynamism of its demolitions and replacements, the jackhammers gouging the streets, and the cranes and towers scraping the sky. That is surely part of our self-image and not without its thrills, but its false first principle is that disruption is an absolute. Such a too-licentious willingness to tear things down complements another assumption of current planning: that density, too, is an absolute. This particular idea—which is surely channeled, in part, by Carl Weisbrod, the real estate operative who is director of the New York City Department of City Planning (DCP)—has become neoliberal writ and is bolstered by a cadre of academics, including the enabling enthusiasts for "hyper-urban development" at Columbia's Center for Urban Real Estate, which has advocated, without apparent irony, filling in New York Harbor to annex Governors Island as a massive development zone: the numbers are impressive but the premise is nuts. More recent studies of where to put new housing units are—like those of the DCP—diagrammatic to a fault, tiny massing models devoid of any non-quantifiable considerations of character: whatever the question, density is always the answer.

Housing affordability is at a crisis stage, a symptom of a more endemic inequality that de Blasio's progressive agenda and impulses seek to redress. The vital questions now are whether the inherited strategy of using subsidies to cajole philanthropy from developers will continue to work; whether the existing stock of affordable housing can be protected; whether a widespread policy of uneven development can be managed; whether planning coordination of new housing with necessary transport, educational, cultural, recreational, and environmental improvements can be achieved; and whether the form of this new approach will be equitable and urbane.

This will be tested all over the city, and there are reasons for both skepticism and hope. Skepticism because of what seems like a doubling down on former mayor Mike Bloomberg's development deals and rampant up-zoning. The element of the de Blasio protocols that's receiving the most pushback from mainstream preservation organizations and progressive public officials is a zoning amendment that will allow up to a 31 percent increase in height in so-called contextual districts. According to the official definition, "contextual zoning regulates the height and bulk of new buildings, their setback from the street line, and their width along the street frontage, to produce buildings that are consistent with existing neighborhood character." The consensus among the opposition is that this densification will be a double negative: The increased size of new buildings will disrupt a neighborhood's formal character, and enormous pressure will be placed on existing buildings by offering incentives to their owners and developers to tear them down and replace them with bigger, more expensive structures—producing, in the end, a context of no more context.

The reason for hope is that the mayor is supporting some very good, indeed progressive, policies: renewal of the rent laws, permanent housing for the homeless, and additional protections for tenants facing harassment and eviction. More, he has just announced a comprehensive initiative to bring public housing— a huge store of affordable housing that the city directly controls —back from the fiscal and physical brink. Nothing could be more urgent, given the widespread deterioration, mediocre

design, poor community integration, and unfortunate location of a large number of projects in flood zones (damage from
Hurricane Sandy was severe). But here, too, the proposal is not
yet more than a numbers game, with virtually no attention paid
to questions of place and character.

The plan begins with a variety of administrative streamlin-
ings (and an effort to collect rents from the approximately one
quarter of tenants who are in varying degrees of arrears), and
only time will tell if these tactics will realize their projected fiscal
turnaround. But its central proposition is to utilize "vacant" land
within the projects for new construction, applying the general
densification policy to fresh terrain. That such land exists is due
to the architectural approach behind the projects—the high
modernist vision of "towers in the park," which in the case of the
New York City Housing Authority includes not simply copious
landscaped areas but a large number of surface parking places.
(The reduction of parking requirements is one of the sensible
aspects of the administration's general housing policy.) Because
of this, many NYCHA projects are built to densities that are less
than the underlying zoning allows, leaving what is technically
a buildable surplus—free air. Any addition, though, will both
change context and add to the pressures for new services and
infrastructure. De Blasio's proposal is, at the "structural" level,
the same as what Bloomberg bruited: turning over this "excess"
land and space to private developers.

Whatever the developers' plans, they will certainly transform
the character of the projects. Opinion about these places has
shifted somewhat in recent years. A reflexive, Jane Jacobs–ean
animus to their sterility has been overshadowed by a more
nuanced appreciation of their bowered, campus-like interruption of the street grid's dense regularity. This bucolic view is not
without limits: The projects direly need an admixture of nonres-
idential uses, serious attention to their public open spaces, and a
redesign of their inhospitable and grim lower floors. And, their
uniformity, utilitarian detailing, cheap finishes, and uninspired
architecture desperately want reinvention. This is not a problem
that is exclusive to New York, and cities around the world
must consider the patterns that will both renew and succeed

the millions of units built according to this model. A number of hopeful prototypes for recuperating these places (as opposed to demolishing them and leaving their tenants with vouchers or just the finger) are beginning to emerge.

Because any general case against densification remains contested, the question devolves on how to do it and for whom. I have a fairly knee-jerk animosity to the handover of public property (and rights) to narrowly private interests. These deals are only viable when developers feel they have more to gain than they must give back, and so each of these exchanges is, by definition, a bad deal for the public. But, given the deficit in public revenue—those housing projects were built with federal money that has long ceased to flow—the municipality is forced into bed with the only people with cash. If one accepts this premise, as de Blasio has, then the overriding issue is the resulting mix of tolerance and the proportionality of the trade-off.

For a straight housing deal during the Bloomberg years, the price point was 20 percent affordable units for the strictly voluntary bulk bonus. De Blasio is looking to increase the price to 30 percent and make it mandatory (although there's no move to implement this so far). And he's looking to do better still with the projects. Here, the proposal is for a two-tiered system, including one in which NYCHA land would be leased (in a number of as-yet-to-be-specified complexes) to developers who would be obliged to provide 50-percent affordability, and another in which land at three complexes (two in Brooklyn, one in the Bronx) would be leased to developers for $200 million in a ten-year deal, for which they would build 10,000 "low-rent" units.

Many details bedevil this arrangement. What will attract developers to accept a cross-subsidy from market-rate housing in neighborhoods in which there's no market for it? What will happen to the 10,000 units after ten years? How can the administration lock in affordability after its term expires? And, to get back to the place where I began, how will the design of all this construction and amendment help secure not simply the financial health of the NYCHA but environmental excellence and healthier, more livable and complete neighborhoods? The just-released report contains only the vaguest, most notional images of transformation and none that even begin to suggest how the huge quantities of new housing will be placed in the chosen sites.

The fiscal tail is wagging the design dog, and this is what unites the transformation of the projects with that of Tribeca. Just as the blight of luxury towers rising around Central Park or Grand Central is really no more than the decorative extrusion of the underlying lots, the pure monetization of space, the city risks treating place as a matter of speculation rather than care, finesse, and the medium of true *distributive equity*. Besides, it isn't clear whether the massive displacements, demolitions, and reengineering of our class and spatial structure will result in any increase in affordable housing: we've been losing it at a rate that far exceeds even the rosiest predictions for its replacement.

(2015)

20

Sow's Ears

"If you want to build a bad building, hire a good architect, and if you want to build an outrageous building, hire a *distinguished* one," goes the old saw. New York is suffering a rush of global starchitects energetically putting lipstick on a rash(er) of enormous pigs.

The "billionaire's row" of hyper-tall apartments rising along Fifty-Seventh Street is Exhibit A, not simply for its wanton hijacking of the skyline and the chillingly long shadows it will cast on Central Park, but also for so literally mapping the heights of our crisis in housing affordability. Stratospheric prices reserve these *pieds-à-ciel* for oligarchs and the shell companies that anonymously park their money (and the occasional Rolls Royce) in safe havens. Most owners will spend scant weeks in residence each year, tenancies calculated to minimize local tax burden.

Although the names of famous architects are attached to these buildings, they're actually designed by lawyers and accountants, their form the outcome of negotiating the arcana of the city's zoning system to exploit its bonuses and breaks and assemble "air rights" purchased from adjacent and nearby lots. Last summer, the venerable Art Students League sold the void above its winsome 1891 French Renaissance–style digs (designed by Harry Hardenbergh, of Plaza Hotel and Dakota

Apartments fame) to Extell for $31 million. This windfall may secure the school's future (although the sale was delayed by a lawsuit by League members who argued that the price was at least $300 million too low), but the cost will be the Nordstrom Tower, an eighty-eight-story "neighbor" cantilevering over the tiny school like a "giant poised to squash a poodle," in Michael Kimmelman's indelible phrase. When completed to the plans of Adrian Smith (of Burj Khalifa fame) it will be the Northern Hemisphere's tallest *residential* structure, clocking in at 1,775 feet, one foot shorter—"out of respect" says the developer—than the city's (and the country's) current highest tower, the hyper-homely One World Trade Center.

It's estimated that sales of Nordstrom's condos will net $4.4 billion. Such empty extrusions are the nearly pure monetization of land, and the increasingly precise resemblance of our skyline to a bar graph of real estate prices is no coincidence. The most succinct such hollow architectural signifier is 432 Park Avenue by Rafael Viñoly, which, at 1,397 feet, while a shrimp compared to Nordstrom, is nonetheless 146 feet taller than the Empire State! 432 Park—visible from almost everywhere in the city (and probably from the moon)—has its admirers—both for its slimness and for the relentless, Sol LeWitt-less minimalism of its facades, gridded like graph paper (and bearing a strong resemblance to Skidmore, Owings & Merrill's 1965 Brunswick Building in Chicago, a pioneer of the look).

Evaluating these buildings devolves almost entirely on the quantitative, and their architecture is judged statistically. Preening competition for height is joined by the slightly more arcane standard of *skinniness*, which tests both engineering chops and stages the battle of habitability. Is the building stiff enough to resist wind, earthquakes, and other non-market forces? With the core subtracted, will the plate still yield useful amounts of space for actual apartments? Current leader of these svelte-stakes is 110 West Fifty-Seventh Street, designed by SHoP, and touted as "the slenderest tower in the world." At 1,428 feet and eighty stories, it will hold a mere sixty apartments (forty-six full-floor units in its upper reaches to assure park views over surrounding clutter, and fourteen in Steinway Hall, a landmark seconded as its base to provide air rights and cachet). Prices will top out around $100 million.

It's an open question whether the starchitect labels on these buildings actually add much retail value. First-born of this litter, the klutzy 1,005-foot One57—an earlier Extell product designed by Christian de Portzamparc—has been derided by critics, especially for its psoriatic skin (its shape bears a strong resemblance to a '70s-era Helmut Jahn, if without the finesse), but still commands insane prices. Jean Nouvel's 1,050 foot 53 West Fifty-Third Street—"Live above the Museum of Modern Art in a striking expression of architectural strength and grace"—will be more butch, with its brawny cross bracing and tapered shape but, really, does anyone care? The architect's brand is just one among others, a fillip added to the super-luxe appliances, the slather of onyx and bubinga, the exclusivity, the ostentation, the location, the Olympian views, the sense of superiority and self that only comes from spending the equivalent of the GNP of Burundi on an apartment.

On a visit to Yale, Frank Lloyd Wright was asked where he'd want to live if obliged to pass time in New Haven and elected the Harkness Tower, a neo-Gothic spike. When his interlocutor wondered why, he replied that it was the only place in town from which you couldn't see the Harkness Tower. (Guy de Maupassant was said to have eaten in the restaurant of the Eiffel Tower every day so his meal wouldn't be disturbed by a view of it.) Unfortunately, there's almost no place left in New York to hide from this plague of designer pork.

(2015)

21

Lost at Sea

I taught in Boston in the spring semester and commuted from New York City on the shuttle. The university discount applied only to the lower-rent, US Airways version, which meant that the free in-flight reading material was somewhat limited and, as a result, I was stuck with the *Wall Street Journal* and the *New Criterion*. Why the Right is more inclined than our side to gratis distribution to this particular commuter demographic is a mystery, but I dutifully took my trips on wings of freebie reaction.

The *New Criterion* published two articles about architecture during the term, and, curiously, *both* were about museums designed by the Italian architect Renzo Piano: the Fogg Museum in Cambridge, Massachusetts, and the new Whitney Museum of American Art in New York City's Meatpacking District. The magazine had previously enthusiastically supported Piano, covering his "masterpiece" addition to Fort Worth's Kimbell Art Museum in 2014 and his "splendid" modifications to the Morgan Library in 2006. But something's changed. The review of Piano's upgrade and expansion of the Fogg by Peter Pennoyer (a New York architect practicing in the "classical" manner) is chilly. Focused on the suture of modernity and "tradition," Pennoyer—bemoaning "exquisitely detailed stone aedicule balconies" threatened by the proximity of a new handicapped ramp—overvalues the tepid 1927 building, itself much of a muchness with other Georgianoid construction from Harvard's roaring twenties boom.

To his credit, Pennoyer also decries another ramp—on the back side of the building—that's a wretched and trivializing extension of the great bifurcating distributor of Le Corbusier's masterpiece next door, the Carpenter Center, and he nails many of the Piano's deficits: its crude negotiation of the old/new seam, the graceless facades, indifferent finishes, and tepid circulation (although calling the main stair "anti-humanist" is over the top— *too narrow* would do). He also rightly points out that the most habitable new space in the building is the conservation area under its huge glass roof, a spacious working environment with killer views, far more "functional" than the rather dour new galleries.

Tarring the whole by praising the incidental success of some function ancillary to the actual display of art (the staff quarters, the views, the café, the comfy sofas) is a critical strategy that recurs in almost every piece written about the Whitney, including one by *New Criterion* executive editor James Panero. His animus is freer floating than Pennoyer's, perhaps because there's no literal victim to be defended. In lieu, he idealizes "the museum" as a place of "elevated design," embodying "coherence, symmetry, and a sensitivity to materials." The Whitney thus fails on two counts: as a flunky within a Platonic category and also because it falls outside it; it's a building of a completely different *type*. "Whatever this construction resembled ... it clearly did not look like a museum ... Instead hospitals, prisons, cement plants, Fukushima, and Eastern Bloc government agencies all come to mind." Although Panero lands a few commonplace blows about the behavior of the building, his architectural argument relies almost entirely on whimsical simile: the Whitney can't be a decent museum because it *looks like something else*.

This argument is crude. Truly invidious, however, is Panero's classist—indeed racist—critique by association: the *wrong money* is behind the Whitney. None of its founding board members were "A-list"—"not Rockefellers, Morgans, Fricks, or Mellons, but Kozlowskis." For Panero this déclassé tradition still abides in money for the new building from the lesser of the Lauder brothers and from the likes of "Neil Bluhm, a self-made real estate and casino magnate whose suit jacket was stuck in his pants when he began his opening remarks during the museum's press preview. As a prominent Obama campaign bundler, Bluhm's political contributions, no doubt, did little to hinder the museum's successful effort to get an inaugural blessing from the first lady."

While this is odious, architectural criticism must account for a full range of building's affect and effects: social, functional, aesthetic, and contextual. Provenance matters. But Panero's piece—with its defense of "elevated design"—is clearly also meant as riposte to the functionalist aesthetics that has dominated virtually *all* the critical coverage of the building to date: the *New Criterion's* flatulence over symmetry and coherence is not simply neocon nostalgia for the loss of eternal artistic verities but reflects a more general impoverishment of critical interpretation. Critique of the Whitney has made this problem particularly clear by its tendency to heap praise on the galleries while expressing indifference or hostility to the building *as a whole*, a schizy split often reflected by a division of editorial labor in which an art critic cheers how great the art looks and then hands off to an architecture critic to trash the structure that houses it.

This focus on mismatch between inside and out is ubiquitous. Holland Carter divvies thus in the *New York Times*: "From the outside, Renzo Piano's new Whitney Museum of American Art, set beside the Hudson River, has the bulk of an oil tanker's hull. Inside is entirely different." Pete Wells's review in the same paper of Untitled, the Danny Meyer restaurant on the ground floor, repeats the trope of the marginal building as container for marvelous art: "All the energy and beauty … are on the plates." In her *Times* piece, Roberta Smith loves the inside, asserting that the building "accommodate(s) art and people with equal finesse … Art looks better here, to my eyes, than it did in the old Whitney, and it is amazingly comfortable to be in." Back on the sidewalk, though, Smith writes that "the outdoor staircase epitomizes the operative and symbolic logic of Mr. Piano's design," calling it "the most aggressive part of the multiple components that make the building a kind of architectural assemblage. From the street, the switch-back juts over the building's east face like a fire escape on steroids or a fragment from an aircraft carrier." This seems a pretty un-valenced idea of *assemblage* and the elusive, compound wholes it seeks, but she sees instead— perhaps because it's *architecture*—something put together with the wrong parts and assembled into the wrong thing.

This idea of faulty assembly is given an even stronger workout by Justin Davidson in *New York* magazine (in a piece juxta- posed with a rave from art critic Jerry Saltz). While Davidson is happy inside, praises the wide-open galleries' potential for cre- ative curating, finds the current installation inviting, and relishes the organization of circulation and the stepping terraces (never mind the de rigueur references to cruise ships and fire escapes), he is much vexed with the ungainliness of the physical ensemble, an "awkward kit of protruding parts and tilting surfaces," and describes the building as something "that might have arrived in an IKEA flat pack and then been prodigiously *misassembled*" (my italics) into a "deliberately clunky building." Davidson, a far subtler and gifted critic than Pennoyer, also finds the build- ing overwhelmed by the ancillary, a "symphony full of rests," a "wonderful place for people who get easily bored by art."

The *Times*'s admirable architecture critic Michael Kimmelman is more tempered but also falls back on generic tropes. Seen from the west, the museum is "ungainly and a little odd, vaguely nautical, bulging where the shoreline jogs, a ship on blocks alluding to one of New York's bedrock industries from long ago." On the other hand, "from the north, it resembles some- thing else, a factory or maybe a hospital, with a utilitarian wall of windows and a cluster of pipes climbing the pale-blue steel facade toward a rooftop of exposed mechanicals." Fire escapes also get the obligatory mention. (I myself find the outdoor stairs *unlike* fire escapes, which—in their classic New York incarnation —are grafted directly to the vertical surface of a building.) Kimmelman is a bit easier on the seasonality, discomfort, and disconnection of the circulation but is—correctly I think— skeptical of the constraining "flexibility" of the big gallery spaces. Indeed, in the opening show, these have been converted into a totally standard-issue set of enfiladed Sheetrock rooms, with pictures hanging on the walls. Kimmelman also invokes old/new-money class warfare, noting that with downtown's financiers, "Hollywood stars and other haute bourgeois bohemians stand in for the old Social Register crowd." Nu?

Virtually all the criticism I've read sees the Whitney's social effects either in this sort of passing parsing of patronage or as the consummation of the gentrification of the Meatpacking District and Chelsea, on par with the High Line, for which it provides a literal culmination. Barry Schwabsky, writing in the *Nation*, riffs on a 1971 Hans Haacke documentary takedown of a slumlord included in the show and, in a displaced lament, discusses the gentrification of his old neighborhood on the Lower East Side. Peter Schjeldahl concludes his piece in the *New Yorker* by observing that the museum will quash the chances of any "young artists, writers, and other creative types" to live anywhere nearby. Holland Carter too invokes this eliminationist trope, describing Chelsea as "the precise opposite of being an artist neighborhood ... a gated community." And, for good measure, he mentions that there's only one Native American included in the show.

But let's get back to Roberta Smith's aircraft carrier. I found it surprising that no critic has mentioned the gigantic example twenty-five blocks upriver: the *Intrepid*. Closest was Robert Bevan in *Architectural Review* who (while also comparing the building to a "swish hospital"—what's up with the hospital thing?) writes that "the model is not, as some have said, the post-industrial loft or even the white cube but the aircraft hangar." Indeed, the *Intrepid* does have a vast, column-free hangar deck—with a capacity of many Whitneys—and also harbors, on the flight deck "terrace" above it, a brace of aircraft that we assimilate—in their inoperability—as functionalist "sculptures" of tremendous refinement and even beauty. The *Intrepid* is a genuinely floating object that can unmix the prolix critical/nautical metaphors directly. In service for many decades, its elevators, stairs, gun emplacements, antennae, radars, conning towers, and other appurtenances encrust the smooth symmetries of the hull, having been added—*assembled*—seemingly at random but rigorously calculated not to disturb the ship's balance and therefore offering a genuinely functionalist working method with a resulting visuality—always also tested by its operational efficiency—that is completely succinct, by definition.

Virtually every critique of the Whitney founders here, by confusing functionalism's aesthetic of pure consequence with some other formalism. Because the Whitney cannot be easily compared to any ready-made icon, each critic thinks, if sometimes restively, within the nominal confines of functionalist aesthetics while seemingly blind to the fallacy of trying to account for the good-galleries/bad-building argument within it. Such confusion is a testament to the Whitney's actual functionalist successes: like the *Intrepid,* it yields disquieting and unfamiliar formal results. Schwabsky, perhaps, gets closest, finding the building "neither visually dazzling nor particularly elegant; nor is it the sort of shape-as-logo design that makes its mark on the city as a graphic silhouette. It is not architecture trying to be sculpture." Although he describes the museum's appearance as "nearly anonymous," Schwabsky finds the galleries impressive and, without inconsistency, calls the Whitney the "best place to see modern and contemporary art in the city."

The problem with the compositional reading of functionalism is that it is completely at odds with functionalism's nominal aesthetic—with "form follows function," to coin a phrase, the idea that the succinct, economical accommodation of some set of literal operations is the ground on which appearance is constructed, understood, and judged. By these lights a diesel engine, a band saw, or an assembly line could care less about harmony, proportion, rhythm, coherence, symmetry, or any valorizing criterion drawn from the other arts, say music or poetry or old master painting. In fact, few functionalist architects—proudly declaiming their inspiration by non-architecture—have had the courage of this particular conviction. "Functionalist" architecture has been dominated not so much by a genuine machine "aesthetic" but, on the one hand, by the minimalism of the undecorated and repetitive mass-produced building block (imprisoning some robotic fantasy of subjectivity degree-zero), and on the other, by the aesthetics of a very specific category of machines: aircraft, ships, and automobiles—devices in which there's a premium on the smooth curvatures of hydro- or aerodynamic streamlining. Criticism that insists the Whitney cannot be described sui generis, that the only way in is by comparison to either another kind of building or another kind of object, ends up treating buildings *as sculpture,* as form stripped of any actual function save to be looked at.

The true high-water mark in Whitney-crit has to be Ingrid Rowland's shipwreck in the *New York Review of Books,* which completely drowns in nautical-metaphorical overdetermination. "Piano has repeatedly described the Whitney project as a ship. A native of Genoa, the hometown of Christopher Columbus, he knows a thing or two about navigation; thus his latest structure's similarities to a seagoing vessel are neither casual or superficial." Rowland doesn't actually specify why this is the case, save to suggest that "the building, like a ship, is made of a steel frame, sheathed in steel panels" which, of course, also makes the building a lot like … a building. In the more directly mimetic realm, however, she's more precise: "Approaching from the east side … it looks like a cruise ship." But "from the harbor side … the museum reads as a container ship piled high with the portable freight units, dazzling in their simplicity, that have transformed international shipping." She reminds us too—with weird redemptive imputation—that "the *Titanic* was to have moored just a few blocks to the north (and along this much altered riverside my family and I boarded an ocean liner bound for Naples in 1962)." The metaphor pitches as it burgeons. Rowland writes that the building "was designed from the inside out"—precisely *not* how a ship is designed—claiming that "the interiors make more sense as isolated individual units than as an exterior shell that sometimes looks as stern and irregular as the upper parts of a battleship—for the Whitney Museum is a bit of a seagoing destroyer as well." Cruise liner, containership, battleship, seagoing destroyer: I'm swamped!

But she's barely underway.

Ships must be sleekly streamlined to slip thought water, but the water also buoys them up, cushioning them from the pressures of gravity. In its landlocked position, therefore, the Whitney is another kind of vessel, forced to sustain its stack of containers between land and air; if this terrestrial ship is going to sail at all, it must anchor its airy steel-frame galleries to something substantial.

(By which, of course, she means *the ground* and one hopes the anchoring will be sufficiently robust to keep the building from actually floating away come the next Sandy.) Rowland sails on with her unpacking of this stability/motility conundrum, calling out the building's "array of columns, some hollow some solid" and other structural features, including a concrete core that "rises visibly like a bunker on the building's north side" before declaring that it is precisely Piano's decision *not* to pack the museum's interiors "into a more compact, ship-shape arrangement" that prevents it from having "a more coherent profile on the New York skyline."

The rather modestly described functional gain is that having the "variegated pile of separate pieces is a good-enough solution to the basic problem of showing a great profusion of artworks." Rowland finally concludes that because of the *absence* of "the company of the ocean liners that once docked along the Hudson, slotted into their massive steel piers, the Whitney makes for a more striking object in the cityscape, but it is, despite its bulk, a relatively quiet presence." Rowland works the image to the end— with pauses to describe the "outdoor stairs that deliberately evoke the fire escapes that zigzag across the red brick facades of onetime meatpacking facilities" (this just after describing how the museum's frame has "been painted a pale shade of robin's egg blue, to harmonize with the sky"). She's totally gripped by ships—like that poor soul tied to the mast of the *Hesparus*—and even the Whitney's inconsistencies send her cruising: "On any ship, some decks are more glamorous than others" (that class thing again!), and, on SS *Whitney*, perhaps most fabulous of all is its "concrete heart, where the thrum of the engine room keeps this whole gigantic vessel on course." Well, perhaps not so glam as the eighth-floor café's balcony, "where you can, if you like, stand in a tiny crow's nest and pretend that you are Leonardo DiCaprio and Kate Winslet breasting the North Atlantic from the deck of the Titanic."

Critic overboard! *(2015)*

22

Getting Together

There is no shortage of colossal egos in New York. One of them has a *huge* desire to be president. On October 10, two others, Governor Andrew Cuomo and New York City Mayor Bill de Blasio, put aside their long-simmering acrimony and came to terms about the city and state sharing the costs of the current five-year, $29 billion Metropolitan Transit Authority (MTA) capital plan.

With apologies to the forest, I printed out a copy of the plan and found it to be encouraging and depressing. Those billions are primarily intended to keep the system in a functional state of repair in all its inspirational, if spotty, vastness. Much sleek new rolling stock is to be acquired, but it will mostly replace railcars and buses that have reached the end of the line. Just 20 (out of 469) subway stations will be renovated. A fair amount of money is earmarked for a couple of long-underway projects that extend the system, including the Second Avenue Subway—first proposed in 1919. Service is predicted to commence on part of that line next year, although, as part of the deal, it will stop at Ninety-Sixth Street with completion of the vital segment to One Hundred Twenty-Fifth Street delayed until at least 2020 (perhaps some of El Chapo's people are available to accelerate the job). The other big addition is the "East Side Access" tunnel that will enable Long Island Railroad trains to stop at Grand Central Terminal, not only Penn Station. Altogether, "improvement," as opposed to replacement and repair, amounts to 15 percent of the budget, a respectable sum for a big, old, and long-neglected operation.

Yet for all its urgent remediation of a transportation network marvelous in its extent, the plan's overall philosophy is miserly. The MTA has once again bypassed literal and conceptual expansion of the system in the name of "necessity." It's a plan for people accustomed to hearing the word crumbling right before the word infrastructure, and for politicians who tend to look at capital expenditure on mass movement as either jobs programs (shovel ready!) or merely the means of securing the continued viability of a system ever at the point of collapse. It's also a plan for people who don't question why the private car is still the engine of our national transportation budget. The stupid fracas between New York State and New Jersey over the construction of a new railway tube under the Hudson River, arrested for years by the shortsightedness (masquerading as fiscal responsibility) of Governor Chris Christie, is an especially egregious example of the foolishness in which any big, non-highway public project is held suspect. In China, Japan, and Europe super-fast trains zip from town to town while here Amtrak is perennially derailed. Shanghai alone has built over 350 miles of subways since 1986; during the same period New York City has managed to extend the 7 line by one stop.

The MTA plan is also informed by the larger mentality of traffic engineering, of simply getting from place to place rather than *getting together*, the real basis for mobility. Seeing cities as vast engines of economic productivity, the priesthood of traffic reduces the travelling subject to little more than a package to be speeded on its way as economically as possible. The airlines subtract another inch between seats, subway stations grow ever grottier, and the mediocrity of their design—in one of the world capitals of creativity—becomes more of an affront every day. I'm charmed to see sweet art by Tom Otterness at the Fourteenth-Street A, C, and E stop, but I'd sooner the station be clean and ventilated.

Though it is the work of an old guard, the MTA plan announces itself with some research that makes a remarkably compelling case for expanded investments and the creation of an even larger system. It presents the familiar—if seemingly counterintuitive—statistic that the most energy-efficient state in the union is New York, despite inclemencies of climate and the most voracious consuming class outside the Saudi Royal Family or the Kardashians. This is for one reason alone: its denizens' wildly disproportionate—and rapidly increasing—use of public transport. New York City's low rates of car ownership and predilection for mass transit translate regionally into an annual reduction in greenhouse emissions of around 17 million metric tons, a benefit equivalent to what would be achieved by planting half the area of the state with saplings.

In his delightful new book *Street Smart* (2015), Samuel "Gridlock Sam" Schwartz attributes the brisk national rise in transit use over the past decade (and the corollary decline in the use of private cars) to a particular cultural shift, which he identifies with the so-called Millennial generation. The statistics are persuasive but the cultural account—Millennials' disgust with suburban numbness and endorsement of their own parents' complaints about cars—not so much. Never mind: there's little doubt that postwar youth—a historical concept which must surely embrace us boomers—have acquired a special connection to cities as loci of consumption and conviviality, as antidotes to specifically suburban forms of alienation and anomie, and, most critically, as places where the collective practices of democracy are best enabled. While Millennials may be especially adept at forms of digital assembly, the evidence—from Tahrir Square to Sherry Turkle—seems to be that Twitter merely facilitates the real action, which takes place face-to-face and that, finally, exclusively digital communication is having dire effects on deep sociability and its engendered politics.

The de Blasio/Cuomo deal was negotiated during the mayor's short-lived attempt to rip up the pedestrian precinct that has transformed Times Square into an actual *permanent* public square for the first time in its history. Six years ago, de Blasio's predecessor, Michael Bloomberg (and his remarkably enlightened transportation commissioner, Janette Sadik-Khan), tamed the area's congested streets by installing plazas, first captured temporarily with beach chairs, picnic tables, and planters, now durably paved in stone. Not only did this draw crowds of sitters and strollers; pedestrianization effectively *speeded* traffic, reduced accidents, and increased retail sales and real estate values around the square's periphery. Weirdly, when this remarkable public gesture attracted actual public use—including a proliferation of street performers—de Blasio saw a *public nuisance* and concluded that the plazas had to go. But the mayor was after more than just busker removal. Hectored by police chief William Bratton, he wanted to give Times Square *back to cars*!

A great problem for New York City—and its region—is the fact that its facilitators of mobility—MTA, Department of Transportation, Taxi and Limousine Commission, Amtrak, Parks, Uber, Lyft, business improvement districts, New Jersey Transit, bus lines galore, private cars, Citi Bike, private bikes, ferries, helicopters, planes, elevators, and on and on—operate as fiefdoms. Modal diversity is critical to a metropolis as complex as New York's, but the failure of coordination is pathological (tried to go LaGuardia Airport lately? Across Brooklyn?), and it surely harkens back both to the private, competitive origins of virtually all these systems and to the history of aggrandizement (and control of revenues) brought to such a state of dictatorial perfection by Robert Moses. Why must half the space of our streets be used to *store* private vehicles? Why can't we regulate the numbers that enter our gridlocked centers? Why must a biker take her life in her hands to ride down the block?

There is one absolute in the creation of good city form: giving pride of place to people on foot. This is not simply to maximize individual autonomy (of course, human locomotion must be abetted by freedom of movement and access), but also to assert that the human body remains a fundamental constituent of the body politic, and that any impediment to our capacity to gather must be viewed with deepest suspicion in any part of the city that is public, that belongs to us all. This is not to confuse public space with absolute sanctuary for any activity, although the prejudice must always be for latitude rather than constraint. In general, behavior in public can, as the Supreme Court has repeatedly affirmed, be subject to restrictions in "time, place, and manner." Fighting words, obscenity, too much noise late at night, "purely" commercial activity, mugging, and other departures exceed the automatic perquisites of public space, although the Court has shown both confusion and nuance in parsing this. For example, it has held that the litter that arises in consequence of leafleting is not sufficient grounds for curbing this form of speech.

Perhaps the most frequently cited high court opinion affirming the right of assembly is *Cox v. Louisiana*, decided in 1965. That case arose from a picket organized by a group of civil rights demonstrators in 1961. The Reverend B. Elton Cox staged the protest in front of a Baton Rouge courthouse, and at a legally designated remove from the building itself, where a group of students was being held after their arrest for picketing a segregated restaurant downtown. The protesters and the students joined their voices in song, Cox gave a speech, the sheriff ordered the demonstration dispersed, and, when nobody left, cops teargassed the crowd and Cox was arrested, tried, and convicted.

The Supreme Court, in overturning this verdict, defended the use of public streets as sites for assembly and the exercise of free speech but also affirmed the viability of certain of those time, use, and manner restrictions. Indeed, the majority opinion, written by Justice Arthur Goldberg, stated the no one may "insist upon a street meeting in the middle of Times Square at the rush hour as a form of freedom of speech." The case is controversial. The Court was split five to four, and, according to a much-cited analysis by the late Professor Harry Kalven, the decision was particularly fractured and "bristled with cautions and with a lack of sympathy for such forms of protest." Interestingly, the majority expressed special concern about the implications of the case for labor union rights to picket on public property (Justices Black and Clark cited this specifically, and Goldberg had been counsel to the AFL-CIO).

Kalven writes that the core of the case concerned the question of "whether the citizen using the street as a forum and not as a passageway is making an anomalous use of it." This particular conundrum of appropriate use reached a level of special and especially germane dementia in the mid 1960s when a number of Las Vegas casino owners—including Kirk Kerkorian, Steve Wynn, and that celebrated civil libertarian, Sheldon Adelson—attempted to *eliminate* public sidewalks in front of their establishments, replacing them in some cases with *private* sidewalks, largely in order to thwart labor demonstrations against the non-union shops they were seeking to impose. Indeed, Kerkorian's MGM Grand, after having persuaded the Clark County Commission to allow it to privatize its sidewalks, almost immediately had union demonstrators arrested for "trespass." It's a story that kept repeating itself in front of the Mirage, Treasure Island, and the Venetian, but with results ultimately frustrating to union-busting management, because the courts have consistently ruled, on First Amendment grounds, that attempts to distinguish public and private sidewalks (when, in each instance, they are the *only* sidewalks) are unconstitutional. The still-definitive ruling was handed down in 2001 by the Ninth Circuit in a case brought by the American Civil Liberties Union.

However, the struggle over sidewalks in Vegas continues. Both the casinos and the municipality are trying to figure out a way to banish a cohort slightly more pertinent to the Times Square issue: people handing out leaflets advertising sex services, a shocking affront to the wannabe family-friendly aura of the new Vegas. Privatizing—or eliminating—sidewalks was the initial approach but, to date, this has been thwarted by the Constitution. Other strategies have been contemplated, including attempting to use the 2000 *Hill v. Colorado* decision—which regulated aggressive leafleting in front of abortion clinics via the imposition of an "eight-foot rule"—but this seems a fatuous gambit. And, there are various tricky openings in the laws governing restrictions on commercial speech that will doubtless be explored.

Which brings me back to Times Square. I cross it reasonably often and must admit that I have never been approached by Elmo, Minnie, or one of those *desnudas* the mayor got himself into such a lather about. Indeed, if Nazis can parade in Skokie, I'm not sure why our "progressive" mayor is so worried about the Cookie Monster or the Naked Cowboy. The fracas does seem an especially richly ironic recapitulation: sex is, sort of, back on the Deuce, repackaged for family fun. And, of course, after we've railed for years about the Disneyfication of the place, that politicians are getting their knickers in a twist over the presence of people dressed as Mickey Mouse does seem a bit rich. Finally, the idea of striking a blow against crass commercialism at its very epicenter can only be seen as an assault on the crassness of the small fry on behalf of the supersized. No doubt the city's legal eagles will eventually find a way to corral these prurient affronts.

But there seems to be something beyond prurience that had de Blasio and Bratton going Vegas. Given that Times Square is not only the beloved "crossroads of the world" but also an intense nexus of public transit accessibility (and curses on the truly crappy, incoherent, interminable, and incomplete "renovation" of the station—which doesn't rise to the quality of the public restrooms on the Jersey Turnpike), the mayor's attempt to wipe out the ground-level space of assembly was simply antidemocratic. The reflexive impulse to curb speech by eliminating the space of public assembly both affronts liberty and thwarts the progress made under Mayor Bloomberg in the direction of a system of movement and access that places walkers further toward the top of the mix of motion and rest. De Blasio and Bratton forgot that what happens in Vegas should stay in Vegas.

The Times Square fracas also reflects the myopic failures of coordination in the way the city is planned. The Department of City Planning does nothing but *zone*; the Department of Transportation seems to have lost the will to reconfigure our streets and sidewalks to abet walkers and bikers; the MTA is barely able to keep the system in a reasonable state of repair and the sums spent on a few glossy projects—$2.5 billion for the 7 line extension, $4 billion for the Calatrava PATH rapid transit station, $1.5 billion for the Fulton Street Station—beggar the imagination: nice places but deeply skewed priorities. Estimates for the cost of a mile of dedicated urban bike lane range from about $150,000 to $500,000. Let us assume the extreme top-end, bells-and-whistles version. The $8 billion spent on these three projects could provide 12,000 miles of safe bike lanes. Fortunately, the total length of the city's streets is only 6,000 miles which leaves enough money for ... you do the math!

The streets (should) belong to the people!

Special thanks to Chuck Gardner in Las Vegas, a champion of the First Amendment and the right to the street, for generously steering me to much vital information.

(2015)

23

The Cathedral
at Ground Zero

Proportion—the relationship of parts and wholes—only makes architectural sense when it's joined to scale, the actual dimension of things. For millennia, from Vitruvius to Leonardo to Le Corbuiser, an idealized body has made this connection, serving as the metric for proportioning systems. The commonplace phrase for explaining all this is "human scale," merging aesthetic and practical desires. These are clearly revealed in forms and feelings at the extremity, like the half-height floor in *Being John Malkovich,* too tiny to stand up in, or Albert Speer's Great Hall of the German People, big enough to hold an army and generate its own weather.

That the sweet spot in human scale isn't fixed suggests spaces have to be socially and psychically proportionate, whether to conduce feelings of cozy domesticity or induce shock and awe. The churches built by the conquistadors were meant to dazzle the natives into docility much as the great European cathedrals celebrated the mightiness of the divinity and the smallness of its subjects, dwarfed by vaulted ceilings reaching to the heavens. This capability isn't always negative; it can also celebrate and inspire with grandeur, loftiness, and numinous space without end. Chartres is indisputably fabulous and without it culture would be bereft. But, while it may be wonderful as an architectural absolute—much as the pyramids were to their age or the interstates to ours—a Gothic cathedral's utility is limited by its relative unsuitability for secular purposes. We would not, instinctively, think about building one for, shall we say, the entrance to a local stop on the Interborough Rapid Transit. Or would we?

In Flaubert's *Dictionary of Received Ideas* (1913), the entry under railway stations states, "Always go into ecstasies about them: cite them as models of architecture." With the completion of Santiago Calatrava's Oculus—the remarkable creature at the World Trade Center that's effectively an entrance pavilion for the PATH transit station and several subways—the utility/expression chestnut is set for a thorough roasting. Finally open after a decade of construction and the expenditure of at least $4 billion (including $665 million for "administrative costs"), the Oculus is at once incredible and infuriating. It's a black hole for bucks, a stunningly autonomous monument, and a medium of displacement—a vortex that's absorbed the creative energy that might have been expended on its surroundings (the vanishing Ground Zero arts center or those mediocre office towers) or elsewhere (a new Penn Station and Port Authority Bus Terminal, the renovation of 500 subway platforms, or the desperately needed renewal of the system's creaky nineteenth-century technical infrastructure and frail capacity). The Oculus struggles to symbolize both the purity of its strictly artistic utility (which is to say, its lordly *functional* superfluity) and something more cosmic still.

Calatrava has produced a building that is singular but not recondite, a train station *and* a cathedral. It's a glistening white steel ribcage, 160 feet high and 365 feet long, enclosing a nave-like space with a volume greater than Grand Central Station's, and a singular surmounting crown. Dense rows of vertical ribs alternate with lofty glass to envelop the great room and then turn outward to become gigantic spikes—pituitary versions of those radiating from the Statue of Liberty—that fly away from the building like enormous porcupine quills or the bones of a pterodactyl's wings. The mixed metaphor (it's a bird, it's a plane, a phoenix, a stegosaurus!) locates the irresistibly biomorphic character of the building and its formal originality: it's a real rara avis, albeit one with a strong family resemblance to other members of the Calatrava bestiary.

The Oculus sits at a canny remove from scenes of both spirituality and mass movement, at once neutralizing and absorbing their purposiveness. The 9/11 Memorial pits and a new Greek Orthodox church (also designed by Calatrava) are not simply across or down the street but inaccessible from *within* his gleaming lantern. This arm's-length distance makes the Oculus's spirituality pagan: it occupies the space initially meant to have been evanescently illuminated by Daniel Libeskind's Wedge of Light, a marker of time offered as equivalent to Abu Simbel or Stonehenge but trivialized by the banality of the erstwhile framing and enabling office tower architecture that contrived its solar slot. Likewise, the Oculus is not exactly a train station but a centroid that organizes pathways to a series of more autonomous stations at varying distances and relations, a distributed aggregation of tracks that may equal Penn Station's but which, individually, are miniatures in relation to the huge space. Much of the energizing power of the Oculus comes from this disproportion: the enormous and beautiful un-columned space that shelters the little stairways down to the five tracks of the PATH, with the Broadway Local crossing overhead in a massive tube supported by monster trusses.

But let's set aside the "build a battleship or 10,000 schools" argument that's been at the heart of virtually everything written about the building to date: that argument is both conclusive and concluded. Instead, let's consider the poetics of its assembly and tectonics. I really *like* the fantastic big beast as both object and space, and already feel sad about its imminent squishing between the two crappy towers that will flank it. If only it could just walk or fly away! In fact, Calatrava had originally wanted its wings to flap, animating the animal, and I sympathize with his disappointment that this motility was value-engineered into stasis.

Calatrava is both beloved and reviled for the anatomical literalism of so much of his work: the balance, joinery, rigidity, and rhythm of the skeletal. Because the Oculus is so expressively "ornamental"—larded with enormous, and not so enormous, flourishes that do nothing but please the eye—it fudges the boundary between architecture and sculpture: it's *architecture in an expanded field*. The building begs some of the same questions as the work of that high priest of art-world avoirdupois, Richard Serra, which demands to be seen as more than merely sculptural in its modulations of space and passage, and also derives much of its power from the threateningly massive heft of all that corten steel. As with the Calatrava, much of the impact of Serra's sculpture has to do with the chest-thumping *weight* of those torqued ellipses and precariously leaning, *dangerous* walls. But Calatrava and Serra riff differently on functionalism's asymptotic parsimony: with pieces like Tilted Arc, Serra goes for the massively minimal; Calatrava madly multiplies structural members and coyly conceals and reveals which ones are actually bearing the load.

The very careful—even maniacal—engineering of Calatrava's designs suggests a crucial difference with Gothic cathedrals. Although they frequently collapsed during, and after, their construction, those churches were far and away the most structurally advanced architecture conceived for a period of close to two millennia, right out there at the edge of the possible. Their height, span, complexity, and *lightness* were amazing and —given the pure seat-of-the-pants, trial and error, structural calculation involved—astonishingly daring. Despite its visual and spatial affinities, the Oculus behaves in quite another manner. Calatrava, who trained as both architect and engineer, has always stressed the expressive import of structure, most famously in his often-magical bridges and stations, works which embody the engineer's highest technical and artistic aspiration: the succinct economy of "elegance."

By these lights, this bird's a turkey. It's so expensive, heavy, and dense with structure, so excessive, and so willing to blur the line between the functional and the decorative that understanding it in terms of the prosody of its own construction also requires an accounting of its extravagance. The design of the Oculus is not simply highly conservative in terms of its relationship to risk (balancing risk and means is the key dialectic of structural performance) but is flagrantly, *expressively,* profligate in its conservation of materials, an inescapable responsibility in any twenty-first century construction. According to the *Times*, the amount of structural steel used to construct the transit hub weighs in at a humongous 36,500 tons with more than 15,000 plus going to the Oculus alone and another 12,000 to the PATH. This aggregate is roughly comparable to the "mere" 40,000 or so used to build One WTC, the continent's tallest building. The distinguished structural engineer Guy Nordenson argues that this gives Calatrava's building what may effectively be the largest carbon construction footprint per unit volume of any building on the planet. And—Donald and Bernie take note—all that steel comes from Europe!

But let us say for the moment that there is some virtue in extravagance, and that the Oculus has redeemed the artistic potential squandered at Ground Zero. And let's further assert that vast expenditure on public works is a hallmark of a great civilization and that the game's not zero-sum, that the savings that might be realized by removing a quill or two would not be applied to a supportive housing project in Brooklyn, that the thing can be artistically judged sui generis. Still, the time and expense laid out *do* count in that critical calculus: after all those years and cash, the thing should be close to perfect. Here arrive my reservations: I find the Oculus tremendous and beautiful but *not quite right*. I am disturbed that, about two-thirds of the way out on the rows of quills, there's a steel tube that joins them all together, a stiffener and a spacer. Really? Billions spent on that imported steel and those ribs cannot fly solo? And what about the funky fireproofing that kills the precise angularity of the metal beneath? And the proliferation of inaccessible beams and crannies that are sure to turn the pristine thing into a permanent museum of dust?

As structure, the building is made like a bridge—although it doesn't function like one—and perforce becomes a slightly ironic reflection on the techniques of bridge building. Each of the long sides of the building holds a structural arch, and the huge ribs that appear to support these arches lean in to provide a hybrid of walls and roof, before—as they pass the line of the arch—taking a dramatic outward turn to form those sideways soaring wings/ quills, a pure, flamboyant, "superfluous" expression, although weighing thousands of ornamental, structurally challenging tons. However, although the arches are symmetrical, the quills are not: each side is different, reversing the pattern of the other. This eccentric loading and the variable length of the ribs as they rise to meet the curve of the arches mean that much computer power has been spent on the design of the hidden base: an oval tension/compression ring embedded at grade that acts as the bottom chord of a giant Vierendeel truss to stiffen those walls against the wind and for self-support.

The most self-consciously witty aspect of the structure is the continuous, operable, glass skylight that runs the length of building's ridgeline, forming a gap between the two arches (for my money, this should have been left unglazed like the eponymous oculus in the Pantheon in Rome). These are actually joined, and carried, only at their ends, where they land on massive buttressing knuckles, the push-me, pull-you, beasty heads through whose mouths the building is entered at street level. The long sky-lit slit defies the visually induced expectation that the *ribs* are holding things up and that the two long sides of the building should therefore be joined together across this seam to form a series of A-frames, a very sturdy and conventional configuration that would be made stronger still by the arches linking the row of frames together. The absence of this joinery reveals that the arches really are bearing the load that one assumes is being carried by the ribs. One imagines, too, that the ribs and flying quills are in near equipoise, relieving the expected rotational stress on the ring-base caused by those long cantilevers. Calatrava gives plenty of further hints about the limited role of the ribs by not bringing them down to the lowest level of the building and instead delaminating and bending them into a rhythmic filigree, a curlicue caesura that appears (there's a winking gap that belies a hidden flange) barely connected to the walls! Here Calatrava plays cheerfully with the line between the fussy and the butch, deliberately marking his system—in which the transfer of the load is often hard to follow—as very different from the compressive clarity of a cathedral's buttresses, which bulk up progressively as they head earthward and plunge resolutely into the supporting ground.

The Oculus is further distinguished from Chartres in its organization of movement. The main circulatory action in a cathedral is singularly directional. Enter at the back of the nave, move toward the altar, pray, reverse. There's generally a secondary route around the perimeter—lined with shrines, confessionals, fonts, chapels—that can be accessed without traversing the main axis (an array prosaically repeated in the Oculus with a two-tiered ring of shops). Whereas cathedrals—towers and crypts notwithstanding—are invariably slightly elevated continuations of the ground plane, the primary grade of the Oculus is two levels *below* the street. The privileged movement plane is subterranean, and the Oculus functions diagrammatically as the head of an octopus with tentacular extensions radiating to four transit nodes (including the much more concentrated nexus at Fulton Street, its own ambitious dome made ever so sad by the drama down the block) and to the lobbies of surrounding buildings, often over fairly long distances. And, unlike a cathedral, for which the ground is a single plane, the multiple levels of this space are inelegantly joined by a plethora of escalators and stairs that look seriously under-scaled. This is nowhere more unsatisfying than at the ends of the nave where entries from ground level lead to klutzy cantilevered escalators that, switching back and forth, are more tease than celebration of the glorious axial view. Many wedding couples will be photographed on the intermediate landing.

I admit to being among those who'd argued for a no-build solution at Ground Zero, for turning the entire site into a great space of public assembly—a wanton display of democracy's greatest physical freedom. My concern about the partition of commerce and commemoration is not relieved, alas, by the final results. However "spiritual" Calatrava's astounding building may be, thick demising walls separate, without acknowledgement, the money changers from the more literally sacred environment of the adjoining temple—the memorial and museum. All those glistening Italian marble corridors that the Oculus organizes are lined with retail, retail, and more retail, their deluxe white in blinding contrast to the memorial's somber black. Conceptually, the complex is a glorious reinstatement of exactly what existed there before 9/11: an underground shopping mall brought to us by our old friends at the Westfield Corporation. Step aside, Woolworth Building: this is the true cathedral of commerce!

And yet ... I was able to tour the site a number of times during construction, and the sheer ingenuity of the logistics and the fiendishly complex technicality of dealing with the massive ruin, with trains that ran across the site without surcease, with an astonishing tangle of infrastructure, with the mammoth twenty-four-hour movement of people and materials—this is a breathtaking achievement. Perhaps it's the dedicated workers and engineers, who made this transformation possible and whose contribution invisibly undergirds all that hypertrophied form rising above the surface, to whom we should truly turn in gratitude, admiration, and celebration.

(2016)

24

A New New York, the Same Old Story

When our family first got television, the program we most faithfully watched together was "Sergeant Bilko" starring the immortal vaudevillian Phil Silvers—the legendary "King of Chutzpah." The show ran from 1955 to 1959 and was set on an imaginary army base in Kansas, where Bilko ran the motor pool, presiding over a motley crew of characters who engaged in antic, if penny-ante, schemes of advantage and insubordination. Our favorite member of the platoon was the hapless Private Doberman, a lovable, remarkably homely schlemiel played by Maurice Gosfield. In one sublime episode it's announced that Doberman will receive a visit from his sister, and Bilko—somehow persuaded by the mantra "the uglier the brother, the more beautiful the sister"—prepares for a rendezvous with carnal destiny. She turns out to be Doberman's identical twin.

Needless to say, the "sister" is Gosfield in wig, dress, and heels. It's an image that—in one form or another—constantly returns to me when looking at New York City's recent architecture. The "renaissance" that has brought us our current boom in starchitect building reflects a refinement in the global real estate market in which status is attached to this giant inflection of the "name" brand. While architecture has always been an aspirational object of consumption, the winds of fashion have truly reached gale force of late with the creation of an international market for replicate luxury goods, whose broad track embodies the homogenizing logic of planetary neoliberalism. Here, the emblematic emporium is the airport duty-free shop, its shelves groaning with product that is at once pricey and commonplace: Dior, Gucci, Prada, Glenfiddich, Cohiba, Burberry, Godiva, and so forth. In the architectural world, an upper-crust mobility formerly the province of interior decorators has spread to a cohort of jet-setting architects. (By comparison, deluxe practitioners of the past century whose brands continue to sell in New York—McKim, Mead, & White, Rosario Candela, or Emery Roth—were fundamentally local or national practices, and their currency was not so easily convertible.)

The sheer visibility of this transformation is astonishing and now dominates much of Manhattan. The gaze over Chambers Street from our bedroom window in groovy Tribeca encompasses an exemplary devolutionary prospect. From right to left I see the apartment building where Herb Muschamp and my friends Satya, Vyjayanthi and Sundar used to live: the fifty-four-story Tribeca Tower at 105 Duane Street, built in 1968 to designs of the prolific SLCE (erstwhile Schuman, Lichtenstein, Claman, and Efron, the journeymen behind a multitude of starchitect construction documents as well as their own galaxy of commercial blah-chitecture). Although extruded straight up, 105 is articulated in plan to produce some ins and outs—including bay windows—to variegate views, and to give a little extra shape to the smallish, cookie-cutter rooms within. Next door is John Carl Warnecke's 1974 windowless pink granite monolith for phone company switches, allegedly built strong enough to keep pre-cellular land and sea lines open should an A-bomb fall in the neighborhood. Shaped in a largely vain attempt to make itself less looming, the structure tests the envelope of the "sculptural" in architecture, probing the meaning of form which is virtually bare of any content save raw enclosure. It does provide neck-craning befuddlement to many out-of-town visitors who can't comprehend what it can possibly be and an abashed admiration for its maniacal indifference.

Next over is Herzog and de Meuron's just-finishing tower at 56 Leonard Street, a formal and conceptual hybrid of its two predecessors. Admittedly a pretty winning object from many angles and robustly *now*, it still feels like a period piece, stylistically very much of the era that produced the Tribeca and Tel towers, sharing exposed slabs and infill with the one and formal, push-pull moves with the other. Certainly, the conceit of stacked boxes is very sixties (think Rudolph, think Safdie), and whenever I look at it I feel myself carried back to the pre-computer studio of my own architectural education in the day. Equipped only with Mayline and Rapidograph and influenced by the relative ease and "objectivity" (all dimensions to scale) of the style of projection, I did many a project in axonometric drawings and 56 Leonard looks for all the world like it was designed that way too. This reciprocal relationship between form and representation (currently embedded in palaver about the deeper meanings of "parametric" design) will recur until architecture—via its increasing preoccupation with appearances and branding—finally arrives at a state of total virtuality.

These three Dobermans—built over a span of forty-plus years —almost completely describe our current architectural repertoire and suggest the essential irrelevance of trying to unpack its meaning via purely visual standards. From my perspective (supine, in bed), the treble towers all have exactly the same effect: subtracting sky from the view. While the Leonard Street shaft might look great *somewhere else,* it lacks fundamental urbanity, a sense of cooperation and comprehension, of situation. Like the blight of super-tall towers in Midtown, it's all about seizing views both from within and from a distance, the narcissism of privilege: look at me looking at you. On the street, its effect is clear in the hip Downtowner's lament: gentrification. While many deride this as the mating call of the limousine liberal, the process on the ground is the core site of the criticism's value. American liberalism understands the good society—and the good city—as a place of mix, where opportunity is not simply aspirational but everyday. These buildings reduce mix to a single class (business class!) of both subjects and objects, subtracting its most vital dimension: the social.

Chambers Street is itself a fine register of this kind of winnowing. Bisecting the island from the Municipal Building to the Hudson, it crosses virtually every subway line in the city, and the stations along its length disgorge the daily ebb and flow of commuters who work in our civil service, a model employer offering opportunity to an authentically diverse population. It's contested territory, and the rising gyre of rents victimizes predictably but not a little inscrutably. Is there really so much custom for mani-pedi that the street can support a salon per block and many more on streets nearby? And that big new "European" waxing parlor—who goes there? I get the high-end restaurants and the high-volume fast-food places down by the community college. Certainly the persistence of those holes in the wall that couldn't support a use beyond the sale of gum and lotto makes sense. But in the more mysterious ebb and flow of discount stores, sports bars, dentist's offices, and military recruiters, the street offers a fine archaeology of our cultural economy and its fine-tuned sensitivity to the circuit of capital. Gone are the hot dog stand and bodega and hardware shop. Welcome the oligarch-funded condos and ten thousand Miele appliances!

If the aggressive stylishness of the 1 percent is the most visible manifestation of the tectonics of the income gap, the most important effort to bridge it is the attempt—first in the Bloomberg administration and now more ardently in de Blasio's —to promote housing affordability via the medium of "inclusionary" zoning. The strategy is at once heroic and depressing: Heroic because it is an honest effort to protect and to house a population at risk of being completely priced out, citizens who have every right to share the city and on whom its functionality depends. Depressing because even should the effort succeed to the max, there will be a net loss of affordability as the market devours opportunities at a far faster pace than losses can be replaced. And still more depressing because of the Peter/Paul deal making that pervades the mentality of so-called "public-private partnerships," as if that principle weren't the fundamental basis for our democracy.

It's a very Republican mentality, the idea that every endeavor, whatever its value may be beyond the bottom line, must be subject to an extremely localized test of its ability to, in effect, self-finance. The results range from the construction of condos in the middle of the new Brooklyn Bridge Park to the weird—and resisted—hybridities that are bringing "market-rate" housing to the surplus terrain of our Housing Authority projects and to struggling neighborhoods where there remain questions about both the profitability of such building and, conversely, about whether the price increases it might bring will do more harm than good to the existing supply of affordable housing nearby. It's also the motivating idea behind the legion of business improvement districts and conservancies (classic cases include the Grand Central Partnership and the Central Park Conservancy), self-taxing schemes for "public" improvements that disproportionately favor rich neighborhoods.

New York's architecture has long been founded in a dialectic of form and formula. Gaming the system—whether via the kind of subsidies and tax benefits that have so benefited the Family Trump and other developers or in the morphologies that emerge from canny manipulation of the arcana of the zoning code—continues to produce works of both genius and horror. Our urbanism, for both better and worse, is exactly one of negotiation, the architecture of the deal, and the deal is always between public and private interests. While this is right and proper, the question is always who holds the strongest cards. The deck continues to be stacked against the public and the sum is never zero.

(2016)

25

Manhattan Transfer

"Follow the money" is the immortal, if apocryphal, phrase uttered by Deep Throat, offering the key to unlocking the mysteries of Watergate. Understanding cities requires similar forensics. Urban morphology maps the flow of cash with concrete precision and the New York skyline is a literal bar graph of investment and return. The manufacture of real estate (what some quaintly refer to as "architecture") is our leading industry and the art of the deal the epicenter of our creativity. Money not only talks, it *designs*, and "planning" in most American cities is almost entirely devoted to refining the process of spatial arbitrage.

There's a project underway on the Manhattan waterfront that spins this tangled web with a remarkable combination of clarity and opacity, exposing the freakish, calculated collusion of intentions and outcomes that shapes the city. The story begins in September 1985, when the death knell was sounded for Westway, a lunatic land manufacturing scheme to shove the Manhattan shoreline four hundred feet into the Hudson all the way from Fortieth Street to the Battery. Beneath this massive fill was to have been embedded an interstate—the most expensive per mile ever constructed—replacing the terminally rusted West Side Highway. Planners were *looking for* the most extravagant scheme possible and were strongly supported by public officials (including Rockefeller, Koch, Cuomo the Elder, and Moynihan), the development community, and the construction unions.

Visionary rhetoric and seductive greensward images notwithstanding, it was all about the money: the Feds would have picked up 90 percent of the $2.1 billion ($10 billion in today's dollars) price tag and the resulting 220 acres of new real estate—100 for a park and the rest a free-fire development zone—would have been the most spectacular piece of physical fiscalization in the city's history. But if the magnitude was singularly impressive, the impetus was widely shared. Cities all over the country had been committing urban suicide—ramming highways through their yielding tissues (often of color)—to get their hands on that government cash, and New York—cresting in the Robert Moses era—had been an absolute champ.

Westway was opposed by a coalition of environmentalists, mass transit advocates, community activists, and progressive pols but was finally killed by a federal court ruling that its sponsors had failed to consider the landfill's potentially adverse impact on the Hudson's striped bass population. This narrowly decided opinion nevertheless proved a turning point in the urban highway wars: in its aftermath, Bella Abzug–sponsored legislation allowed a trade-in of highway money for mass transit (to the great benefit of our subways, buses, and pedestrians), and other cities—from San Francisco to Seattle—began tearing down their waterfront highways, a continuing trend.

Today, instead of Westway, we have a surface "boulevard" that—if billions cheaper, tree-lined, and lit by ornamental luminaires—is still too much of a surrender of this precious edge to traffic. Along the road's waterside, though, runs the lovely, if incomplete, Hudson River Park which—while far from big enough to meet demand—offers great pleasures as it struggles toward durability and completion. Instrumentally, the park both reproduces and inverts the Westway principle. Westway proposed to use public funds simultaneously for public benefit (a highway and a park) *and* to create opportunities for the accumulation of private wealth, which would, in theory, yield further public return in the form of income from land sales and real estate taxes. The current park, on the other hand, although built substantially with public funds for public use, is not exactly a public work, inasmuch as it is obliged to finance its own future by directly attracting private capital. This parlous paradigm of the "public-private partnership" has, in our Republican age, become the default strategy for "public" development and has deeply embedded the culture of the trade-off (literal pay-to-play in the case of the park) in our civic life.

The genius of progressive taxation for "general revenue" is that, in theory, it embodies that equitable proposition, "from each according to his ability, to each according to his need." If the US system is wildly distorted on both collection and distribution sides, ability and need are nominally meant to be determined democratically. Unfortunately, when democracy lurches toward plutocracy, the distortions on both ends grow to the inevitable detriment of public needs. As the system becomes more and more regressive, the question of public benefit is increasingly situated in the elective territory of philanthropy—optional altruism—rather than collective responsibility. A tax code designed to favor private fortunes (with the corollary commonweal reliant on trickle-down) begs the question of their public disposition: ceding this to individual interest, itself answerable to charity, guilt, avarice, deductibilty, and political power in varying degrees, depending on whether the fortune belongs to the Koch brothers, Bill Gates, Andrew Carnegie, sundry Rockefellers and Fords, or the Clinton Foundation. The demonization of shared—"redistributed"—wealth is a trope as abiding as it is rank: one reason that Bernie was ultimately unsuccessful is our generalized hostility to high tax. Scandinavian-style "welfare states" (every citizen a welfare king or queen!) and the sapping canard of the individual initiative-killing effects of "hand-outs" from big nanny.

Even in "liberal" New York, we've long since internalized Trumpism as policy: everything's a deal. "Return" on public investment must not simply be quantifiable (gross municipal happiness anyone?) but literally *monetized*. This calculus under-girds the arcane systems of swaps and bonuses that radically territorialize and delimit our practices of urban planning and improvement, with the result that we now insist that virtually every public enterprise demonstrably *pay for itself* (save, of course, warfare—although Trump's neo-imperialist, spoils-to-the-victor proposals might bring this, too, under the umbrella of self-finance). Thus, instead of public construction of housing we have inclusionary zoning, instead of public education we have charter schools and rising college tuition, and instead of public healthcare we have the confusions and insufficiencies of a rapacious marketplace. And, littering New York, we have those oxymoronic POPS—"privately owned public spaces"—a sad archipelago of plazas and lobbies (Trump Tower's among them!), purchased in a currency of lost light, air, revenue, equity, and pride.

Any trade begs the question of who gets the better of it. Are the view-blocking luxury apartments now built in its midst too high a price for the excellent Brooklyn Bridge Park? The conundrum lies less in the answer than the question, with its predicate in a fragmented, discontinuous idea of public space. Its further, and all too legible, implication is that the location and quality of such spaces depend on their realization in places where they can graft values from *already successful* environments nearby. Precisely because the investment is both self-serving and easily recouped in the vise of adjoining real estate prices, private money pours into Central Park, those condos go up in Brooklyn, the High Line flourishes, and Barry Diller wants to build a Fantasy Island on piles in the Hudson—just beyond the window his office—in the "undeveloped" waters between the piers of the park.

Like Brooklyn Bridge Park, Hudson River Park is administered by a trust, a legal arrangement in which someone's property—in this case New York City's and New York State's—is managed by someone else. The Hudson River Park Trust was created by the state legislature in 1998—during the Pataki administration —and is nominally controlled by a thirteen-member board of directors, five appointed by the governor, five by the mayor, and three by the Manhattan borough president. The Trust's board, however, is backed by another larger and perhaps more important one: the self-perpetuating "Friends of Hudson River Park," charged with fund-raising for ongoing construction and maintenance and largely comprised of investment bankers and real estate types (as well as—for cultural leavening—Martha Stewart and David Chang, of Momofuku fame). Both boards are dominated by Madelyn Wils, the Trust's president and CEO since 2011, a shrewd and well-connected operative with long executive service on the city's Economic Development Corporation, the Lower Manhattan Development Corporation, and—as chairman—Community Board 1, in lower Manhattan.

It has fallen to Wils to deal with the fact that the park, legally obliged by the terms of the trust to self-finance, is stone-broke. Her duties thus include not simply supervising the operation of the park but, most crucially, fulfilling the Trust's mandate to "ensure the park's future financial self-sufficiency by developing the remaining commercial nodes." These "nodes" include both the actively commercial piers under its control (the Chelsea Piers sports complex, the New York Waterway ferry terminal, the Intrepid Air and Space Museum, and so forth) as well as the unrealized potential of other undeveloped piers (or deals for new ones like Diller's island). Its largest such asset is the fifteen-acre Pier 40, former terminus of the Holland America line, which occupies a charismatic spot between Greenwich Village and Tribeca, west of burgeoning "Hudson Square," an area recently rebranded and rezoned to incite development and supersede its industrial past by attracting "creative" and tech uses, luxury housing, and a froth of Portland-sur-Hudson amenities to go with. Pier 40 currently accounts for approximately 30 percent of the Trust's revenue—mainly from parking nearly 2,000 cars (a truly idiotic use for one the city's most wonderful sites)—but is crumbling and urgently needs extensive rehabilitation. It's best known by locals for holding several large—and much beloved—playing fields in an area that is one of the most underserved with recreational space in the city. Cash must somehow be milked from this alpha cow.

Thus, on her arrival, Wils and Board Chair Diana Taylor took control of the then-moribund "Friends," loading it with wealthy donors. This move was not without turbulence, including the 2012 purge of uber-developer Douglas Durst (who did not go quietly), nominally over a fight about the Trust's intention to build housing on Pier 40, which Durst thought might be more profitably exploited by something more commercial. Indeed, over the years, a variety of contentious schemes for the pier have been mooted, including construction of offices, housing, shopping malls, theme parks, a permanent home for Cirque du Soleil, more parking, the expansion of NYU, and other not-exactly-park-like uses.

However, this being New York, the pier also offers possible monetization through the sale of its very *lack* of development: by cashing in on its air rights. The main impediment to this has been that New York's air rights regulations restrict their transfer to another site *within* a single block or zoning lot, technically obliging the pier's rights to be fully exploited on the pier itself. Reenter the state legislature. In 2013, the Hudson River Park Act was amended to permit the transfer of the park's air rights (in toto around 1.5 million square feet) to "receiving sites" within a zone a block deep on the *other side* of West Street, the park's landside boundary, running from Fifty-Ninth Street to Canal Street. This amendment was crucial both in establishing the park's most potentially lucrative revenue stream and in enabling a particular deal already in the works between the Trust, the city, the state, and a consortium of developers (one of whom—Michael Novogratz—who subsequently and profitably sold his share—just happened to be the *chair* of the park's "Friends"): the transfer of 200,000 square feet of development rights to a site directly across West Street, now occupied by the ginormous, three-block-long St. John's Terminal Building, erstwhile end point of the High Line (and, interestingly enough, with Bloomberg LC its major tenant).

Throughout this multi-party negotiation, the key intermediary was the PR firm of James Capalino. Capalino is a long-time donor, fundraiser, bundler, and pal to Bill de Blasio who, in 2015, somehow made more money ($12.9 million) than any other lobbyist representing clients to the city. Capalino is much in the news these days, implicated as the fixer in the lifting, by the city, of a deed restriction on the (now former) Rivington House AIDS nursing home on the Lower East Side, allowing it to be converted to upmarket condos. Capalino represented the building's owner—VillageCare, a nonprofit—which sold the building to the Allure Group, a for-profit nursing home company that, with the restriction lifted, flipped the building to the Slate Property Group, realizing (per the *Wall Street Journal*), a profit of a cool $72 million. Capalino now works for the Chinese developer Dalian Wanda, itself a partner of China Vanke, part of the consortium that bought Rivington. At the end of August, de Blasio—although claiming to know nothing about the deed deal approved by his administration—cut his erstwhile fund-raiser loose: "I have not been in touch with Mr. Capalino ... I do not have contact with him anymore."

According to a timeline put together by the excellent Danielle Tcholakian of *DNAinfo* based in part on documents obtained under Freedom of Information Law requests, Capalino e-mailed First Deputy Mayor Anthony Shorris in late January 2014 (just after the mayor's inauguration), with a copy to Carl Weisbrod, who was himself appointed commissioner of city planning *a week later!* The e-mail:

> Tony, for the past twelve months, my firm has been working with Madelyn Wils on a proposal to secure a $100 million contribution by our client, Atlas Capital, to the Hudson River Park Trust to fund the cost of rehabilitation/stabilizing Pier 40 for continued recreational use. We are in discussions to have the residential project over St. John's Terminal become an ESD (Empire State Development) project through a State sponsored general project plan.

In fact, the Trust, Empire State Development, and the developer had *already* inked a secret memorandum of understanding in December of 2013 that fixed the scale of the project and the $100 million price for the enabling air rights. According to *Crain's New York Business*, this had been signed-off on during the waning days of the Bloomberg administration by Robert Steel, the deputy mayor for economic development. Bloomberg (as well as Wils and Weisbrod) apparently also supported the use of the "general project plan" to be overseen by Empire State Development, a process which the developer was eagerly seeking (via copious lobbying by Capolino's firm) as a means of circumventing the city's more rigorous Uniform Land Use Review Process (ULURP), an end-run the developer believed could save many years (and bucks) in obtaining approvals.

Negotiations between the state, city, Trust, and developer—lubricated by the continuing ministrations of Capolino—were proceeding briskly in camera until May of 2015 when the secret memorandum of understanding became public. Consternation from Manhattan Borough President Gale Brewer ("Shocked is an understatement for how we all felt"), Assembly Member Deborah Glick (a leader in the fight against building housing on the pier itself, but also an original sponsor of the Albany transfer legislation, believing it the only hope for saving the pier), the media, and the public, resulted in an about-face by the de Blasio administration—with the immediate agreement of the developer (who clearly knew who his friends were)—to renounce the memorandum and the General Project Plan route, and to go through ULURP.

ULURP—now nearing its conclusion—runs a statutory 200 days from the submission of the developer's plans and Draft Environmental Impact Statement. During ULURP, these are reviewed, successively, by the affected community board (CB2), the borough president, the City Planning Commission (which is obliged to hold a public hearing and did so on August 26), the City Council (which *may* hold a public hearing), and finally the mayor. The community board and the borough president are authorized to make recommendations (including rejection) but these are entirely nonbinding. The Planning Commission, the Council, and the mayor have actual power, but, in the case of this project, the planning commissioner, the ambitious local council member Corey Johnson (who now has great position in the endgame), and the mayor have long since come out in strong support of the deal, and it's unclear whether pushback from CB2, Borough President Brewer, a few members of the Planning Commission, and many in the community (including the energetic Greenwich Village Society for Historic Preservation, which has been trying hard to use the deal to leverage its own struggle to preserve a large swathe of Greenwich Village just north of the site) will materially affect the final outcome. Indeed, their concerns had little impact on the Planning Commission, which in October of 2016 voted to approve the project without substantial modification.

Since the proposed development departs radically from the site's existing zoning, the Department of City Planning (a government agency that reports to the politically appointed City Planning Commission) prepared a revised zoning map to define a "Special Hudson River Park District" that could receive—and advantageously use—the transfer by greatly increasing allowable bulk, changing designated uses, permitting additional parking, and building in exceptions to the "contextual" strictures that govern the scale and character of construction nearby, including those revised to create the Special Hudson Square District a block away. The parameters of the new receiving site, to the administration's credit, would also bring the project under the mandatory inclusionary zoning regime, which obliges the developer to provide a meaningful percentage of affordable housing in the mix but which also further ups the site's permissible bulk. The end point of ULURP is approval, rejection, or modification of these zoning changes, which—if passed—will provide the legal space for the deal to be consummated.

And the project? Its design is a particularly ripe variation on the "form follows finance" mentality at the core of the way New York City plans and is larded with bluff (a big box store, vast amounts of parking, extremely tall towers, plus a truly grotesque "as of right" alternative scheme (a standard-issue developer threat that could be built without special approvals, should this deal come a cropper). The plans have been skillfully reverse engineered from the Trust's primary imperative to realize the $100 million from the deal and are driven by its better-get-it-done-now recognition that public resistance to any further transfers into CB2 will be strenuously opposed, ditto possible transfers to other communities elsewhere along the waterfront. Indeed, recent pushback to the plan from CB2 and the borough president has specifically demanded that transfers from the park to the adjacent neighborhood be strictly capped at 200,000 feet.

Architecturally, the plan (albeit the work of good architects) is a bad one, both in its general outlines and in its particulars. Most strikingly wrong is the almost complete disconnection of the special district—on which would rise by far the largest project *ever* constructed in CB2—from its surroundings (including Pier 40 itself), and its total failure to anticipate and guide future changes, including the much-wished restoration of the street grid obliterated by the St. John's Building and by the equally long, single-story, UPS facility running parallel in the blocks behind it. The vigorous development taking place on all sides (as well as future advances in logistics technology) will eventually create pressures on UPS (and nearby FedEx), and provision should surely be made to restore the streets now erased, and to think about—to *plan* for—what will happen on these newly created blocks, including parks and schools.

The plan placed on the table was clearly an opening gambit, stuffed with calculatedly negative capability in the form of too much stuff but also with a series of artful deficits that might open avenues for more positive demonstrations of cooperation. For example, the public space component is, by the developer's own arithmetic, so sparse that the project will produce a net *decrease* in local public space per capita. The draft environmental impact statement is also deeply suspect and blithely concludes that this humongous erection will have virtually no seriously adverse impacts on traffic, solar access, public services, and other critical infrastructure. Equally irresponsible is the developer's long-standing resistance to including a school to serve the kids among the thousands of new residents. Finally, the plan is noncommittal about its internal distribution of the mandatory affordable dwellings (as well as the actual degree of their affordability), although it appears they're going to be primarily small units for seniors and concentrated in a single building, facing the UPS garage. (The presentation package—full of street-level perspectives rendered to obscure the mammoth bulk of the buildings looming out of frame—disingenuously depicts a rare apartment at the back of the building with a water view through a wee gap in the surrounding condos.)

All of these issues might be addressed in a revised proposal and both CB2 and Borough President Brewer have demanded adjustments. But there's a sad, deckchairs-on-the-Titanic quality to even the strongest of these, which, in the end, fall for the plan's artful misdirection. The salient, undeniable fact is that the project is *vastly* over-scaled. The tallest of its towers—at 420 feet—is three times the height of the surrounding built texture and certain to have a deeply deleterious and distorting impact on the neighborhood that it and its companions will overwhelm. The complex will also irrevocably alter the profile and rhythm of the Hudson riverfront as a whole, a contemptuous interruption in a continuous—and historic—low- to mid-rise skyline that now stretches uninterrupted from Chelsea to Tribeca. An authentically "contextual" solution would simply extend the scale of the existing street wall, which tops out at around fifteen stories. Urbanistically speaking, this is clearly the right way to go.

In the report issued by her office, Brewer tellingly—if somewhat wistfully—observes that, given the city's reliance on private development for the direct financing of public facilities, "the developer has a private interest that is paramount to any public interest." Yes, and? Alas, no public body or official seems willing to walk away from the specific public return on this expression of private interests: the $100 million for Pier 40 repairs, the "up to" 476 units of affordable housing, the now-rejected curb on further bulk transfers into CB2's backyard, and support for landmarking the nearby South Village, a decision that rests with another, nominally independent, agency. As the negotiations enter their endgame, a variety of predictable gambits are being played. Westbrook Partners, the majority stakeholder (Atlas still holds a minority share), has just let it be known that it's "rethinking" the project because of a weakening in the residential market and might be forced to revert to a purely commercial, as-of-right, scheme.

More, *Crain's* reports that Westbrook is actively looking for an equity partner for the site, which both suggestively reinforces the threat to abandon residential use entirely and almost certainly reveals the real plan beneath the plan: to get approvals for the maximum project and then flip the whole thing and walk away with the cash.

The public-private daisy chain keeps yielding moments of delirious, if nauseating, irony. The City Planning Commission (chairman, Carl Weisbrod) held a hearing on September 19, during which a few minutes were devoted to listening to the responses of the Department of City Planning (director, Carl Weisbrod) to questions raised about the project at their August meeting. A visibly nervous planner from the Department was obliged to present her answers to a body presided over by her boss, the man who had been most instrumental in structuring the deal now under review! And, while we're still in ironic mode, there's another I find especially hard to overlook: the projected cost of Barry Diller's little entertainment island has now reached $200 million. The design (by Thomas Heatherwick) is tasty enough but the money would surely be better spent (and the island's entertainment program easily accommodated without displacing the ball fields) were it to be used on Pier 40—100 million for repairs, 100 for theaters and trees. And, Diller would have an irresistible counter to Doug Durst, who has been biliously bankrolling lawsuits to thwart Barry's plans, out of some truly pathetic billionaire pique.

I make this suggestion seriously as one of a number of ways to manage and coordinate both direct investment in the park and the sale and use of its air rights. Another would be to expand the Special Hudson River Park District to encompass Hudson Square (and the UPS site which will surely be transformed at some point) and to radically disaggregate the 200,000 square feet into much-smaller increments that could be added as a series of bonuses to the ongoing wave on construction in the area. Yet another would simply be to gerrymander a 1.5-million-square-foot skyscraper (or add just a few additional stories to several already proposed) into the thicket of towers under construction in Hudson Yards further uptown, an area already given over to large-scale building and one that has a huge underbuilt perimeter (including the Javits Center) into which even these enormous numbers could easily be made to disappear.

Our representatives should steel themselves and fight for the big picture, for something much better than this too-many-eggs-in-one-basket contrivance. The project is far, far too big for the bearing capacity and character of its site, and nibbling at the edges of the design—reducing parking, slightly shrinking a tower, eighty-sixing the big box that everyone knows is only there to disappear, redistributing bulk a bit, getting a few more affordable units, adding a wee plaza at grade—will make little real difference. If public money cannot be made available for maintaining the public park (or housing the poor), the question of the fungibility of air rights—if that is to be the Trust's primary asset—must be regulated with much-greater invention and subtlety: having crossed the West Street Rubicon, there's no reason this conjured property "right" cannot be more broadly and appropriately distributed. Indeed, the question of the creation and deployment of these rights lies at the very core of the way in which we define public space. It's our air, after all!

The complete failure of the Department of City Planning, the Trust, or any other public (or quasi-public) body to formulate a rigorous, sustainable, and beautiful plan for this part of town is simply dereliction. Not only have they acquiesced in a completely barse-ackwards mode of defining and financing genuine and general public interests and slighted a truly collective—and expansive—vision of community needs, benefits, rights and desires; their "spot" planning mentality totally ignores a truly mammoth elephant that stalks the room: the inevitability of sea level rise that will almost certainly inundate this low-lying place, piers, special districts, underground parking, twee little shops, and all. While our public servants blithely order another cup of bouillon, an iceberg looms on the horizon. Time to change course!

It's not too late! While the City Planning Commission has voted to approve the plan almost entirely as originally presented, the Council (which tends to defer to the local member) and the mayor can still intervene, although de Blasio is unlikely to oppose a creature he was so instrumental in stitching together. The Commission altered the scheme only in cosmetic or predictable ways: the Big Box is now gone as are the "public" bridges over Houston Street. The developer has also agreed to provide 10,000 square feet of subterranean recreational space that would be publicly "available" on unspecified terms. A little more open space is to be squeezed in at grade. However, no modification of the project footprint was demanded to reconnect the street grid, no guarantees were offered about a cap on transfers into CB2, no reduction was made in height, and nothing was said about the larger context of the project, including the form and use of Pier 40 or the character of the extended neighborhood.

As part of the deal, however, the South Village Historic District has been placed on the Landmarks Preservation Commission's agenda at its regular November 1 meeting for a vote to "calendar" it, launching a process of hearings, deliberations, and possible designation that can last as long as two years. It's likely to be fewer, as the professional staff at Landmarks is expected to offer a strongly favorable recommendation to the commissioners. Although the precise manner by which the exquisite timing came about remains murky, the agreement to hear the case was surely the result of strong—and long—advocacy by the Greenwich Village Historic Society, CB2, Council Member Johnson (who now holds a great many cards), and others; and Andrew Berman, the energetic Director of the Historic Society (with Johnson's apparent support) has threatened to fight to derail the project should the South Village landmarking fail to go forward. Courage to them both! And to those who are opposed to dumping any further floor area ratio into CB2 and to all who advocate for more public space, affordable housing, and rational planning.

Yet, whatever the outcome of the landmarking gambit, the fundamental contradiction at the heart of both project and process looms huge, both literally and conceptually. I've met virtually nobody with a non-financial stake in the new building who supports it as a piece of architecture or planning, simply as the formal resultant of a negotiation for *something else*. This is the heart of the deal: the inevitability that there will be winners and losers. The developer wants to build a gigantic project and has surely calculated its return with precision, using a knowable metric of profit. The city—in all its roots and branches—is obliged to a far-more-notional heuristic for determining the cost of our benefit. Would it be a good deal if it only produced the hundred million for the pier? The hundred million plus the affordable housing? Pile repair and housing plus the South Village Historic District? Should the developer be offered another 100,000 square feet to build a school? To decrease the building footprint by going higher still?

That we have tipped so far to inducement rather than obligation as a planning strategy is a tragic, indeed Trumpian, marker of the decay of the commons. This collusive failure of imagination, responsibility, and democracy is staggering, if all too typical. Time to demand a vision that grows from our shared "right to the city," planning that looks beyond a contracting, bottom-line approach to the possible and sees our architecture not simply as an outcome but an aspiration.

No deal!

(2016)

26

Preserving People

New York's most important piece of preservation legislation was passed in 1942: our rent regulations. These laws were designed to offer tenants additional security during wartime, to protect them from economic travail and dislocation as they bent themselves to a collective—and urgent—good. In 1947 the regulations were institutionalized in their current form. What was literally "protected" were rent levels, but what was effectively secured was tenure. Although winnowed, our rent controls continue to be bulwarks of community, cementing diversity and thwarting destruction of human habitat: these laws landmark lives.

Our architectural landmark laws don't. Even district-wide styles of preservation are enabled almost entirely by purely formal criteria and by a preference for memory over vitality. Ancillary impacts remain a matter of dispute. Developers and owners resent the implicit "taking"—seizure of property without "just" compensation—when the law forbids them to demolish or alter their buildings. Others argue that these protections have the opposite effect, serving as fulcrums for gentrification. The law itself—and the commission that extends it—are little interested in the lives currently led or the fragility of the human ecologies that inhabit these places. Indeed, a recent attempt by a group from my own, heavily landmarked, neighborhood to argue for the enlargement of the district, based on the prospective inclusion of a large number of long-standing rent-regulated tenants whose buildings would be saved from demolition, was met only with indifference.

But the law, in its conception, does offer some slack for extra-architectural considerations. One of the most recent landmark-ings in New York was the Stonewall Inn, a little building of no special architectural quality that was the scene of the Stonewall rebellion, a heroic moment in the struggle for LGBT rights. Here, the commission held that the *events* that had taken place at the inn were so consequential that it deserved protection. In effect, the Stonewall was accorded the status of a battlefield (which, indeed, it was)—the setting for "great" human occurrences. And the commission has also been ready to extend the mantle of consequence to scenes that are more generally emblematic. Tenement buildings have been preserved. The Garment District—where remnant manufacture is under the squeeze of sky-rocketing rents —is up for discussion, and the arguments for its importance already far exceed the architectural.

But how to measure such non-architectural significance? Clearly, one key to an expansive view is that what's commemorated is often collective: the Stonewall triumph or the Triangle Shirtwaist fire tragedy were about groups of people. We readily preserve the homes of seminal individuals and the sites of their accomplishments, transferring the auras of both lives and events to the material settings in which they unfolded, and the principle is easily expanded to embrace both larger cultural forms and expressions: New York already preserves districts found beautiful or "historic" in ensemble. Landmark laws celebrate non-architectural human accomplishments by protecting the physical environments that sheltered—even nurtured—them. Even when their design is ordinary, certain classes of buildings are held, via this transference, to possess rights, principally the right to remain, itself an enshrined *human* right. This enfranchisement of the inanimate might disquietingly remind one of the weird outcomes of the Supreme Court's *Citizens United* decision and its conclusion that, from a legal standpoint, corporations are people. While this surely seems to be a promiscuous category error in its sinister displacement, it's not an entirely unfamiliar one. The standard of venerability, for example, is a widely felt, even reflexive, source of respect for both people and objects, and the idea that a collective entity should have some of the privileges of an individual is not bizarre.

However, the nuance in the distinction between preservation and conservation (the latter understood as the tool that enables the former) suggests that national parks are a better model than battlefields for thinking about the application of landmarking to neighborhoods that are still dynamic but threatened by other (mainly market) forces. I can recall a trip to Kraków, where the Jewish quarter is "preserved"—including kosher restaurants (with ersatz "Jewish" waiters)—in the virtually complete absence of Jews. The conservation of the ghetto is both a form of guilty redress and a particularly grotesque example of the meaning-stripping, neutron bomb approach of traditional architectural preservation. The real question is not whether preservation laws can cast the past in amber, but whether they can help protect real neighborhoods without looting them of life.

Although the original intent behind the national parks may have been couched in a combination of cultural, scopic, and romantic regimes, it has secured these territories not simply for spectatorship but as *ecologies*. We defend them in this complexity via the extent of their space, via the prohibition of activities thought inimical, and via various practices of "conservation"—some of which (like firefighting) are arguably forms of interference with "natural" processes. But the very size of the parks—their real vastness—surely suggests that much of what they preserve is quotidian, that they are fields of diversity with an ark-like aspiration to taxonomic comprehensiveness for all of the nature within them—something that was, at the time of their founding, conceived as fundamentally other than human and required protection from our instinctual rapaciousness. (The meaning and intent of contemporaneous Indian "reservations" is another subject.) But people are organisms too, and the city is our increasingly predominant habitat.

The exteriors of approximately 33,000 buildings are land-marked in New York City, but only slightly more than 100 interiors are protected. This divide is clarifying, reflecting not only a reticence to interfere with private activities (and an attempt to divorce architecture's public, civic face from them) but also a useful means of exclusion of their *current* uses from the preservation agenda. It's time to re-understand the remit of landmarking in a way that embraces far more than artistic criteria and to give it a robustly sensitized role in how we plan, making it part of the toolkit of techniques we use to cultivate and protect our indigenous urban life-forms. That is, we must make preservation alive to the "internalities" of its too-purely architectural preoccupations.

Which brings us back to rent regulations. New York—like the rest of the planet—is caught up in a radical and growing inequality, which manifests itself as, among other things, a crisis in housing affordability. Our municipal administration is struggling to expand opportunities both by increasing supply and by preserving existing sites and strategies. In too many ways, though, our landmarks policy contradicts this larger policy of social preservation. Is it absurd to think that these two ambitions might be harmonized? Alas, the opposite seems to be happening as the city deploys the blunt instrument of increased density to create added real estate value that it will then attempt to capture as trickle-down to fertilize its social programs. Meanwhile, precious buildings are saved, but the benefit to the environment is, more and more, reduced to mere prestige, camouflage for the cruel cleansing of gentrification. It is time to link architectural preservation to human preservation. Neighborhoods are people too!

(2017)

Elsewhere and Otherwise

27

Need to Know?

We're suffering from a surfeit of information. It isn't simply that we're lost in a deadening deluge of tweets and texts, that elevators and airliners are filled with people chained to their devices, endlessly transmitting and receiving useless data—honey, we're pulling up to the gate; honey, the door is open; honey, I'm on the jetway—the real problem is that the wrong people are producing and manipulating too much information.

This begins with the "state" and its surrogates but extends to a series of shady parallels deployed by self-interested individuals and corporations, entities that increasingly have human rights and characteristics: as Mitt Romney reminds us, corporations are people too! These increasingly use our private communication as the means of acquiring ever-enlarging dossiers of data not simply on our habits, preferences, and proclivities but on our real-time behavior, our location in space, what we're eating, saying, buying, doing, feeling. Where once we feared the growth of the surveillance state, we now find that the government is merely the tip of the iceberg, taking semi-pornographic snapshots of us as we pass through the airport security screen, but basically fronting for the corporate data mining that grows exponentially out of control. The sainted Steve Jobs utters a coy "oops" when it's discovered that our beloved iPhones have been covertly fingering our movements for the benefit of a more perfect market. That's the way the cookie crumbles!

I was writing this on the day the papers trumpeted the "taking out" of a couple of Americans—Anwar al-Awlaki and Samir Khan—in Yemen, the latter primarily for the expression of free, if hateful, speech. The papers reported the spot of the assassination with crosshaired precision but were discreet about the secret installation from which the drone began and ended its mission, "somewhere on the Arabian Peninsula." The murderous robot is accorded both freedom of movement—the most "architectural" of our rights—and complete privacy, while the rest of us are endlessly situated and stripped, deprived of our most fundamental freedoms in service of somebody's idea of the greater good.

Some years ago, I started a nonprofit and engaged an ex-student of great computational skill—a first-order netizen—to collaborate in its work. After apparently suffering an oedipal crisis in which I became the object of his rage, he disappeared precipitously and set up a practice with virtually the same name as my own. From this position, a stream of denunciations were issued as were projects that shaded work we had been doing for years. His "practice" multiplied under name after name designed to create confusion with the original, and he dogged our every move with threatening letters and viral bile on the net. He retained a private detective to harass colleagues and friends with defamatory suggestions about me and my project, and in the last month we have been obliged to devote many hours getting counterfeit Facebook and Twitter pages removed from the web. I have, to my great chagrin, acquired my own private Javert.

The point is that the power of information is not a neutral matter: the putative leveling of the playing field has tremendous potential to distort. While not everyone, as I have, has had to deal with the problem of lies and defamation posted in the guise of objective information on his or her Wikipedia page, we are all paying the price of the social insinuation of information that is skewed or mendacious, information that eludes the checks and balances that are natural to democracy or even sound academic practice. I know that this complaint walks on thinnish ice and that the clarion call for information to be free is something we accept as an item of faith. But we also have to remember the old saw about the press being free if you happen to own one, and that this empowered age, in which a raging adept—in Yemen or Brooklyn—can so exponentially multiply a lie or a threat, is one in which the connection between freedom and responsibility must be defended, insisted upon, addressed.

In particular, the question of the simulacrum in the era of Photoshop seems to very deeply problematize such questions, and this has been recognized for over a century—articulated as this replacing that (per Hugo), the work of art in the age of mechanical reproduction (per Benjamin), and other anxious formulations. Our response to this loss of "authenticity" or "aura" cannot be a doubling down on the slippery slope of the infinite malleability and dissemination of texts and images: the exponential expansion of the field of access begs an elastic relativism where the fact of a post or a picture is assumed to have authority simply because it exists. We risk a Great Soviet Encyclopedia of the mind, an instrumentalization of the truth in which it will cease to be verifiable by anything but prejudice, special pleading, or the empty attractions of the image. The degree to which our public discourse is fogged by Holocaust and climate change deniers, by birthers and creationists, by aggressive ignorance and lies, by a free-floating malevolence that defies understanding, is scary as hell, and the time may come in which we are all marked and circled by our own dedicated Predator drones or adolescent assassins.

Our problem is not the lack of an answer but of an audience. Sorry to say, but the information age demands of us that we increasingly recognize that there are limits to tolerance. The politics of information forms up in the cultivation of an intolerance of lies, an insistence that the great parity engine of the net is, in fact, an instrument increasingly dedicated to the occlusion of importance, to the proposition that every stupidity and lie should find an advocate, that what assumes the *form* of an encyclopedia perforce compiles the facts, that an algorithm that simply multiplies has the weight of evidence, that morality is a purely private matter, that the freedom to hate is absolute.

As architects, our first obligation is to the idea that the environment can be made better and that this improvement can be more and more inclusive. But we mistake our project if we fail to understand that the physical environment is sited in the human, that we shape ourselves first. Our power is rooted in our ideas, and there are good ideas and bad. We should inform both ourselves and the world of the difference.

(2011)

28

A Reminiscence of Hollin Hills

Like so many others, my parents moved to the suburbs from the city to fulfill a fantasy of better living. Fantasies are historically produced, and the one that drove them to Hollin Hills was surely very much of its time. They would have a space of their own, their little increment in the American territorial project. The climes would be healthful and the child would have the freedom of the yard, the neighborhood, the woods and pastures beyond. The school would be decent and the neighbors convivial sharers of these values.

And there was that agrarian fantasy—partaking in perhaps equal parts of Thomas Jefferson, Theodor Herzl, and Marie Antoinette—of raising up a crop of carrots and azaleas, making that bare hilltop bloom, sitting down to dinner to consume a salad raised by the sweat of their brows. And mine. They were remarkably committed to this, and gardening—the creation of their own private state of nature—consumed a major portion of their leisure time. This was always somewhat mysterious to me—dreading as I did my role as reserve labor army, pressed into onerous duty weeding (most horrible) or lawn-mowing (a little more Zen). Better were the trips across the street and under the barbed wire to fetch pails of manure from Popkins Farm, which still functioned as a dairy during much of my childhood, although it was many years ago, alas, parceled into lots for decidedly un-modernist McMansions.

Those houses, with their traditionalist styling and little windows, were flagrantly other, not simply in terms of a battle of architectural styles, but in occupying the landscape differently. One of modernism's best fantasies—and one that surely characterizes the architecture of Hollin Hills—was of the free flow of space within buildings and the breakdown of the distinction between inside and out. This idea—and the means by which it might be realized—arose from many sources. The early modern movement and its extravagant simplicity was founded in reaction to the stifling, overstuffed interiors of the Victorian and Edwardian eras and against forms of domesticity that were seen as hierarchical, rigid, uncreative, oppressive. At the same time, the very idea of a distinction between the city and the country was being questioned—by Karl Marx among others—and this historical trend toward the urbanization of the countryside had a reciprocal effect in the rise of the idea of the garden city— proposed most famously by Ebenezer Howard—as an antidote to the industrial metropolis, a new kind of place where these old distinctions dissolved. Undergirding this all was the Romantic movement's religion of nature, which itself was intertwined with the birth of the practice of landscape architecture in the eighteenth century, modernity's true point of origin.

The idea of the superior virtue of "getting back to nature" depended, of course, on this invention of the *idea* of nature and exponents of the superiority of the "simple" natural life—from Rousseau to Thoreau to William Morris to Grizzly Adams to the Unabomber—have been somewhat split as to the architecture appropriate to being at one with the great outdoors. Likewise, modern architecture's relationship to the natural—one of its sturdiest tropes—worked its way into design in a number of ways and via a variety of means. The branch of the family that produced the houses of Hollin Hills descends from another great eighteenth-century creation: the greenhouse. Enabled by the manufacture of glass in large quantities and at low prices, greenhouses proliferated wildly toward the end of the eighteenth century, culminating in the erection of Joseph Paxton's immense Crystal Palace for the Great Exposition in London in 1851. As constructions, the more—er—garden-variety green-houses were like Hollin Hills houses in their use of walls of glass supported by lightweight, modular frames. Of course, the genius of the greenhouse is not simply in its transparency but in its ability to flip the relationship of inside and out—the garden is now within—and in their ability to defy climate, to produce the tropics in Kew—or Kiev.

The invention of the greenhouse also parallels the rise of landscape architecture in the project of domesticating nature for purposes of art and enjoyment. (We have been domesticating nature for purposes of food, fiber, and fuel for millennia.) In the, as it were, potted history of landscape architecture I was taught in school, there's a primary split between two styles of this domestication: the English romantic manner and the rationalism of the French, the one favoring the look of the wild, with its ha-has and ersatz ruins, the other the rigid order of geometry and topiary discipline, trees trimmed to resemble Platonic solids—boxwood cones and spheres and cubes. The organization of American space has long been engaged in a sometimes-tense dialectic between these spatial outlooks. Jefferson, our premier exponent of the rationalist side of the Enlightenment, divided the expanded American territory into a mile-square grid, perhaps the most prodigiously successful—and visible—spatial act in the history of consciousness. This Cartesian ordering was not simply about disciplining space but about understanding the nation as a map of property, prepared in increments ready for transaction. The commissioners' plan of 1811 that laid out the New York City grid obviously moved in this same spirit, with its rigid organization of both city blocks and the building lots within them: divide and prosper. The New York plan, however, left a remarkable exception at its core, the great void that was to become Central Park.

It is here that the heroic figure of Frederick Law Olmsted must be introduced, the man who—with Calvert Vaux—not only realized Central Park but who founded the American paradigm for artificial nature that dominates our consciousness to this day. His ideas of a mingled informality and precision descend in a fairly direct line to Dan Kiley, who inspired, and in many cases designed, the landscape of Hollin Hills, a remarkable piece of work in which each house was equipped with a plan meant to induce—via cooperative adherence to what was suggested in his drawings—the growth of the development into a seamless landscape whole. While obedience to the precise details of these plans has been spotty, the overall spirit has surely emerged, producing a reading of Hollin Hills not as a series of bounded lots but as a single park space into which houses have been placed. This insight is very much of a piece with a number of park-like development ensembles done by the Olmsted firm in the late nineteenth and early twentieth centuries, which, in effect, reconfigure the dualism of Central Park and the grid into a unity.

To me, this is what was always most remarkable about Hollin Hills. If you look at a plat of the individual lots, god's little half-acres, you will surely see the divisions that are characteristic of contemporaneous suburban development, much of which is, like Hollin Hills, organized with topographic informality, cul-de-sacs, and curving streets. But in the actual version of Hollin Hills in which I grew up, the increment of property was repressed, the boundaries blurred in favor of the space of a single landscape, augmented by parks that insinuate greenery, foment collectivity, negotiate sensitive topography and hydrology, and buffer the community from the olde-colonialoid weirdness beyond its bounds. This fantasy of an innocent state of nature, not inappropriately, gave children particularly privileged access to its flowing space, and we were habituated to vectoring ourselves across lots, using yards, not streets, as our primary circulation armatures, at least when we were on foot. Hollin Hills was a pedestrian paradise for those who were least equipped to motor, and we wild children felt especially free.

As a semi-communal experiment buttressed by the vibe of nature, Hollin Hills was also an inheritor of the specifically American version of the garden city movement, exemplified most classically in Radburn, New Jersey and the small number of greenbelt towns built during the New Deal—including Greenbelt, Maryland. A number of early Hollin Hills residents were émigrés from Greenbelt, who, in the prosperity of the postwar, sought out the possibility of a house and yard, moving on from Greenbelt's apartment units and more-thoroughly collectivized green spaces but still retaining the vibe of progressive planning. And, it's surely true that modernist architecture, self-identified with that same progressive political project, was attractive to those who thought that way. The remarkable liberalism of Hollin Hills, at least in the early days, was certainly attributable both to the look of the architecture and to ideas about planning that celebrated the collective, the common ground of the landscape as defining the nature of what it meant to settle together.

My mother subscribed to the *New Yorker* to her dying day and grew up reading the Skyline column, written by Lewis Mumford. Mumford is a key figure in the development of the garden suburb—or what might better be called the planned community—and stands in a line that includes Olmsted, Ebenezer Howard, Patrick Geddes, Clarence Stein, Henry Wright, and the big interwar movement for the idea of regional planning; she was, apparently, the driving force behind our move to Hollin Hills, winning out over my father who apparently had the retrograde desire for a basement. But it was always clear that both of my parents moved to Hollin Hills in search of an idea about community that was predicated both in the rationality of planning and in a kind of repudiation of the messiness and, for them, claustrophobia of city life. It's an idea I share—as an idea—although I am confronted by an urbanist's horror vacui when I hit the burbs, even my beloved childhood home.

There is, of course, always at least a little trouble in paradise. As an architect, I am very fond indeed of the elegance of the houses—especially the big butterflies—of their very sensitive siting, the efficiency of their internal planning, and, indeed, the expansiveness of the views they provide. But they are—and here I will insert the obligatory remark about mid-century modernism—very much of their time in their overly abstract relationship to the natural environment, something understood perhaps too much in terms of its visuality. In truth, from the perspective of what we know about sustainable construction nowadays, the houses are problematic: almost uninsulated, those expanses of glass creating insane solar gain, the little, low-operable windows not making much contribution to cross ventilation, and—of course—an entire community predicated on using the car to shop, get to work, go to the movies, for nearly everything. Interestingly, the absence of sidewalks in old Hollin Hills—and the tenacious resistance to their installation—acted, I think, as a kind of displacement, a further ruralization of the garden city idea to get around its special fetish for separation of vehicular and pedestrian "traffic." The Hollin Hills fantasy was that there was actually *no* traffic. But finally, in its real and total dependence on the car, Hollin Hills is a suburb like any other.

And yet, it is also a suburb like none other. A suburb full of beautiful ideas.

(2012)

29

Back to the Burbs

I grew up in the suburbs and so address this gathering with a combination of expertise and jaundice. In fact my experience was in many ways pleasant, due in large part to the specific character of the suburb in which I was raised. Located in the then-bowery and semi-somnolent climes of Fairfax County, Virginia, the development of my youth—Hollin Hills—was an island of modernity in the rising tide of cookie-cutter split-levels. Designed by Charles Goodman with a landscape plan by Dan Kiley that included extensive community parks and green buffers, the place was almost apparitional in its otherness and, to many in the area, somewhat threatening. Begun in the late '40s, its frank and glassy modernism attracted a particular breed of buyer, educated and liberal (although one must remember that the model liberal government agency in those days was the CIA, and we had many neighbor spooks).

This sense of exceptionalism—and beleaguerment—gave the place identity and deepened bonds. There arose both a community of interests and a kind of compensatory communalism that did not exactly derive from spatiality but certainly had it as one of its roots. This sense of shared social, political, recreational, and organizational interests was continuous with the idea of

The brief for the MoMA show and conference at which this chapter was presented took the form of a platonic dialogue.

modernity—and its communal aroma—expressed in the architecture. There was a "sitter's pool" for collectivist babysitting, a lively newsletter, a swimming team, collective picnics, amateur theatrics, and organizing for Adlai Stevenson. A feeling of galvanizing otherness was reinforced both by a sense of political isolation in an era when Jim Crow was a local default and by a certain indifference from the organs of local governance. When surrounding roads were running smoothly, snow remained unplowed for days and days in Hollin Hills.

Of course, it was not. In the early days there was a restrictive covenant on deeds that lasted well into the 1950s, when a house was finally sold to a black neurosurgeon. Later Roberta Flack lived down the street. There were many and refined struggles over the dream at the nexus of the formal and the social. A faction that wanted squash courts in addition to the shared tennis courts and swimming pool was spurned for the elitist vibe of the game. Sidewalks were rejected as a denial of the (new) frontier fantasy. And, the design committee that vetted the numerous additions for compliance with the overall architectural tone was not always a source of harmony. On the other hand, the widespread building of additions—and some houses were multiply expanded—was a sign of literal and conceptual investment in the community, and a dedicated and creative response to the fact that many of the houses started small and to the tractability and flexibility of the type. While I don't compare this to other self-help paradigms—like the romanticized squatter settlements that so figured in the thinking of my generation—I do feel that the idea of formal, social, and functional malleability is a key to the prospects for the utility of the suburban.

But let's step back for a minute. Since this has been billed as a debate, I think I am meant to represent the view that there is something irretrievably failed about the suburbs, and I'd like to work through the brief for the dark side with which, I must admit, I have some sympathy.

Pure Evil

I am awake—insomniac even—to the possibility that the American suburb is the breeding ground of a terrifying malevolence. When I cruise these places, part of me believes that each basement rec room holds its bound and bleeding JonBenét, that *Fatal Attraction* bunnies boil on every stovetop, that kids contemplating Columbine lurk in the shadows, that spousal abuse in perverse profusion abounds, that George Romero zombies await behind the bushes for the fall of night to their move on the mall. The diffuse and leaky spaces of suburbia, the failures of comfortable enclosure and propinquity, the nonadditive quality of the strip, the communities gated against a spectral other— all stoke a sinister disquiet. I remember too that during the Cuban missile crisis, when the debate blew about whether one would shoot the neighbor trying to get into the bunker where one's nuclear family was sheltering from the nuclear bomb, the suburbs felt like a homeland of holocaust. Angry at my parents' seeming sangfroid, I went out to the yard and began to dig.

Alienation Factories

Between the mother's little helpers and bowling alone, the suburbs are a petri dish of anomie. We all await the far-too-long-delayed return of *Mad Men*, which is, inter alia, a rumination on suburbia at its high point. Natty admen and their alienated wives drink gallons of martinis to numb the pain of seething meaninglessness. Ties fray and temptations are taken. The routinized behaviors of getting and spending, Little League and PTA, accumulate into a lexicon of nothingness. It is clear that people are unhappy in the suburbs, and only a chosen class—men—is liberated to voyage to the fulfillments of the city. Even these, though, are often illusory because the pact of eternally trivial pursuits—and advertising is surely the ultimate expression of the truly empty—has been signed and signified by that ticket punched to Greenwich every evening, save those when escapist betrayals are consummated in town. Listen up Socrates, the mall is not the agora.

Racism and Regulation

The suburbs were, of course, the destination of white flight, and the dire binarism of sprawl and urban renewal is their expressive morphology. The veteran's benefits that stimulated the suburbs' rapid postwar growth were restricted to whites and sealed the bad bargain. That the suburbs effloresced on a rhetoric of freedom and autonomy persuaded tens of millions that that was actually what they were experiencing. This idea that freedom was the reserve for the white chosen also reflexively produced the penal stylings of urban housing projects (let us remember that Athens ran on slavery). The two models had many formal affinities, with a predicate in the idea of single uses, schematically separated: housing in its isolated estate, shopping clumped in dogmatic concision, work at a distance or not at all. And to the monochrome of race were added the exclusions of class. Just as the suburbs were carefully segmented by incomes, so too the architectures of urban renewal were meant to reify the economic isolation of neighborhoods of color. Likewise, the suburban "neighborhood" school was code for segregation, and the redlining of the "slums" served to buttress schools that were deeply deficient in quality, resources, and variety. Interestingly, the post–*Brown v. Board of Education* remedy for the segregated schools of suburbia was the introduction of that quintessentially urban modality: public transportation, in the form of bussing.

Here, though, there has been some progress both in the recycling of the inner ring for a far more mixed population and in the slow progress of integrating the middle class itself. At the end of the day, this late buy-in to the historic spatial practice of middle-class America has to be seen as a step forward, as must the reoccupation of the city center by the children of those who had fled.

Distended Infrastructure

A standard-issue critique of the suburbs, but a telling one, is the analysis well made by Myron Orfield in his classic *Metropolitics*

(1997) and by others in the simple proposition that low densities produce higher infrastructure costs. This is surely true and represents one of the innumerable subsidies that give the lie to the delusion that this pattern somehow embodies the Jeffersonian fantasy of free yeopersons sitting securely in their sustaining increments of property. But here is surely the site in which there is an opportunity for meaningful reform that computes on the sides of both equity and sustainability. The most-easily argued logic of densification may not be social (at least in the psychological sense) but economic, a way of more efficiently marshaling resources that are growing more scarce and expensive. That the social life of the street may flourish is a corollary that cements but does not animate the deal.

Creature of the Car

I recently saw a fine film about Victor Gruen, erstwhile father of the shopping mall (*The Gruen Effect*, 2009) that was awash with footage of the high-suburban days of the 1960s. The scenes of roads crammed with cars were amazing, mesmerizing, weird. The Baroque excesses of the automotive stylings of the time were totally mind-blowing and it's hard to believe that I grew up in the midst of this particular taste culture. For all their charm, these gas-guzzling, unsafe-at-any-speed, what's-good-for-General-Motors behemoths harbinger the death of civilization, the clotting of the planet by a technology that has outgrown its usefulness.

The history of the modern city is fundamentally predicated on a game of catch-up played with movement technologies that were invented with no thought of their impact on the cities they would serve. The industrial city found its form around the demands of the railway, which propelled its vast extension but had dire local consequences: the vast cuttings and yards, the belching smoke, the fire and noise, the other side of the tracks. The same is true of the car, another vehicle for the annihilation of "traditional" urban values—the easy adjacencies, the pleasures and practicalities of the street and its life. Cars demand suburbs, the material condition of their easy operation. The automotive system is an efficient distributor for a population living in points fixed and dispersed, but density renders it dysfunctional. The successive scaling-up of the system into trunk roads and highways was never able to keep up and, in its distortions by the compressed diurnal cycle of commuting, only operated against its inner logic as a system designed for an even equilibrium.

Certainly the strategies of suburban redress must include a serious critique of the car and its environmental and human inefficiencies. Ongoing attempts to reconceptualize the suburbs in favor of a pattern of "transit-oriented developments" are surely on the money and, indeed, seek to repattern suburbanism along the lines of one of its originary motivators, the streetcar, itself the victim of a conspiracy of automobile and oil-company collusion. What's good for General Motors and Standard Oil is frankly not good for us. But we should also remain wary of any technologically based magic bullet: high-speed rail is not urbanism.

The Hidden Subsidy

Although the suburbs are bruited as the quintessence of Americanness, an alleged compendium of individual responsibility and resistance to the interventions of the collective, this is a shuck, camouflage for the massive public subsidy that sustains them. It's a typical bit of Republican hypocrisy, the idea that your subsidy is socialism and mine is simply priming capital's pump. The suburbs were produced by a variety of handouts, government interventions designed for a dramatic reconfiguration of American space. Low-interest FHA loans, mortgage deductibility, accelerated depreciation on commercial property, direct subsidies for road construction, and the endless dough required to sustain sewers, electric lines, and other infrastructure all provide disproportionate advantage to the pattern of sprawl. Socrates and Glaucon have made similar observations, and I do understand that this project seeks to nurture publicity in the field of the private.

Not the Least Green

Again, density and cooperation are the sine qua non of sustainable urban form. In their patterns of distribution, movement, and consumption, the suburbs are an affront to all that is green, despite the camouflage of all that lawn, however xeriscaped. The car truly is the villain of the piece, the enabler of the suburban habit. It is a technology that has run its course, and not simply because it is part of the ozone-depleting, cancer-inducing petrochemical system but because it commands spatial practices that are simply no longer sustainable on a planet of almost 7 billion souls. Compaction and convenience are the quintessence of green urbanism, and the car and the suburbs are the enemy.

Festering Swamp of Ill Health and Indolence

The exponential postwar growth of the suburbs correlates precisely with the rise of the televisual system. Indeed, the suburbs represent a kind of cultural and morphological pixilation of their population, a series of bounded monads that collude in producing meanings that always wind up, on the one hand, as an argument for stasis, and on the other, as a series of incitements to consume, to make the system go, through sallies to the mall to stock up on the massively processed provisions that will allow the domestic economy to thrive in its passive, interiorized, couch-spud way.

Our grotesquely obese and afflicted population has been gestated not simply by the generally purposeless character of our national culture, and by its appalling disdain for intellectual and other socially beneficial forms of human achievement, but also by the styles of indolence inscribed by the suburban televisual-automotive-consumption apparatus—increasingly the American raison d'être. We are alienated from the body, which becomes a symptom to be cured only by the futile but hugely profitable ministrations of the diet, gym, surgical, fashion, and lifestyle industries. Does anyone doubt that the reduction of walking to a species of entertainment, the elevation of the tube (and its exponentially growing web-kith) to the absolute default for the intake of information, and the pervasive isolation of suburban life have had a dramatic disembodying impact, that life has become more and more virtual, that we are prisoners in a system that relegates us to farther and farther recesses of a chain of mediation, leaving us ever more remote from the individual bodies and minds of our neighbors?

The Suburb Is Not a City

For a final point, let me intercede with my old drinking buddy from the Hemlock Tavern, Socrates. I've been arguing that the suburbs are not a species of the city, however degenerate, but its antithesis. Claims for the idea that they represent a variation might either come from a statistical conceit based on contiguity or, conversely, from the claim that they have, via the putatively nondependent relationships of the edge city, become an autonomous realm. Such arguments, though, slight spatial, political, social, and other qualitative descriptions of the city's particularity. While I warmly support the aspirational slogan "Change the dream, change the city," it begs, as an idealist like Socrates would tell you, a fantasy of the good city, a theory of city-ness. For me, the city is a special conduit for the meeting of bodies in space, full of serendipity and friction both. Theories of urban form and density, of modes of movement, of the public realm, are all derivatives of this primary motive. And this is what the suburbs—in their disembodying retreat into monadic privacy— annihilate. Precisely what participants in the foreclosed project must address.

Underneath the lawn, the sidewalk!

In Conclusion

Enough of the riot act! We are gathered today not to lament the afflictions of a set of spatial patterns and practices that have gone wrong but to seek solutions via new logics of sociability, sustainability, and political economy. Much crucial and ground-breaking work has been done, and we are increasingly well equipped to offer suggestions for the reform of a pattern gone wrong. Data from the 2010 census, too, reveal that the current pattern of suburban growth is focused on the inner and outer rings, with the "mature" suburbs between them, the suburban locus classicus, developing more slowly. The reasons are relatively clear and in some ways encouraging. Reinvigoration of the first ring seems due at once to its friendliness—largely derived from devaluations of aging property—to poorer, more mixed populations and from its proximity to rebounding cities and to public transportation.

At the other end of the scale, the outer, exurban ring has grown at a phenomenal pace, over 25 percent in the past ten years. The reasons lie in development economics—cheaper prices at the periphery—as well as, apparently, in a recapture of the lower densities of the classic suburbs in their early days, still desirable to many who just don't like city life. It appears, too, that the "cost" of these lower prices is greatly reflected in commuting times ("drive until you qualify"), the devil's bargain the suburbs have conventionally demanded. From the standpoint of the critique above, this is clearly mixed news and a situation that is differently susceptible to morphological suggestions, save at the largest scale: no amount of gentle prodding or persuasive pro forma is likely to have the effect of an absolutely enforced growth boundary or of differential taxation that would seek to recover the greater public cost of distributed development.

Here is my actual suggestion for those involved in this project: do not limit your proposals to architecture. The forces that created the suburbs included a powerful fantasy of the good life, but it was a life that would have been little achieved without the wide variety of financial, legal, and social institutions that were the practical enablers of this enormous cultural and spatial transformation. We now need to rethink our pattern of settlement at a similar scale, making sure whose dream we're actually advancing. This means thinking way outside the little ticky-tacky box.

(2012)

30

Architecture without Capitalism

Crammed into Zuccotti Park last year, Occupy Wall Street tried to imagine an architecture without capitalism, even in spite of it—the possibility of standing *outside* the system. It proved difficult. The insurgent little city, founded in equity, vamped the real one all-around—and simultaneously acted as an inverted special free trade zone for decommodified speech—but eventually it got cold and the cops came. That community, however short-lived, was indelible and its message received: how you choose to assail the system is a product of how you understand it. Occupy understood it at once precisely and diffusely. As the slogan evolved into "We are the 99 percent", though, the critique of capital became articulate, and the struggle was quantified, secured to the primal political tether: distribution.

All architecture distributes: mass, space, materials, privilege, access, meaning, shelter, rights. The inevitable nexus of architecture and capital is one of its core fascinations, one of the reasons it can be so efficiently and abundantly *read*. That the legibility of the ostentation all around Zuccotti Park—and the deployment of every conceivable police technology to assure Wall Street's perquisites remained unassailed—is only the zillionth instance of architecture's insistence on making its role perfectly clear. In the main, architecture only abets the transparency of capital's inequities. Even the most robust architectural revolutionaries seldom do more than currency conversion, exchanging the material for the symbolic.

What is to be done? Can architecture live without capitalism? Possible approaches:

1. The old-timey vulgarity of simply looking at architecture as reflexive superstructure on the economic base yields nothing practical. The Man's capacity to co-opt races ahead of our ability to invent and we, enamored of invention, buy a ticket to ride. Architectural form has completely lost its power to be dangerous, and only its absence—or its violent destruction—threatens anyone. This lesson is not lost on a variety of both state and non-state combatants, including those who created Occupy's reciprocating other across the street at Ground Zero. As ever, though, the question is: who will be left out in the cold? Connoisseurship is not exactly the enemy, but its promiscuity can be, especially when seduced by the sublimities of extent. Just because we can understand, and/or deconstruct, any taste culture doesn't mean we must approve of it. The semiotics of evil is not the same as those in *Architectural Graphic Standards*, which embodies a central predicate of resistance, in its case to gravity.

2. Or, the occupation could actually proceed down its own implicit highway and—instead of throwing up encampments on the real estate surplus designated "public" space—move into the trading rooms and live there. Why acquiesce to the ossified production relations inscribed so vividly in the city made by the market? A progressive politics is irrelevant without the courage to demand redistribution. However you parse capital in its historical formation, whether this is the era of late capital, global capital, or Bain Capital, the descriptor is merely convenience. All economies are distribution engines, and we vet their moral adequacy via the ethics of appropriation and sharing. What's wrong with the Park Avenue apartment or the Aspen condo is

not a matter of the crown molding or the wainscoting; it's the unequal aggrandizement of space, convenience, and privilege embodied and represented. This is obvious, less so what to do about it. In the classic articulation in *The Housing Question* (1872), Engels suggests that the solution is not the meager compensation of meanly built worker's terraces at the blighted end of town but moving into the surplus space on Central Park West, a highly economical solution.

3. We might test the pathways of renunciation, the sustainable, Gandhian austerities of simply refusing to play ball with consumption, ceasing to be the Strasbourg geese of capital. Indeed, the exponential rise in American obesity threatens to turn each of us into architecture, big as a house. We've certainly been down this path before, but there are those, Amish and anarchists and ashram-dwellers, who make these alternatives work, who do (more or less) opt out. Localism is worth thinking about if it can offer a riposte to the "have it your way" co-optations of the multi-nationals. In its modern incarnation via our "Enlightenment," politics originated in some state of nature, whether mean and brutish or paradisiacal, where everyone emerged blinking from their precapitalist primitive hut. No coincidence that the ubiquity of this figure—whether Semper's, Laugier's, or those recorded in the intrepid sketchbooks of the explorers in the great age of European colonial expansion—was part of this great era of historicism and linearity, the necessary origin point for someone's foregone conclusion. It's an act that keeps getting repeated, as in the twentieth century discourse of the *Existenzminimum,* the primitive hut of modernity, with its redolent distributive and tectonic simplicities establishing both an origin point and a zero degree. Back to the trees?

4. We might truly look into the nature of informality, in its perpetual state of negotiation and pushback with the law, as the medium of permanent resistance. Recent thinking has demonstrated that informal operations in the urban realm are not simply a "state of exception" in which the marginal ply their alternative spatial methods while scrounging for a droplet of

trickle-down. Rather, as Ananya Roy and others have argued, informality is an "idiom" that is practiced at every level in places like India or Brazil, a form of planning that uses legal hermeneutics, evasion, passivity, and violence to continuously remake the landscape of both construction and rights. On the one hand, this idea of a spatial tractability that is the subject of continuous contention offers a promising situation, one in which the disenfranchised can continuously find strategic openings for the inscription of their desires and rights, and one in which needs can be modeled at more and more levels, wrested from the terrains of marginality and brought to the center of town. On the other hand, the inbuilt insecurities of such a field of operations give scope for no end of "creative destruction" as strong powers arrogate—via shifty legalism or outright expulsion—the territories they wish to infuse with surplus value.

5. We assert another formula for our rights, the right to the city, the best axis available nowadays. If this means, first, that we demand that property retreat before our demands of access and assembly, then we find a vital tractability, a space of *occupation*. If it means that capital reconfigure itself to accede to our dreams of other ways of living, other relations, other cities, other fantasies, we will have so interrupted and bedazzled its prospects that we can restart the engine of history and ride it down the line. The relevance of utopia is always in its ephemerality: you can learn a lot from dreams.

6. Is there an insurgent style of assimilating/encountering/being in the city? Modernity as a mode of life and the city have both emerged as an intertwined articulation, and the city has spun itself around the variety of perceptual apparatuses that have allowed us to love it, consume it, know it. We've been flaneurs, cruising the boulevards with ostentatious purposelessness. Shoppers, liberated from our private confines to mingle with spectacle and otherness unguarded. Drivers, with that fast seriatim view of a space of radical elongation. Filmmakers, with our recombinant synthesis of spaces that both are and never were. *Derivistes*, with our blithely deliberate detachment trying our

best to experience an aleatory authentic, a chart of the unconscious, that space of nearly no accidents. Stoned. Kidnapped. Caught in a shower. Is there a perceptual appliance that turns the capitalist city into its other, flips it, a real *détournement*? Let's keep looking, bumping into strangers, staging random events. Success will always be evanescent (attempts *are* the outcomes) but failure is always completely clear: if every route across town brings you to McDonald's, the apparatus is defective.

7. OK, then, we *really* celebrate our visionaries. This category is defined by the *present impossibility* of what it alerts us to. It is, of course, necessary to be critical about the condition of impossibility and to be clear about the necessity for limits. A vision that does not include our bodies is ruled out as not-architecture. We fight capital's big plans by defending our own corporeal construction. There's certainly a conspiracy to make habitation and haberdashery commutative and we must take care not to let the Man camouflage us from ourselves by dappling us with art-for-art bromides and celebrity, studding our skulls with diamonds. Nor should we surrender to our own side's dour, paternalist theories (so often produced between sips of Sancerre as if the way we live our lives is just incidental) and simply assume that all iconoclasm is just another strategy of bourgeois repression. Call it negation if you insist. We cross the bridge of irony or cynicism at some risk: Who wants a joyless revolution? Why overvalue Archizoom at Archigram's expense? Why the preference for silence over laughter? A decisive hammerblow is unlikely but death from a thousand jokes stands a chance.

8. We wait for the contradictions of that vaunted creative destruction to prove exactly how uncreative it actually is. If the system seduces and abandons its every subject, enslaves us each to a mortgage and leaves every house underwater, everyone will have to move to higher ground, which means saying "fuck it." Marx dreamed of just this kind of collapse. What happens to building when capitalist relations of production are subtracted? Let's find out! Socialism in one dorm room? Crash pad? *Werkbund*? Neighborhood? Town? City? Country?

Planet? To find out we must continue to confront a dilemma scarcely unique to liberalism: how much state is enough? I know this much: a welfare state beats a warfare state.

9. We enter the communism of disembodiment, download our entire capacity onto silicon or its successor and, becoming pure mind, defeat the very palpability of property. Well, maybe this is a step too far: mental architecture is just a metaphor. Let's leave it at that.

(2013)

31

Informal Formality

Informal settlements don't actually exist. Not that vast "unplanned" territories in Lima, Cairo, and Mumbai aren't visible and distinct, but they're not discontinuous with the cities and societies in which they are embedded. This is both because the "formal" culture deploys a variety of informal means in its own development—Ananya Roy identifies the nominally formal planning regime in India as almost entirely the outcome of fundamentally informal strategies—and because nobody living in an informal settlement can exist entirely outside the routines of formality. Their lives hybridize a wide variety of economic strategies and relations: a resident might work in the formal sector by day, return to housing in the informal, conduct commercial activity in a combination of both, and hold an informal second job. This porosity is also characteristic of the continuous transformation of so-called informal settlements by various schemes for upgrading, some imposed from the "top," others self-initiated from the "bottom."

For sympathetic observers, informal settlements are admired for their spontaneity, for the intricacy of their social networks, for their capacity for economic and architectural improvisation, for the drastic economy of their sustainable characteristics, and for their ability to eke out benefit at the economic margin.

While the idea of informality is the subject of intense debate—in the work of scholars including Roy, Janice Perlman, Asef Bayat, James Holston, and others—that seeks to situate its styles of regulation, its legal status, and its social meaning within the larger circumstances and practices of settlement in places like Brazil, Egypt, or India, the functional and architectural character of "informal" communities is, despite being constantly contested, more conceptually transparent and a potential source of speculation—and inspiration—for building more generally.

Of course, as Roy and others point out, there is great risk in detaching the physical qualities of these settlements from their social, political, and economic complexities, in particular, from the debate about the proletarianization of their inhabitants and the ways in which they're caught up in the routines of neoliberalism and the globalization of capital. There is a particular danger both in the "aestheticization" of these places—in what Roy suggests is a version of pastoral nostalgia—and in the impetus to judge them via their relationship to mythologies of rationality that have shaped the discourse of the "modern" city. These views have led to a variety of often well-intended efforts at "upgrade" that are simply palliative, that neglect the complex of non-architectural determinants of their form and life, and that participate in their assimilation to dominant routines of property, sociability, and exchange—effectively shifting the burden of survival onto the shoulders of the poor via the one-dimensional celebration of their "entrepreneurialism."

Nonetheless, there are arguments for the conceptual and activist utility of insisting that informality is both an illusory condition and a useful one. Clearly, the phenomenon of the "squatter settlement"—places that combine poverty, minimally built housing, big deficits of infrastructure and other services, high rates of non-wage economic activity, lack of social mobility, and a very mixed picture of formal ownership and tenure—is something that's easy to recognize *on the ground* from Karachi to Jakarta to Rio. While these places may be characterized as slums, they invert the typical pattern of the poor neighborhoods of Brooklyn, Detroit, or South Central Los Angeles, in which the trajectory is often the progressive deterioration of market-produced stocks of housing, with the poor arriving at some pivotal movement in the downward spiral. Informality's movement, on the other hand, is from zero toward a more rationalized environment. It seems more "natural" to associate heroism with the curative forward motion of bricolage, and we value informality precisely for its resistance in creativity and its potential to question the undergirding assumptions of the modern city, to collapse the artificial distinction that relegates the informal to a frustrated and unfulfilled, even impossible, aspiration to modernity, an incompetent otherness.

From the architectural perspective, this relationship is surely complicated by modernism's own insistent conflation of physical and social action, and the forms of the informal have long resonated with many of modernism's own aspirations. Seen from a distance, the prismatic assemblages of houses on the hillsides above Rio evoke both its Mediterranean ideal and, for those in rebellion against it, the picturesque, "irrational" order of these settlements—a bracing antidote to the schematic rationality of modernism in decline, linking formal variety, meandering, medieval geometry, and the liberating vibe of an "architecture without architects." Indeed, this was a big part of the dream, a way around the complicity of the architectural profession in a classist, command mode of spatial production, a restoration of the liberatory aspirations of modernity.

The idea of informal, user-generated, and restive practices of settlement also aligns with a renewed focus on the idea and value of neighborhoods, the displacement of the quantitative schema of modern planning (with its neighborhood "units") by a more nuanced and qualitative view. Casting about for a concept to assimilate place and culture, this elastic increment— the neighborhood—seems to be a non-prejudicial, global, descriptor that embraces dimension, ecology, and community. This analysis was typified by Jane Jacobs, who posited a collaboration between the formal and the informal *within* the modern city and celebrated strategies for vitally mixing people, uses, and forms in a variety of contexts. For her, the contest for the soul of urbanity was between the one-dimensional authoritarian urbanism represented by Robert Moses—the deracinated, un-textured architectures of urban renewal—and the informal styles of neighborliness and cooperation that could only arise by local diversity and the accumulation of social—and spatial—capital.

Informal communities have simultaneously distressed and fascinated observers for decades because they offer a set of practices and possibilities that illuminate larger questions about the future of the city, not simply because the exponential growth of these settlements has made them the literal future of global urbanism, but more importantly because so many have read into them a nearly utopian horizon for self-organization, an urban state of nature. The now dominant axis of appreciation stems from the proposition, first articulated by Henri Lefebvre and later taken up by David Harvey, Don Mitchell, and others, of the *right to the city* and, more specifically, the right not simply of access and use but of the *production* of the city, something literalized by the legions of self-help and autonomous builders who create and transform the urbanism of informality.

But can the lessons of informality be inculcated in the development of the modern city, the historic paradigm for growth and form that dominates not simply Western practice but that continues to be the replacement model—the medium of annihilation —for the informal city around the world? I don't wish to repudiate modernist ideology in its entirety. Indeed, there is something vexing about the *pejorative* reading back of certain modernist design ideals onto informal spaces, the thought that such fundamentals as sunlight, clean air, greenery, personal space, hygiene and other touchstones must be viewed as inimical to freedom, autonomy, and difference. Is there a potential for exchange between these worlds of illusory binarism?

In my student days, we were deeply fascinated by squatter settlements, informal urbanism, and "self-help" housing. There was a group of earnest investigators at MIT—John Turner most prominent among them—who were involved in what was a classic straddle of the sixties, bridging the roles of activist, investigator, and designer. Latin American informality in particular was a touchstone for architects and planners struggling with the mode of production being taught in our universities, a contest between increasingly arid formal investigations and the sense of social purpose that was not simply an artifact of the times but lingered as a category in the sputtering modernist enterprise that formed the ideological core of most American architectural schools. "Housing" and "advocacy" were the key frames of our pushback, and we were legatees of the movements for housing reform that arose in the nineteenth century, which themselves were the ideological substrate for the modernist project to house the world, a contradiction we sought to unpack.

The idea of "housing" as an urban or architectural category implied *mass* housing, which, in turn, suggested a condition in which a particular form of subjectivity was identified and foregrounded, and in which those subjects were seen to have a special species of rights and particular formal requirements, figuring a clear communal gestalt. The ideal subject of this formulation was a mythical urban proletarian, and the architectural polemic that emerged to describe his or her rights compounded ideas about uniformity, economy, and style. The revolutionary vector of equality translated itself—in the architectural field—into a precise and insistent measure of both literal and visual parity and in strategies for the seriatim reproduction of endless uniform habitations. It insistently begged the question of the minimum, a theme that arose out of the confabulation of shortage and an ethics of parsimoniousness that was meant to suggest a righteous working-class solidarity, but which was produced from a perspective of bourgeois charity. This was wrapped up with the idea that housing could be produced as an industrial process, and the debate over the idea of the *Existenzminium*—the irreducible quantum of housing—continues to this day.

Both in the nineteenth-century formulation and our own, the issue that defines the idea of "housing" as a category—and the broader idea of the informal—is that of scarcity. There continue to be two main approaches to shortage: redistribution and economy of means. The classic reading of the redistributive side is Friedrich Engels's *The Housing Question* (1872), which argues that the shortage is not in housing but equity, a situation that persists today, both in the unequal distribution of property and in the uneven consumption of resources and production of waste. This begs the second question, which lies in the connection between the technical and the ethical, the "small is beautiful" approach to our moral and environmental commons, a doubling back with a new data set. In this sense, the idea of the *Existenzminimum* can be seen as the expression of sustainability *avant la lettre*, an early address to the finitude of global resources.

By the time I encountered "housing" as a problematic, it was already deeply inflected with the negative. Housing was for the poor, for the unemployed, for people of color. It incarnated segregation, a new form of ghetto, a prison, an unproductive and criminal place, a symbol of the failure of a marginalized population to gain any purchase in the system. Against this monolithic, repressive, and ugly architecture, the idea of the informal or squatter settlement seemed a bracing alternative. A key value of progressive architecture (and the politics that informed it) was the idea of user control, of a physical environment rendered more and more personal and tractable by "appropriate" technology and by a pervasive idea about "flexibility." This took various forms that associated freedom and righteousness with concepts of impermanence, mobility, and malleability, if more often understood in terms of consumer rather than democratic choice. In an atmosphere where the promise of property was under question, romantic cachet attached to the idea of ephemerality via a growing environmentalism that celebrated the use of found materials and off-the-shelf solutions. To be sure, this was a way for first world architectural discourse to extend the basic parameters of functionalist minimalism by arrogating the luster of the struggles for justice in the third. But, while there was an envious—even colonial—component in this view, it was also an expression of genuine solidarity and a recognition that the problems of both scarcity and runaway urban growth were not parochial but planetary.

The response in the "Western" architectural community organized its applications both at home and in systems of rationalization directed at the transformation of developing-world settlements in situ. Manifestations of this ethos as alternative practices took several directions, scales of informalities differentiated by level of professional expertise and culture of inhabitation, expressed both literally and representationally. There was fairly extensive, quasi-formalized, squatting of abandoned buildings and tenant takeovers of neglected properties, and I enjoyed a brief experience of this in early '70s London. These squatters were, clearly, the children of Engels, and for "illegals" in Earl's Court or the Lower East Side, the occupation of empty buildings was at once a strategy for survival, redress, and propaganda. Like the squatters of the developing world, confrontations with the authorities focused both on questions of property rights and on the provision of services like water, power, and sewage.

The Occupy movement is an heir to these tactics and begs both the question of housing inequality (thrown into great relief by the mortgage meltdown) and the linked issue of what constitutes public space, the formal matrix of community. Understanding that ideas of public and private are always produced reciprocally —and that sorting out rights and responsibilities for this differentiation is a matter of spatial proprietorship—lies at the core of the imbrication of the idea of housing (and the city) with the idea of freedom. Informal housing cannot be approached without addressing the nature of property, and the classic point of departure is the private appropriation of public land (although this is becoming less and less the predominant model as the informal is progressively "rationalized"), as opposed to the movement—whose most prominent advocate is Peruvian economist Hernando de Soto—to establish some form of individual security of tenure through titling. But it is perhaps even more crucial to secure deep connections to the webs of public infrastructure that formalize the relationship and establish the particularity of the social construction of place.

Using the experience of the long sixties in the United States as model for working out the reception of these third-world practices, the other main vector was another elective form squatting, the communalism of alternative communities, many of which involved self-executed building of relatively simple shelters. Of these, one of the most memorable was Drop City, an exemplar not simply of a minimum-consumption lifestyle, but of an economy that both sat outside of disdained formal arrangements and produced an architecture embodying the ethos of material minimalism and reuse that has been central to that aura of informality embraced by first-world observers.

Drop City was known for the visual excitement of its so-called "zomes," Fuller-esque geodesics fabricated from the recycled carcasses of automobiles under the guidance of guru Steve Baer. "Bucky domes" were then the object of almost mystical reverence because of their succinct geometry, their modularity, and their rich imputation of universality and economy. The use of abandoned cars—detritus of the Fordist economy and symbols of the military industrial complex—carried a swords-into-plowshares vibe that added a patina of the political to the enterprise. There is, to be sure, a Marie Antoinette, faux-farm-girl aspect to many of the intentional communities of the period that grew exactly from the *degree* of their intentionality, the fact that most of the inhabitants of these alternative communities had other alternatives. But the right to the city *must* include the right to shape its form according to our artistic desires and to reject the joylessness that can't find inspiration in acts of "empty" creativity.

Along with this form of communal living arose a related culture of nomadism, an elective version of the impermanence that characterized, on the one hand, the flows of refugees and the economically displaced into both camps and squatter settlements, and on the other, the dramatically increased mobility forced on participants (including the undocumented) in the American "formal" economy. For both our middle-class nomads and communards, this polemical positioning situated somewhere between politics and art—in that treacherous terrain of so-called lifestyles—at once sought to assimilate the qualities of social life imputed to the improvisations of the deeply constrained poor and to offer a critique of the forcible character and miserable circumstances of the settlements that were the result. The exploration jibed well with a more general feeling about the need to create "responsive" environments that could be transformed to accommodate both immediate user-needs as well as more general demographic trends, including the accelerating metamorphosis of our living arrangements—particularly the decline of the nuclear family as the predominant increment of residential demand. It is one of the ironies of the day that the informal practices of customization and addition, rampant in the suburbs where our parents lived, were only later absorbed into this lexicon of freedom.

In the years of decline in the appeal of modernist ideas of mass housing and government responsibility, infrastructure has displaced housing as the official locus of public purpose in architecture. The reasons for this shift include the apparent political neutrality attached to the idea of infrastructure, a semi-visible but suggestively universal system of support that defines both the limit and the obligation of the public realm. This line reproduces itself in the dual approach to improving informal settlements: on the one hand, to provide basic municipal services as part of "upgrades in place," and on the other, to offer titles to slum dwellers to secure the private control of the environments at the end of the water hookup. While many question titling and argue that it simply draws the poor deeper into a subservient relationship with the institutions of predatory capital, this critique does not gainsay the crucial element of environmental control as emblem and means of personal freedom—either in being able to act to manage one's personal future and that of one's private environment, or in freedom from the oppressions of manipulation by power and the dead-ends of the choicelessness that grows from inequality and disempowerment.

A key articulation of the idea of a crossover informality from my student days was the Dutch architect John Habraken's notion of "supports." This theory was characteristic of a certain ambivalence about the relationship between individual choice, the persistence of convention and tradition in the built environment, and the necessity for intervention at a scale consonant with the huge extent of the problem. Habraken offered a system that, in effect, proposed the construction of kind of loft city in which housing was recast as infrastructure—a series of vertical frameworks to be serially inhabited by individuals who would customize their own spaces in conjunction with new kinds of industrial resources in developed environments—within a generic, putatively malleable megastructure.

While never really convincingly depicted, these support structures attempted to channel both modernist fantasies of simultaneity and extent as well as a sense of the "mega-structural" qualities of more timeless styles of building, the continuous morphologies of Italian hill towns, Islamic medinas, and other unitary but serial constructions. In that romanticized view-from-a-distance of the favelas on the Rio slopes, the same idealized collective morphology was conjured by an alien gaze. However, it is a mistake to moralize this reading as totally perni-cious and misaligned. Complexity, variation, the view over, local responsiveness to topography, party walls, expandability, and extremely situational and personal configurations are values in the built environment that enjoy qualities exclusive of their production in conditions of exploitation, shortage, insalubri-ousness, lack of services, and the Big Intractable: inescapability

Habraken's support parti was a useful inversion of the actual conditions of squatter settlements as a means of transmitting what were seen as their positive aspects to more developed situ-ations. Habraken was proposing the provision of infrastructure *before* the fact of habitation, rather than what had become a typical solution to the upgrading of squatter settlements, in which infrastructure followed the basic acts of settlement and habitation. This begged the question of a paradigm of uniform-ity, of very large-scale intervention by the authorities, and of the baseline for replicability of modernist mass housing that it sought to critique. The approach also failed to establish the superiority of elasticity in place over the ability to change places. But still, a useful site of ambiguity between the collective and the individual was opened up, and his frank attempt to merge mass-manufacture efficiencies with the ethos of DIY and self-help was tonic.

Habraken stood firmly on the shoulders of his colleague Turner who, while stridently denouncing the hegemony of heteronomous—"other determined"—systems over autono-mous ones, recognized the ambiguities necessarily embedded in the approach, that the "freedom" he advocated was also a constraint. As he writes, "Self-help, if limited to a narrow, do-it-yourself sense, or even to group construction, can actually reduce autonomy by making excessive demands on personal time and energy and by reducing household mobility." Turner was after a "third way" and argued, if not entirely persuasively, that government should cease "doing what it does badly or uneconomically—building and managing houses and concentrate on what it has the authority to do: to ensure equitable access to resources which local communities and people cannot provide for themselves." His point was that housing decisions should be controlled by households, that "for a viable housing process to exist, local and personal control is essential," and he articulated the necessary contingencies of such local networks, including economic land prices, abundant availability of tools and materials through local suppliers, easy *local* credit and *locally* based supply and organizational systems and summarized, "When dwellers control the major decisions and are free to make their own contribution to the design, construction, or management of their housing, both the process and the environment produced stimulate individual and social well-being."

Applying the inventive character of informality to the modernist city begs the primary contradiction of the idea of the large-scale design of informality. This will always entail not the design of settlements per se but of their circumstances and will embrace a permanent debate about the nature of both subsidy—or support—and freedom. In the van of this struggle is the constitution of the public to which these solutions are addressed and from which they rise. The genius and impossibility of the informal city, however, is that it is authentically dialectical, in a constant state of often-confusing becoming. While we celebrate its possibilities for empowerment, liberation, and creativity—and see its improvisation and spirit of sacrifice and mutual aid as crucial to its sustainability and resilience—we must not forget that these places also have a tremendous capacity to oppress. *That they oppress hundreds of millions with no way out.*

(2013)

32

The Trials of Rafi Segal

In early 2012, the National Library of Israel announced a competition for a new building in Jerusalem. The site was one of special prominence—near the Knesset, the Supreme Court and the Israel Museum—and the project enjoyed enormous national prestige. The competition was sponsored by two entities: the National Library Construction Company and Yad Hanadiv, a foundation funded and controlled by the Rothschild family and the principal funder of the library.

The track record of the Rothschilds in sponsoring Israeli architectural competitions is somewhat checkered, which isn't surprising for a rich and powerful organization participating in processes where the outcome is, theoretically, beyond its control. In the case of the Knesset competition (also financed in large measure by Rothschild money), the controversy surrounded the undistinguished composition of the jury and the visibly mediocre quality of the results. When, in the 1980s, Yad Hanadiv got involved in sponsoring the contest for a new Supreme Court building, it was wary of entering a process over which it lacked final say and resolved—once burnt—not to risk the embarrassment of the Knesset affair. Writing in the online business magazine *Globes*, and drawing on research by architect Yaniv Pardo into the Supreme Court competition, Meirav Moran has explained (quoting Pardo) that Yad Hanadiv tried to protect itself by playing "the game in such a way as to fulfill their interests while appearing to be fair." It wanted "to control all stages of the project while being the sole authority for planning and implementation and satisfying all bodies ... and to make it look as if public conduct was proper." The manipulation came in the form of an attempt to stack the jury and also to add a clause to the terms of the competition allowing the foundation to cancel the jury award under "an exceptional circumstance." This was a blatant conflict with national regulations that required an anonymous tendering process from qualified architects, to be judged by a group of professionals. Fortunately, in this case, the jury was able to agree on a winner—Ada Karmi-Melamede—who went on to complete a building of high quality.

When the library competition was announced, it almost immediately became mired in similar issues of power and manipulation. Like many such contests, it was conducted in two stages: a general call to Israeli architects (which ultimately produced eighty-one entries), with the intention of winnowing the entries down to twelve for more detailed development in the second stage. However, the sponsors also decided to invite four well-known international offices and four leading Israeli firms to proceed directly to the second round. Allowing such a free pass is not entirely unusual, although with the library Yad Hanadiv turned the idea of an "open" competition into a charade: two-thirds of those advanced to the finals skipped the first round, making the odds for the rest of the participants far longer. Almost immediately a storm of criticism arose, including a petition signed by many Israeli architects calling for the competition's cancellation. Arad Sharon, an architect who helped launch the protest, was quoted in *Haaretz* saying that "the terms of the competition constitute a death blow for the architectural sector. This ... is a colossal humiliation."

And yet on it went. Four Israeli architects were chosen to compete against the eight "big names," and all of them developed and submitted projects to a jury composed of three distinguished international personalities in the field (the critic Luis Fernández-Galiano and the architects Rafael Moneo and Craig Dykers), as well as two Israeli architects (Gaby Schwartz, former municipal engineer of Jerusalem, and Elinoar Komissar-Barzacchi, the Jerusalem district planner at the Ministry of Construction and Housing), two members of the Rothschild family and two representatives of the library. And then something remarkable happened: in September 2012, Rafi Segal—a very talented young Israeli architect—became the jury's enthusiastic choice. His elegant, subtle, site-sensitive scheme was described by the jury as "modest yet original and unique." And so it was. Organized around a series of courtyards on a challengingly proportioned site, Segal's building was a highly functional deployment of a complex program, extremely well considered climatically, and elegantly expressed in austere, yet striking, tectonics.

Then the assault began. First came an attack on Segal by Yair Gabbay, an attorney from the Jerusalem municipality Planning and Building Committee, who threatened to thwart the permit process for the new building unless the National Library board promised to "cancel the results of the tender and start a new process to choose a worthy planner for the National Library from among the Zionist architects living in Israel." Gabbay's beef with Segal had to do with the latter's authorship a decade ago (with Eyal Weizman) of an important book *A Civilian Occupation: The Politics of Israeli Architecture* (2003), which succinctly examined the spatial specifics of Israeli settlement policy. In a letter to the prime minister, the mayor of Jerusalem, and the media, the hyperbolically frustrated Gabbay wrote, without a whit of self-consciousness, that the book "reflects the depths of insanity plumbed by frustrated people who can't get their way via democratic means" and insisted that no architect should benefit from public funding while "spitting on Israel all over the world."

This was only the beginning. Accusations began to circulate on the web that Segal had plagiarized his design for the project from one in China done by a colleague at Harvard, where Segal was then teaching. To be sure, the works share a motif—an inclined roof section surrounding a void—but so do half the courtyard buildings built over a millennium or so in China, Italy (a source cited by Segal in his presentation to the jury), and elsewhere around the world. Segal had also used the motif in earlier work. In scale, use, materiality, and expression, his library was altogether different from the Chinese building—itself very beautiful—by his fellow faculty member, who raised no objections of his own. In fact, the abstracted allusion to this widespread traditional form (a common source for many projects) was part of what gave the Jerusalem scheme its special resonance.

But the Harvard Graduate School of Design can be a treacherous place, and the next attack on Segal—by Bing Wang, a colleague who teaches planning and real estate—provided the pretext that the library used to change course. Wang's claim was a more serious one: not that Segal had poached from her previous work, but that the library design was as much hers as his. Her aggressive insistence on intellectual property rights as an "equal partner" was quickly—and, it seems, unreservedly—accepted by the client, which decided, scarcely three months after the jury had made its original decision, to dump the winner. This reversal has been greeted with gales of protest from the architectural community, perhaps most strikingly from the Israel Association of United Architects, whose support for Segal represents another reversal: it was the IAUA that had commissioned *A Civilian Occupation* from Segal and Weizman as the basis for the Israeli exhibition at the 2002 International Union of Architects Congress in Berlin, only to suppress it after finding that the work ultimately produced was contrary to the organization's political interests. But regarding the library affair, the IAUA has publicly demanded Segal's reinstatement and called on the architectural community not to collaborate in any new selection process.

Having attempted to be reasonable with all concerned, Segal has been forced to go to the courts to counter both the manifest injustice he has suffered and the sponsor's own retreat into the narrowest (and phoniest) legalism, and to demand that he be reinstated as the winner and offered a contract. I've been sorting through the claims and counterclaims and have spoken with Segal, corresponded with Wang (as well as the library and several of the jurors), and read the legal submissions to the sponsors and the courts. What is clear is that Wang supported the project with funds and office space, and that one of her employees—Yonatan Cohen, an Israeli friend of Segal's, who does seem to have done much of the heavy lifting to produce the final drawings—was shifted to reduced pay and worked on the scheme in Wang's office. Wang also provided a variety of other office services, including the hiring of a freelance computer renderer. Finally, Wang asserts that Segal failed to inform her that the competition was open only to Israeli architects and that, in effect, her contribution was secured under false pretenses.

Wang's central claim is that Segal had promised her equal credit as one of four authors: herself, Segal, Cohen and Matan Mayer (another young Israeli architect, who provided substantial assistance and, along with Cohen, has signed a document relinquishing any claim to rights for the project). Cohen has also written a letter to the library stating in part that "it was perfectly clear to all persons involved in the planning that the work was the creation of Rafi, who is the architect of this project and who is the superior authority in anything related to planning, from small to large details. Rafi was the one who presented the initial concept of the planning by way of a set of sketches that were very clear, and any decision related to planning derived from that set of sketches." To be sure, it appears that Wang's firm, the HyperBina Design Group, was not properly cited in the initial press release of the results—though on its website, HyperBina takes credit for the project and lists Segal as a collaborator, somewhat undermining Wang's claims of interest in equity. But beyond the question of being credited for her support, Wang insists that she played an important personal role in the creation of the design, not merely in helping to enable its documentation. Segal, for his part, continues to assert that he was the author of the scheme (and contractual documents pertaining to Wang's involvement clearly establish his ultimate authority over it); that the requirement for an Israeli license (which only Segal possessed) was clear to Wang and a matter of public knowledge; and that he was always prepared to recognize the contributions made by all the members of the team.

Rafi Segal is a friend, and I haven't the slightest doubt that he was the intellectual and creative author of the scheme. His submission to the court includes reams of drawings that show his painstaking development of the project. Even as specified in her legal brief, Wang's claims of design participation are almost negligible. Moreover, I've seen no graphic or other evidence to bear them out: while her assistance in facilitating the entry is clear, it is equally clear that this was not in the form of a contribution to the actual *design* of the project. This view is shared by Preston Scott Cohen, the chair of Harvard's architecture department and himself a distinguished practitioner. In a letter to the director of Yad Hanadiv, he wrote: "Ms. Bing Wang does not teach and has not taught architecture at the Architecture Department and to the best of my knowledge is not a practicing designer. Her expertise is urban planning and real estate development." He goes on to explain that Segal's

winning competition proposal clearly bears the marks of his previous work and thus represents his design authorship. It is very consistent with his sensitivity to the urban context, both in terms of the site and the larger historical context, his use of simple geometric patterns, the inclined plane and "cut out" strategy, the abstracted and restrained exterior and several other architectural features which are reoccurring elements in his work.

Furthermore, conceiving of and resolving a project of this complexity requires years of experience and active design practice. In short, Wang's claim to authorship, which would mean that she personally served in a collaborative role, acting jointly as a principal designer, is clearly unfounded."

Cohen also explains what those of us with experience in competitions of this type know all too well: they are always somewhat frantic, collaborative, midnight-oil undertakings with strong affinities to barn raisings or spontaneous performance pieces. A team is gathered in a cooperative spirit and works flat-out to get the thing done against high expectations and low odds of success. People come and go according to the time they have available and their particular abilities and resources, pitching in to help meet the usually impossible deadline. Nearly all architectural work is collaborative, and it is surely always right to credit those who participate for the help they've given; any failure by Segal to adequately acknowledge such contributions must be corrected. However, while it is clear that Wang made an administrative and financial contribution to the project, the question of authorship is not opaque: it belongs to Segal, the instigator of the project, the organizer of the team, and the obvious sensibility—and hand—behind the design.

Did the sponsors of the competition accept Wang's argument because they were looking for a way to get rid of Segal for his politics, or because they were cowed by her legal claims? It's hard to say, but their punctilious insistence that the commission be rescinded because Segal could not reach a legal agreement with Wang is not merely disingenuous but vicious. According to Segal and to documents submitted to the court, there were lengthy negotiations with Wang during which he offered her appropriate credit, a generous financial settlement, and his apologies for any aspect of the competition project he failed to clearly disclose. Throughout, Wang apparently remained unyielding (a document from her lawyer attests that she flatly declined Segal's settlement offer), preferring to pull the temple down around all concerned rather than find an amicable resolution. Wang should remember her prior friendship with Segal, swallow her injured pride, forgive any perceived affront, reach an agreement and allow the project to go ahead. Enough of relying on the law to be the ass it too often is.

In depriving Segal of the commission, the sponsors acted in the worst of faith. Their anodyne assertion that "Segal's proposal was disqualified in light of deficiencies discovered in it" neither addresses the public's interest in the construction of what had been hailed as the best design mere weeks before nor the flimsy core of Wang's charges against Segal. No genuine investigation could have been undertaken in the brief time between the award and the dismissal, and I find it unbelievable that a sponsor—and an immensely powerful one at that—committed to the architect and design it had chosen was incapable of intervening to smooth any ruffled feathers and arrive at an understanding that would have allowed the project to proceed. I find it equally impossible to believe that the sponsors were so clueless about the creative character of the competition process.

Segal, a man of gentle demeanor, has been deeply hurt and humiliated by the affair and has lost the opportunity of a lifetime. Alas, the wheels of justice turn exceedingly slow, and his case will not be heard until May. Taking advantage of this lag, the sponsors have rapidly initiated a do-over and have already released a call for another "competition"—structured much differently and more controllably than the first—which clearly seeks to establish immovable "facts on the ground" before the thing works its way through the courts.

In this new round, the call is not for a design but for a statement of qualifications from experienced Israeli firms (who can presumably partner with the appropriately luminous intergalactic starchitect). They are obliged to demonstrate that they've recently constructed a large public building with a substantial budget, and also to employ a minimum number of architects in Israel. The jury has been reduced to the key Rothschild, the chair of the Yad Hanadiv, Komissar-Barzacchi and Fernández-Galiano (whose collusion I find both surprising and disappointing). And it must be observed that a particular segment of the Israeli population—and, presumably, of the readership of the library— has been excluded, as usual, from any participation in the process.

Among the many ironies of this story is that one of the jurors who strongly supported Segal—Craig Dykers of the firm Snøhetta, recently the subject of flattering profiles in the *New York Review of Books* and *The New Yorker*—was himself catapulted to global prominence at a young age precisely on the strength of having won a competition for a major Middle Eastern library: the Bibliotheca Alexandrina in Egypt. The newly configured arrangement—with its dependence on credentials rather than design and the absence of any distinguished practitioner on the jury—cannot by any stretch be legitimately described as a competition, and it will also ensure that youthful or nonmainstream designers do not participate. Indeed, the sponsors have, with calculation, dashed the hope that dances behind every architectural competition: that a brilliant and unexpected design will emerge from an imagination that has not taken the easy path through established styles in order to get to the top.

Esther Zandberg, long the leading architectural writer in Israel, has called what has happened to Segal a "targeted assassination." I strongly urge architects of conscience to refuse to profit from Rafi Segal's misfortune by participating in this grotesque process. I especially urge those architects who were beaten fair and square in the original competition to have the courage to speak up about this affront to both architecture and justice.

(2013)

33

Krier ♥ Speer

In his doss-house days in Vienna, that great-artist wannabe Adolf Hitler made a modest income painting postcards. The most legendary of these was his view of the Michaelerplatz, the little square behind the Hofburg. This was home to the most famous project of the architect and polemicist ("ornament is crime") Adolf Loos, the 1911 building now universally referred to as the Looshaus, a seminal monument of early modernism. Although the lower commercial level is classical in form, feeling, and materiality, the upper floors—austerely white with simply punched windows—were controversial from the get-go, famously cartooned by contemporaries as looking like a sewer grating. Hitler, ever the traditionalist, hated the thing and in his postcard view painted out the elegant little building, substituting its predecessor. His animus could only have been exacerbated by the fact that the client for the building—a bespoke tailor—was Jewish.

Of course, Hitler was later to enjoy far wider scope for his pleasure of obliteration. Cities and towns across Europe were smashed flat. His program of racial purification was—inter alia—understood in terms of a project of beautification, the ugly degenerate Jews and Slavs to yield to the more elegant Nordic phenotype. In the Nazi "philosophy" this collusion of the aesthetic and the ethical was ubiquitous, and much has been written about the fanatical stagecraft of the regime, the fetishization of uniforms and ceremonies, the remorseless décor, the cathexis onto the sleek forms of the instruments of mass destruction, the exultation of the German-ness of Wagner and the operatic trajectory of a nation consigned to flames, the whole nauseatingly policed mythopoesis that suffused everyday life in the Reich, leading to its Götterdämmerung crescendo of mass annihilation.

Hitler's central artistic preoccupation, however, was architecture. I had the ambivalent experience of teaching for several years at the Academy of Fine Arts in Vienna, the school that was long the object of Hitler's ambitions but which, alas, twice denied his application for admission. The thought was never far from my mind as I strolled that weird, amnesiac city, that if only the decision had gone the other way, the planet would have merely been afflicted with another mediocre, power-hungry architect. Unfortunate, too, that Hitler channeled his rage at the rejection into a lust for acceptance, an abiding emulation of the worst kind of academic values—the insistence on the correctness of historic forms, the exclusion of the unworthy, the veneration of authority—rather than in the liberating insubordinations of the avant-garde he so reviled.

As Hitler consolidated power, however, he found a young architect who was the quintessential embodiment of his own desires, and the two enacted a weird transference, developing a codependence that, among other things, measurably prolonged the war, resulting in the deaths of millions. Albert Speer was just the ambitious, amoral, disciplined mediocrity that Hitler aspired to be, and Speer rapidly moved—via a killer combination of technical competence and obsequiousness—closer and closer to the center of the regime, rising from interior decorator to minister of production. Without reticence, he translated Hitler's sketches into built form and presided over the dictator's most exalted projects of reconstitution, the huge monumental buildings, the redesign of Berlin, Linz, and other cities as the stage sets for the anticipated 1,000 years of murderous pomposity. So connected to this fantasy was Hitler that one of his last acts before he fed cyanide to his dog and put a bullet in his head in the bunker was to go upstairs to gaze, misty-eyed, at the architectural model of his fantastically rebuilt hometown in Austria that Speer had constructed for him.

Who among us isn't fascinated by Speer and his deal with the devil? Although Speer's redemptive dissembling has now been stripped away by Gitta Sereny and other historians, the Speerian narrative abides—like that of Werner von Braun—as a central ethical conundrum of the Nazi era: the question of how *people who seemed to be like us* could become mass-murdering criminals. The impossibly illusory answer defines evil itself. Of course, both Speer and von Braun managed their respective rehabilitations by claiming they were really non-participants, merely present, and thus deserved credit for their special technical or artistic competences, which might as well have been applied in other circumstances without opprobrium. Von Braun, after all, took us to the moon. Speer outdid Hollywood with that fabulous searchlight colonnade at the Nuremberg Rally. For his part, Hitler built the autobahn.

The ongoing axis of architectural apologetics made for Speer is a double one. There is a substantial body of argument that suggests that his kind of traditionalist taste (continuous with that of Hitler, who could competently sketch his ideas and is certainly entitled to share authorship) was equally congenial to Roosevelt, Mussolini, and Stalin—that the stylistic affinities between the varieties of "classicism" that were the official getup for power during the 1930s somehow liberates his work from a specifically Nazi referent. This, of course, is the nexus of the *langue/parole* distinction and is exculpatory only if there's a refusal to make any distinction *within* the field of this expression or to consider any integral relationship between form and function. The more outré defense of Speer insists that he is not simply tarred with modernism's anti-classical brush but that he was actually an excellent architect, full stop.

There's actually pretty much only one person on the planet who's willing and eager to make this argument—Léon Krier—and his 1985 edition *Albert Speer: Architecture 1932–1942*—limited to work until 1942, the year of the Wannsee Declaration, and without effort to inquire into Speer's role in the design of buildings that might fall outside the programmatic sanction of familiar types of public architecture—was reissued in 2013 in a lavishly produced volume that includes a preemptive defense of the innocence of Krier's sanction by Robert Stern. Krier's claims to be taken as more than the Kenneth Mars character in *The Producers* are built on his long-standing reputation as a spirited anti-modernist whose rhetoric on behalf of "traditional" architectural form and culture and in opposition to the alienations of the machine has an occasionally appealing William Morris/Werkbund/Kropotkin aroma. His sketches are succinct—stylistically not a million miles from Hitler's—and his propositions for "traditional", hand-hewn, little buildings perfectly harmless, even charming. And—talk about tragedy lapsing into farce—he has long been the court architect for Prince Charles, for whom he continues to work on a little Olde English town—Poundbury.

But why defend Speer *as an architectural talent*? While this is really a question for psychoanalysis, Krier uses Speer—whom he does seem genuinely to revere—to continue a battle against an imaginary enemy, a long-gone modernist cabal that he thinks will find this especially irritating. By choosing to make his metonymic defense of "classicism" via its most egregious exponent, Krier displays a kind of bathetic chutzpah he clearly finds deeply clever and *dangerous*! This is merely infantile. As the immense and waxing volume of scholarly and popular work on the Nazis—from Elie Wiesel to Quentin Tarantino—shows, there is no issue of this being forbidden territory. The more specific question, however, is whether Speer's architectural oeuvre actually has any formal merit. Taking Krier's implicit challenge and imagining Berlin's Great Hall filled with 180,000 Stones fans rather than 180,000 storm troopers and the Chancellery as an office for Jamie Dimon rather than Hitler, I turn to the tome in front of me.

Revisiting this work, I find myself at once bored and creeped-out. It isn't simply that the production of a monster is given the deluxe treatment; the work is flat-out bad and stinks of both human and imaginative death. Speer's designs are uniformly lifeless and dry, without a spark of originality, even within the conventions of the received idiom. The proportions are flat, often compressed, lacking elegance or attenuation. The ornament is not indigenous, simply applied. (Speer claimed he was working on finding a specifically Nazi decorative system, to replace those shopworn triglyphs and metopes.) Materials are used joylessly to impress, like the lobby of a second-rate Park Avenue apartment house with its slather of marble and gewgaw applique. There is no subtlety in plan, section, or elevation (unless you're into really long flights of stairs). The symmetries are dogmatic. The rhythms in the work are uniformly military, unsyncopated, without a grace note, merely repetitive, never complex. The "grandeur" much vaunted by Krier is just grandiosity.

Krier everywhere betrays his deep difficulty in understanding the relationship between form and content, language and speech, and his actual readings of the work amount to little more than brief enthusiastic captions: his claims for Speer are always comparative and he never actually analyzes the work on its merits. He rails against those who hypocritically criticize Speer's megalomanical Great Hall—would-be eighth wonder of the world—because the Hancock building is even taller and the gruesome superdome is just as wide! This is a typical bit of Krierian argumentation, drawing a distinction without a meaningful difference, a limp classification *within* the category of grandiosity, conferring no advantage on Speer, however much he evokes breast-like "maternal" aspects of the monster dome. (Krier also betrays total indifference to the production of gender, glossing over the Nazis' view of women's highest calling signified by that elephantine teat: breeding machines for the master race.)

If Krier defends Speer by asserting that nominally ethical architects have made worse buildings, there's also the constant effort to establish quality by aspirational association: Krier constantly reverts to claims (some made by Speer himself in their conversations) that this work marches in the great defile that that includes Friedrich Gilly, Karl Friedrich Schinkel, Otto Wagner, Carl Asplund, Paul Cret and John Russell Pope. This is not simply to malign these great designers but to reveal either Krier's truly incapable eye or his actual agenda—the defense of

Speer by a conflation of all so-called "classicism" into a completely undifferentiated category that retrospectively justifies his seduction by an "artist" whose true medium was genocide. For this chain of filiation to make sense, it isn't enough to *admire* Otto (or Richard) Wagner; one must learn something. As Hitler himself discovered, aspiration is not talent. And we do remember historical figures for the preponderance of their achievements: who cares how beautifully Heydrich played the violin.

Learning is something almost completely lacking in Krier's analysis. Although the book has the full apparatus, Krier is no scholar. His primary sources are Speer and his acolytes, and it seems—looking at his citations—he has consulted virtually no serious theoretical or historical works for his spirited but deeply dopey gloss. In a rare citation from an "outside" source, he quotes Hannah Arendt's description of the importance of the transcendence of public space invidiously, against her real meaning, in a revolting act of false assimilation—bring out a Jew to defend the Nazi! Although he betrays the occasional flash of ponderous wit, his highest and most self-satisfied form of argumentation is summarized by a foolish syllogism he attributes to his opponents, and with which he thinks he disposes of any criticism: Hitler loved classical architecture; Hitler was a tyrant; Classical architecture is tyrannical. Bada-bing! Who actually believes this?

Am I being unfair? Is Krier actually this grotesque? Here are some typical assertions from the book:

Classical architecture was implicitly condemned by the Nuremberg tribunals to a heavier sentence than Speer.

It was? To be sure, Speer got off easy at Nuremberg, but his status as "classical" architect was part of what saved him, evidence of his alleged greater civility than the other murderers in the dock. The tribunal had nothing to say about architecture. Symbols of the regime were partially—and understandably—destroyed in the effort to "de-Nazify" Germany, though many survive to this day, including the Luftwaffe headquarters (it was actually kinda modern looking), the Nuremberg stands, and much fake

Fachwerk housing. But if there was a war on classicism how did the Altes Museum survive? Sans Souci? The castles on the Rhine? Why were the cathedrals restored?

An influential critic of the postwar German architecture scene fought an emphatic radio campaign to convince listeners of the high moral duty to free Berlin from the symbolic vestiges of "Fascism" in particular the street lanterns designed by Speer.

Let us restore the elegant swastikas too: after all, the ancient Hindus used them. What craziness to impute a sinister meaning to such faultless geometry! Perhaps it might be clarifying to string up some of the bodies hung from those lampposts in the orgy of destruction that marked the city's last days under Nazi control. Surely we can differentiate the dangler and damned.

It is not surprising that architects now consider using classical columns to be ethically more reprehensible than building nuclear power plants.

Really? Which architects are those? While we await Krier's designs for the first ionic reactor, such argument through unfounded hyperbole and limp wit substitutes everywhere in the Krierian discourse for actual evidence. Interesting that, as part of his exercises in expiation, that old Nazi Philip Johnson built a rather handsome nuclear reactor in Israel in a kind of hybrid style: a sculpturally modernist containment vessel, with classically reminiscent arcade around a courtyard for the ancillary structure.

Alongside his burning passion for advanced industrial technology, the Führer had cherished all things beautiful.

What a lovely menorah! That Bess Myerson is my favorite Miss Subways!

Superficial attempts to unmask an inherent totalitarian nature in all of classical architecture only succeeded in obscuring the mechanisms and motives that generated these buildings and this style.

Here is the straw man in the flesh. Who is it that claims the Parthenon is totalitarian? The statement—repeated endlessly— is actually a fig leaf for Krier's absolutist claim of the obverse: all modernism is totalitarian.

Even if classical monuments are reused to legitimize criminal ends, they remain unpolluted.

Guilt *can* come from association, and meaning can inhere in objects. The question is what we do with those that are so burdened by their use that their meaning is indelibly described by it. We retain the *völkisch* gatehouse at Auschwitz not because it is unpolluted but because it is the filthiest building on earth.

Speer's architecture is monumental and colossal, grand and sublime, imposing and embracing, maternal and virile … It is as absurd to blame an airplane for being aerodynamic as it is to condemn Speer's works for being monumental.

Or the gas chambers for being efficient killing machines.

To this day, many people are more disturbed by images of Speer's designs than by those of extermination camps.

On what planet?

A final word about the book itself. It's of stately dimensions and elegantly printed in black and white. Save for two images. A view of Hitler's chancellery building in a sepia-toned shot with what looks like a hand-painted blue sky and an elevational drawing of the unrealized *Marzfeld*, a reviewing stand where 160,000 spectators were to watch military drills. In this otherwise monochrome image, the continuous backdrop of Nazi banners is rendered in vivid red. What are we to make of this chromatic privilege? There would seem to be a message about the consequential symbol.

It's often said that great architecture is the product of a great client. It's no coincidence that Speer's was Hitler.

(2013)

34

Rumble in the Urban Jungle

It's hard to keep up with the musical deck chairs in the disciplines these days. The boundaries of architecture, city planning, urban design, landscape architecture, sustainability, computation, and other fields are shifting like crazy, and one result is endless hybridization—green urbanism begets Landscape Urbanism, which begets ecological urbanism, which begets agrarian urbanism—each "ism" claiming to have gotten things in just the right balance. While this discussion of the possible weighting and bounding of design's expanded field does keep the juices flowing, it also maintains the fiction that there are still three fixed territories—buildings, cities, and landscapes—that must constantly negotiate their alignment.

This has several consequences. The first is that the theoretical autonomy of the individual disciplines remains fundamentally uninfringed. The second is that new forms of a much-needed transdisciplinary practice are stymied by rigid intellectual bureaucracy. And finally, that the opportunities for turf warfare are usefully multiplied. A tiny skirmish has just been unleashed by the New Urbanists in the form of a book edited by Andres Duany and Emily Talen—*Landscape Urbanism and Its Discontents* (2013)—which singles out that inoffensive hybrid for withering opprobrium.

But why? And why now? In their preface, the editors wistfully suggest that this was a book that should have been compiled fifteen years ago. They're right: the project is pervaded by the sense that the nag being flogged long since passed through the glue factory. Their critique is antique—Landscape Urbanism is just the continuation of the Congrés Internationaux d'Architecture Moderne (CIAM) and its anti-urban principles by other means. The collection thus winds up as another—and completely unnecessary—iteration of that beloved chestnut, New Urbanism versus modernism. The current screed is obsessively focused yet again on what is seen as the leadership role in urbanism of a powerful and invidious cabal at the Harvard Graduate School of Design, an effete elite that just doesn't get it. This weirdly fetishistic animus has gnawed at Duany's craw for years What's up with that? Give it a rest!

The *trahison des clercs* schtick—those academic intellectuals are fey and fashionable compromisers without real values—plays repeatedly throughout the book. In puerile dudgeon James Howard Kunstler reaches the startling conclusion that Harvard is a bulwark of the "status quo"! Talen bemoans the Landscape Urbanists for their reversion to misconstructions of post-structuralist, Marxist, and ecological discourses as gauzy camouflage for their designs for world domination and weird uninhabitable cities. That academics would speak in the lingua franca of their own community is hardly more surprising than the New Urbanists adopting the language of developers. Their book is, indeed, full of hard-nosed whinging about the bottom line, which, in the end, is the only substantial riposte offered to actual "Landscape Urbanist" projects. Duany particularly reviles the High Line, which he thinks would have been better—and cheaper—with Adirondack chairs from Home Depot instead of all that "design."

Because there's no real case, there are more straw men in this book than at a casting call for the *Wizard of Oz*. The most cited include Harvard Graduate School of Design professor Charles Waldheim, landscape architects James Corner and the late Ian McHarg, Frederick Law Olmsted, the University of Pennsylvania, and various fellow travelers in the promotion of

... what exactly? The foundational offense is clearly Waldheim's statement in his 2006 *The Landscape Urbanism Reader* that "Landscape Urbanism describes a disciplinary realignment currently underway in which landscape replaces architecture as the basic building block of contemporary urbanism." This is simply tendentious, another way of saying, "It's the environment, stupid." But the Newbies rise to the bait. Let's get ready to rumble!

They've been preparing the battleground for years, insisting they along have found the one true condition of equipoise. New Urbanists defend their superior wisdom in three areas: the preferability of the "traditional" city of streets and squares to the universally discredited Corbusian model, a claim to special access to knowledge of sustainability, and a faux-populist derision of practices that are "avant-garde." None of these arguments is interesting or particularly controversial. No designer of conscience (or consciousness) resists the idea of cities with streets built for people on foot or fails to pay at least lip service to a sustainable—even equitable—environment. Insisting otherwise is just disingenuous.

But there *is* something interesting going on in thinking about the design of cities, informed by questions of sea level rise and climate change; massive pollution of air, earth, and water; and a broad realignment of public consciousness about the limited bearing capacity of the earth. Like virtually everyone in the disciplines, both Landscape Urbanists and New Urbanists recognize this and have produced projects that address it. It's the war over formulas that's a waste. The New Urbanists continue to dine out on the enervated notion of a regulating "transect," a graded wash of conditions from rural to urban, derived from Patrick Geddes, which they serve up with all the nuance of creationism.

But "more or less urban" is only one of many axes by which the city can be discussed, and this idealist structure has been thoroughly unpacked by many writers. One of the key deficits of the New Urbanist model is that their picturesque conceit is both nonlinear on the ground and is disrupted by the transect's own rogue category: special districts, an outlier in the neatly graphed descent. Landscape Urbanists, among others, are excited by the importance of these ubiquitous zones of exception, which include "traditional" parks as well as the "dross-scape" of rail yards, industrial zones, edge-city squalor, and other parts of the city not so easily assimilated to the historic order. Recognition that such territories—an outcome of powerful global forces—constitute a huge component of the built environment locates a truly urgent question for design.

While many usual suspects from the Congress for the New Urbanism contribute to the book, there's a clear divide between unabashed assailants and those with a more conciliatory, even sheepish, position about being provoked into a death match with an opposition that has long since morphed on: many of the book's essayists try to tiptoe away from the bluster. Duany would urgently like the High Line and Freshkills Park in New York and Downsview Park in Toronto to be seen as meretricious, but his cohort is unconvinced. Dan Solomon wisely finds these projects not simply praiseworthy as places but understands they are just parks, not urbanisms. Likewise, Jason Brody sees the valuable discursive contribution of an evolving set of landscape practices, all of which are engaged with an effort to infuse city making with our exponentially increased understanding of the planetary crisis.

If there's a bright spot in the schools and the professions nowadays, it rests in landscape architecture's ability to introduce the urgency of ecological analysis into design's atmosphere and to inventively pioneer forms of representation and meaning that freshly depict territories and phenomena from micro-climates to regions. While McHarg may have gotten it wrong in the end with his overly anthropocentric schema, the ecological insights in his mappings were seminal. The beautiful work done by James Corner and others in bridging the gap between datascapes and landscapes has been critical in establishing the utility of both new forms of analysis and new approaches to planning and building. We all want to be the mother of the arts, but why can't we just get along?

(2013)

35

Working Drawings

James Wines draws with uncanny—dare I write godly?—precision. The circuit from head to page is so amazingly short that the vision seems to spring almost fully formed and find its way into line and wash like some kind of preternatural translation: automatic drawing. We architects fetishize the sketch, the idea that the first thing that appears on the page should be so notional and spare that the contaminations of material form are displaced by the purity of idea. The hand-off from doodle to draftsman is characteristic of many of our masters, and the space between the energetic vagueness of the sketch and the precisions of construction becomes the true realm of invention.

Because Wines is so commandingly—and simultaneously—skilled in depicting perspective, dimension, materiality, setting, atmosphere, and detail, his drawings are immediately authoritative, scalable, and, indeed, ready for the more primitively precise forms of representation that enable building. Perhaps because of his initial formation and practice as a "fine" artist, it's harder to slot Wines into a conventional "architectural" category, and the magic of his technique also places him among a class of frank speculators who drew not to build but to move the meaning of architecture: Piranesi, Boullée, Chernikhov, Ferriss, Woods, Webb, and others for whom a remove from the quiddity of construction has been crucial to their authority. It isn't so much that this work seeks to be isolated from exigent use so much as it demands that its occupation, by never being literal, is left open to both a wider—and a narrower—range of fantasy. This double defiance of limits institutes both specificity and latitude, the eye drawn to formal particulars while free to roam the meaning of inhabiting the uninhabitable.

How does an architect coming from this twinned sourcing in pure expression—from sculpture, from "visionary" drawing—materialize his vision in the world of gravity, climate, dimension, and the frequent banalities of "program." It's probably both an accident and a miracle in Wines's formation that his work has followed a graceful, gradual trajectory from the symbolic terrain to the real. It might also be said that what categorically distinguishes Wines is that he has gone too far—that he has followed an arc begun along with others of his generation to take their art into an "expanded field" but has chosen to cross boundaries that remain merely notional in the work of Heizer, Smithson, Aycock, or other "environmental" artists who have always insistently made space that adjoins but does not accede to architecture. Indeed, one of the characteristics of almost all so-called land art (a very different set of practices than landscape architecture) is that it is purely invested in the scopic, environmental in only the narrowest sense.

It pays to remember that the name of Wines's studio, SITE, is the acronym for "sculpture in the environment" and that this foundation in artistic meaning gives Wines's work its originating specificity. In some kind of primal recapitulation, SITE's work descends from sculpture and its foregrounding of meaning-in-observation over a meaning-in-use. Early projects, like the Ghost Parking Lot or Highway 86—assemblages of found objects abstracted by "useless" immobility and a detail-repressing coating of asphalt or white paint—might be said to be still on the side of sculpture, weighted with artistic expression. Of course, Wines's first critical turn away from contemporaneous practices of "environmental" art is in the frank representationality of his work, a kind of landscape pop, the ironic insinuation of the social. The next step—the true bridge—was the amazing event of the BEST Products commissions. With these, SITE effectively performed an art/architecture graft in which—in fine post-modern style—there was a flip of meaning that produced a form of decorated shed where the "useful" part of the building—the replicable big box of the discount stores—was abstracted into the appearance of mere geometry while SITE operated around it in a deepened zone of expression that was—at once—facade and substance, a thickening of the thin masonry membrane wall that pointed to its own potential for autonomy via expansion.

As this study progressed from those first tectonic pratfalls to the greenhouses and terraria that came later, another flip took place, and the work morphed into *EITS*: environments *in* the sculpture. This was decisive. Where the "environmental" vector in so much art of the time was simply an axis of aggrandizement, the rationale for a more monumental canvas, SITE became crucially conscious of another environmental movement, the burgeoning of green politics and practices that formed a decisive shift in building's epistemology, its transformation from object to actor. Again, Wines found a unique vantage point, a mode of participation that further enriched the work. Architecture is sculpture infused with the performative, and the genius of the BEST buildings is that SITE's interventions—which organized both image and entry—were so manifestly continuous with the architecture as a whole: intensifications rather than ornaments, doing the full range of architecture's work.

There's a twin critique of "green" architecture that decries, on the one hand, a merely statistical approach to environmental performance and, on the other, a fashion that does not exceed decoration, a festoon of planting to camouflage actual functional indifference. Wines understands that the emergence of a "new" and responsive architecture must come from understanding the dialectic of behavior and expression as foundational to the idea of the architectural. Rooted in landscape as a system of productive, symbiotic, *ecological* relationships that define a series of forms and, in effect, conventions, nature has—not to go all Gaia—its own intentions. The kind of architecture that Wines and SITE have invented is an ongoing experiment to investigate how this process can embrace our own needs—as players not sovereigns—and renegotiate the divide—the conceptual and literal ecotone—between the natural and the architectural, surely the central subject for the future of building.

For various reasons, James Wines puts me in mind of Louis Sullivan, of his gorgeous and integral elaboration of building by a system of "ornament" derived from natural forms, of the amazing, lucid fluidity of his line. It goes perhaps too far to suggest that Sullivan truly anticipated either the debates we've been having for the past century about the criminality of ornament or nature's forms of return to architecture, but his building fairly groaned with the desire for synthesis. So too, in another register, did Le Corbusier's famous trinity of architectural desiderata—*soleil, espace, verdure*. This primitive, but extremely succinct, mantra was paired with expressive and organizational preferences that—and here is modernism's most signal failure—were seen as having the weight of both tectonic and moral inevitability. We now know more about how to skin this cat, about nature as substrate, not spectacle.

That we have spent so much time and energy arguing the way in which building can accommodate this is symptomatic both of an authentic struggle to understand architecture's instrumentality and of an eternally narrow debate about the meaning of appearances. Which brings us back to drawing. If modernism sought to capture nature via a kind of scientistic translation into a series of distancing formulas, the reaction must not be an attack on the effort to see buildings as organisms but on a kind of architectural psychology that excluded all but quantitative criteria for understanding their working kindness. The decisive break—and here we get back to Wines's own formation—was not in the silly reversion to denatured classical forms but in the kinds of rebellion that resituated technology in appropriate ways, in architectures, on the one hand, of Bucky domes and recycled industrial detritus, and on the other, in those that drew on the millennia of experience of building developed "without architects." The fantasy here was not of the superior virtue of "simple" societies but of building practices that were predicated in the rhythms of locality and availability and on actually listening to the voices of place.

This idea of such mindfulness has its own predicate in the range of techniques of observation brought by the practitioner. And it's clear that Wines draws as a means of seeing, of understanding the dynamic interaction of growth and form, of climate and light, and of the bridging morphologies he seeks to evoke that lie between the architectural armature and the field of its inhabitants—which Wines enlarges to include a maximally biodiverse population. His drawing is a kind of tropism, the experimental attraction of his hand in the direction of intelligent desire. If Wines's drawings often have a finished look, this must be seen as a form of speculative completion, and his method does not lie in a sequence of essays that begin in the primitive and culminate in the refined, but a seriatim set of well-fleshed propositions that can be eyed, vetted, modified, discarded, or approved.

As a construct, nature is very much our invention. Today, seeking the certification of the value of the natural, many attempt to associate the automations of parametric design to the field of natural process, infusing what they do with a mock-Mendelian rigor, aping genetics. James Wines, a more authentic naturalist, prefers direct field observations (sometimes of his own mind), the sketchbook instead of the DNA sequencing machine. There's a risky territory here in which the authentication of metaphor stands in for the more genuine truths of natural process. Wines's commitment to "nature" as both setting and inhabitant for his work transcends the frail hubris of translation to seek real harmony. His drawings, which trace the line of the reciprocal dissolution of nature and architecture into one another, are a beautiful testimony to an idea of mutuality that is indispensably transforming building.

Wines is *drawn* to nature.

(2013)

36

Cells Out!

Architects have been tested immemorially by the question of where to draw the line, and the choices are not exclusively aesthetic. Because buildings have uses and frame and enable particular activities, their ethical aspect is inevitable by simple association. The connection can be fuzzy or clear. Bauhaus grads worked on the plans for Auschwitz, and someone thought hard about the ornamentation on the facade of the Lubyanka. This was unambiguously wrong. So too was the target of the first explicitly architectural demonstration I ever attended, which was organized by a group called The Architect's Resistance. We marched in front of the headquarters of Skidmore, Owings & Merrill, then at work designing a skyscraper in apartheid Johannesburg. The leaflet handed out suggested that somewhere upstairs was a draftsman designing two men's rooms—one black and one white.

Sometimes the argument is less clear-cut. What about a client who specifies endangered hardwoods in a project? What about using materials with high levels of embodied energy, like aluminum? What of working for gentrifiers, or designing buildings in countries where construction labor is cruelly exploited and forced to work in dangerous conditions? Building is rife with politics, and ideally an architect will always consider the ethical implications of what he or she designs. The scale, of course, can slide: there are presumably also those who will demur at working on an abortion clinic, a nuclear power station, even a mosque.

In this country, much of the leadership on the question of architectural ethics has been provided by Architects/Designers/Planners for Social Responsibility (ADPSR), and since 2004, a focus of its activities has been the design of prisons. It has promulgated a pledge not to participate in any such work. (I signed on long ago.) The reasons for refusing such projects are many: disgust with the corrupt enthusiasm and extravagance of our burgeoning "prison industrial complex"; objections to our insane rates of incarceration; our cruel, draconian sentencing practices; and the wildly disproportionate imprisonment of minorities. Designing spaces of confinement and discipline is also contrary to what most architects imagine as their vocation: the creation of comfortable, humane, even liberating environments.

ADPSR has now focused its efforts on the worst aspects of imprisonment—execution, torture, and solitary confinement—and is in the midst of a campaign to convince the American Institute of Architects (representing about 75 percent of licensed architects) to amend its code of ethics to explicitly exclude participation in designing the sites of such barbarity. This new petition has more than 1,000 signatures, and the Institute's San Francisco chapter has become the first to vote its collective support for the drive. The no-solitary restriction is the most radical revision yet proposed to the code, which already protects unpaid interns and encourages "public interest design" and "obligations to the environment."

ADPSR—behind the energetic leadership of its president, Raphael Sperry—has asked the American Institute of Architects to "prohibit the design of spaces for killing, torture, and cruel, inhuman or degrading treatment," and cites existing language in the code that stipulates that "members should uphold human rights in all their professional endeavors." In particular, ADPSR advocates an explicit refusal to design execution chambers and supermax prisons, which are conceived for the universal solitary confinement of their inmates.

According to Solitary Watch, "at least 80,000 prisoners are in some form of isolated confinement, including 25,000 in supermax prisons." The US average for time spent in solitary is *five years*, and there are, according to NPR radio and other sources, thousands held in such isolation for decades. The destructive effects of this form of punishment have long been widely known. The UN's special rapporteur on torture has described it as "cruel, inhumane and degrading" and urges that it not be used for juveniles or the mentally ill, nor for longer than fifteen days in any circumstances, noting that this is the threshold for permanent psychological damage. In July, *Scientific American*—joining other mainline media, including the *New York Times*—published an editorial that called for a halt to this practice, citing a Supreme Court decision noting that

> a considerable number of prisoners fell, after even a short confinement, into a semi-fatuous condition, from which it was next to impossible to arouse them, and others became violently insane; others still committed suicide, while those who stood the ordeal better were not generally reformed, and in most cases did not recover sufficient mental activity to be of any subsequent service to the community.

The decision is from 1890. The editorial's conclusion: "Solitary confinement is not only cruel, it is counterproductive. The United States should reclaim the wisdom it once held and dramatically limit the practice."

Supermax prisons are exactingly designed to kill souls. Their architecture is antiseptic, barren, impenetrable, regimented, scrupulously ugly. All life is cleared from their peripheries, replaced by fields of gravel, guard towers, concertina wire. A solitary cell (referred to as the "hole" or the "box") is typically between seventy and eighty square feet, and prisoners are kept alone in them for twenty-three hours a day, with one hour alone in a "yard" barely twice the size of the cell, and a shower perhaps three times a week. Practically all human contact is mediated by bars, mesh, or manacles, and many cells are windowless, with an inmate's exposure to the world outside limited to the door slots through which food is passed by the gloved hands of jailers, often in the form of "the loaf," a disgusting pressed amalgam of pulverized food. Cells are, in most cases, deliberately colorless (any "aesthetic" ingredient is considered an inappropriate privilege in an environment that seeks to level all distinctions to the basest) and are—bunks and all—built from bare concrete; the only furnishing is a stainless steel toilet-and-sink combo positioned to deny privacy. The lighting is never turned off.

A number of observers, including Michel Foucault, Erving Goffman, David Rothman and Sharon Shalev, have told the history of the institutionalization of imprisonment, including the fluctuating sense of its purpose and the social and physical organization of its practices. In Shalev's succinct taxonomy, the purpose of imprisonment—and the use of solitary confinement—has evolved from the early nineteenth century; a focus on moral reform and the redemption of souls was superseded by a postwar emphasis on Skinneresque behavior modification, itself replaced by today's practices of "risk management." The supermax represents the almost complete abandonment of the idea of rehabilitation, replacing it with a hypercruelty of convenience.

Much of this history has been written in architecture. In the early days of the republic, an argument raged between the carceral philosophies of the Philadelphia and Auburn, New York prisons. In the former's "separate system," prisoners were held in a state of constant solitary confinement, whereas in Auburn's "silent system," they slept in solitude but mingled in silence with other inmates for meals, work, and recreation. Partisanship was intense on both sides, and Shalev cites an exponent of the separate system criticizing its rival in 1854: "The silent congregated system ... is a great step toward real improvement [but it fails] in reformation of morals as well as correction of the offender, since although the prisoner is prohibited from communicating with others, he is still surrounded by them, and 'the winking of the eye, the movement of the finger, a sneeze or a cough, is enough to communicate what is desired.'"

Hovering over much of both the architectural and social debate is Jeremy Bentham's Panopticon, his 1791 scheme for a prison based on a radial organization of cells with a concealed observer at the center. The much-marked genius of what Foucault called this "cruel, ingenious cage" was that discipline was imposed invisibly: even in the absence of the all-seeing guard, the sense of always being observed was inculcated, transferred as anxiety to the prisoners themselves. This design has had a long life, both practically (many prisons were built on this model) and as a metaphor. It has become a kind of portmanteau for descriptions of the surveillance society of which we are all increasingly inhabitants, even as Bentham's pure geometry of supervision has been displaced by a ubiquitous network of cameras, taps, and search algorithms. The supermax prison is a highly technologized über-Panopticon: prisoners leave their cells for exercise or showers via the sequential opening and closing of electronic doors, never catching sight of another person but ever under the system's inescapable gaze.

The question of why we incarcerate through such alienating means and in such massive numbers continues to trouble and confound. All the arguments are, of course, disciplinary and include the obvious conclusion that the wave of prison construction that began under Reagan in the 1980s—based on a nearly complete abandonment of rehabilitative ideals and a "punitive turn" in corrections—is one of the ugly legacies of the Gipper, Papa Bush and Bill Clinton, a racist project pure and simple: Willie Horton was no aberration.

This prison rush—described by Loïc Wacquant as a switch from the rehabilitation of convicts to the rehabilitation of the prison—has a weird dystopian parallel with the public housing projects of the postwar years; it is a massive scheme to isolate people of dubious class and color and to inculcate in them the habits of order. Indeed, the huge prison-building program of the past decades has been far larger than any public attempt to construct conventional housing. Likewise, the massive privatization of prison construction and administration—much like the current militarization of the US-Mexico border—can be seen as a perverse "peace dividend" for the private contractors whose bottom lines grow wobbly as Washington scales back on bellicose adventures abroad.

It's no coincidence that hunger strikes recently took place simultaneously at Guantánamo and, by tens of thousands, throughout the California system; despite their different practices of imprisonment, these places are representative of the American style of coercive justice and a universalized state of war against the other. Without doubt, solitary confinement is qualitatively the same experience at all of these places and mixes ideas of control and colonization, the punitive and the productive: Guantánamo used the supermax as its model. This production includes information, deterrence, retribution, and correction, whether of the soul or of some specific behavior. But the medium is always discipline and depravation. In all instances, what is produced has been demonstrated time and again to be virtually nothing but cruelty to prisoners and the convenience of the jailer. And whether in Guantánamo or upstate New York, the result is ultimately failure. Supermax prisons are factories of recidivism, rage, madness, and suicide. James Ridgeway and Jean Casella have cited evidence that the suicide rate in solitary is five times the rate of the general prison population.

While there is widespread agreement that solitary confinement is a form of torture, the debate about it reflects the same dissembling that surrounded "enhanced interrogation," as if torture could simply be described away. In the case of solitary confinement, the terms of art include "administrative segregation," "disciplinary confinement," "security housing," and "restricted housing." This rename-it-and-disclaim-it evasion provides the wiggle room for professional participation. The well-documented collusion of psychologists in the design of American styles of torture is shameful and has resulted in a professional pushback which parallels that of architects who refuse to design prisons for solitary confinement. For those psychologists who do participate, the exculpatory ruse is the question of drawing the line at "permanent" damage, and the claim is that they are there to monitor risk, not to administer it.

The interest of architects who engage in prison work would not appear to be altruistic. The back flap of a standard guide for professional prison designers offers this peppy injunction: "Now you can acquire the savvy needed to capitalize on the boom in correctional facility construction and renovation!" A headline on CNN Money is even more succinct: "The nation's 2 million inmates and their keepers are the ultimate captive market: a $37 billion economy bulging with business opportunity." But "boom" scarcely describes it: since the growth of the lock-'em-up mentality driven by the Rockefeller drug laws, various three-strikes formulations, and a general spirit of rage at the poor, minorities, the undocumented, and the dependent that has polluted our polity, the growth in prison construction has been exponential. The number of state and federal prisons rose by 43 percent from 1990 to 2005, with a new prison opening every fifteen days at the peak of the boom; and the country's rate of incarceration in the past decades has grown 400 percent to lead the world. The United States, with 5 percent of the planet's population, has 25 percent of its prisoners and now "controls" over 7 million people, either in jail or under some form of penal supervision. Employment in the sector rivals that of the automobile industry.

The leading prison design firm in the United States is the DLR Group (website motto: "Elevate the human experience through design"), which claims over $3.5 billion worth of work in the field and created the first federal supermax prison, the Florence Administrative Maximum Facility in Colorado (the erstwhile "Alcatraz of the Rockies"). Opened in 1994, Florence was the culmination of a line of development that can be traced from the Arizona Special Management Unit in 1986 and was refined by California's notorious Pelican Bay State Prison in 1989. There is an archipelago of architectural offices that do the work of designing for "justice," and many of them embed this aspect of their practice in lists of other building types, including schools, hospitals, military facilities, and so on. Kitchell Corporation, which claims 150 projects and more than 200,000 beds in its portfolio, cheerily proclaims that "Prisons Can Be Green Too." Other firms with a strong presence in the field include Arrington Watkins, KMD, and the notorious SchenkelSchultz, also implicated in the design of Gitmo.

In Shalev's study—and others—it becomes clear that architects discharge their professional responsibilities by cleaving closely to their clients' demands, rather than by thinking about the human consequences of those demands for the majority of the population housed in their work. Shalev quotes an architect she interviewed as saying, in effect, that his primary responsibility is the safety and comfort of the prison staff and that all else is secondary. Increasingly, the business contract simply replaces the social contract, something reflected as well in the great wave of privatization of prison construction and administration, led by the likes of Corrections Corporation of America [CoreCivic], the GEO Group (formerly Wackenhut), Community Education Centers, Cornell Companies, and the Management and Training Corporation. And big money is to be made not only in design and management but in food service (Aramark is big in both prison and university feeding systems), logistics, and supply.

Just as doctors are enjoined by their oath from the actual performance of state-sanctioned murder, so architects should resist when confronted with the design of death chambers. But today, hundreds of architects are engaged in the design of spaces of living death that defy every precept we should hold holy. These are lines no architect should draw.

(2013)

37

Presidents and Libraries

> Communities [have] to be created, fought for, tended like gardens.
> —Barack Obama, *Dreams from My Father*

Although the presidential library is now as natural a part of our national trove of civic rituals and commemorations as the pledge of allegiance, it is, like the pledge, a fairly new one. The first presidential library was FDR's in Hyde Park, New York. Based on his own sketches, it opened in 1941, one year before the pledge was adopted by Congress and not long after the construction of the Lincoln and Jefferson Memorials in Washington, DC.

The Roosevelt library established a series of precedents that have endured. First, the president himself is, in effect, the author of his own memorial. Second, the project is built with private funds and then conveyed to the care of the national archive. Third, every president gets one. Fourth, the president initially curates its holdings and materials. And finally, its location is completely discretionary; there are no presidential libraries in the nation's capital.

The thirteen presidential libraries (Hoover, envying Roosevelt's, erected his out of sequence in 1962) are part of a panoply of memorializations for the chief executive, including birthplaces, boyhood homes, ancestral mansions, and holiday spots, not to mention airports, cultural centers, and other civic structures. Presidents rated distinguished (Washington, Jefferson, Lincoln, FDR, Eisenhower) are honored with "pure" memorials in the precincts of the Mall. But the presidential library quickly became an executive custom, and each version to date has expanded on a basic formula. The main component is the archive, and these have experienced an exponential expansion in size, from the 17 million documents in the 40,000-square-foot Roosevelt library to the 76 million in Clinton's 152,000 square foot "Bridge to the Future." These massive deposits of paper are now joined by countless terabytes of digital data.

From the start, too, a museum has been part of the parti. These have grown from modest collections of memorabilia and presidential swag (Carter's museum includes a portrait of George Washington woven into a Persian carpet, an unfortunate gift of the shah) to include trinkets as large as the decommissioned Air Force One installed at the Reagan library in California. Another staple is a reproduction of the Oval Office, occasionally at slightly reduced dimensions. *Every* presidential museum has one, save two: Nixon's, which reproduces the Lincoln Sitting Room instead, and JFK's, which displays the furnishings of the Oval Office but without the room. Perhaps the most striking of these is at the LBJ library, where it is built at Disneyesque seven-eighths scale in order to fit in its new home at the University of Texas at Austin, which nonetheless had to have part of its roof blown out to accommodate the height of the room. Johnson, in retirement, used to work in the simulacrum: at its reduced size, it surely increased his own apparent dimensions. The Oval Office has also been reproduced unofficially countless times, including in the house of Tampa millionaires Tom and June Simpson and the lobby of the San Francisco digital start-up, GitHub. One observes the emptying of the signifier.

Johnson's library—which is the most architecturally distinguished of a largely mediocre lot—also expanded the remit and tenor of the institution by being the first to locate on a university campus and to include a school of public affairs as part of its program. This was at once an important expansion of purpose and a riposte by LBJ to the much-resented hegemony of eastern institutions in the training of high-level men and women of affairs. This pattern was repeated by the Presidents Bush, and by Bill Clinton, Jimmy Carter, and Gerald Ford. (Both Nixon and Reagan were rebuffed in their attempts to find universities that would accommodate them.) Johnson might have been frustrated that the mother of all these power academies is the Kennedy School at Harvard, built *after* his own school in Texas. And, vigorous ex-presidents have also used their libraries as the sites for their own ongoing philanthropic and political activities, most prominently Clinton and Carter whose initiatives continue to be consequential.

This idea of a presidential library as a place for *doing good* and not simply facilitating scholarship or the *muséal* appreciation of—or apologetics for—term-time achievements seems particularly relevant in the case of Barack Obama, who will leave office at the ripe old age of 56. He will surely continue to work for equity, justice, and peace through a variety of means as he continues his trajectory of public service. However, his deliberations over the potential site for his library beg another question of service: how can the construction of an institution itself leverage social and environmental transformation? Indeed, President Obama has the opportunity to return to his roots as a community organizer via the infusion of the capital, construction, energy, and purpose his presidential center will represent, and he should seize the moment to further transform the nature of the institution to the contours of his own sensibility, shaking it from the dogmatic slumber of its own creeping Disneyfication, be it playacting decision making at George W. Bush's branch (invade Iraq?) or the life-size statues of Golda Meir and Anwar Sadat at Nixon's.

Obama's choices for a location appear to have been narrowed to Honolulu and to several sites in Chicago. Chicago is clearly to be preferred. Not simply is it the city where the Obamas will presumably live post-presidency, but it is where Obama made his first deep contributions in public service and the place to which he returned to begin and advance his political mission. More, the neighborhoods bruited as choices in Chicago (half a dozen have appeared on one list or another) might all strongly benefit from the injection of institutional vigor and investment. Although there are appealing arguments for several of these possibilities, my own sense is that—far and away—the best choice would be Woodlawn, on the city's South Side, and that several large vacant sites on Sixty-Third Street most perfectly fit the bill.

Woodlawn has, to put it mildly, had a troubled history. Its origins are as a rural neighborhood that—along with adjoining Hyde Park—was annexed to Chicago in 1889. Soon after, the World's Columbian Exposition of 1893, located in what was to become Jackson Park, caused a building boom that rapidly increased the population by 20,000 and brought public transport and large and beautiful green spaces. From the start, Woodlawn's commercial spine was Sixty-Third Street, and the neighborhood developed as a leafy, bourgeois residential zone, its gentility reinforced by the closing of its popular racetrack in 1905 after the city banned betting. Many of the residents were faculty from the nearby University of Chicago, although there was also an early community of middle-class African American homeowners in West Woodlawn.

However, blacks were largely excluded by a restrictive covenant put in place by local landlords in 1928. This officially endured until being overturned by the Supreme Court in 1940 but remained in tacit effect for years more. Beginning with the depression, the neighborhood began to "tip," with increasing housing deterioration and subdivision accelerating after the war. A population that was 13 percent African American in 1930 had hit 95 percent in 2000: from 1950 to 1960, Woodlawn went from 86 percent white to 86 percent black. Total inhabitants rose to a high of 81,000 in 1960 but dropped precipitously to 27,000 by 1990 and hover around 25,000 today. By the mid seventies housing abandonment was widespread, commerce had fled, and—in a misbegotten piece of planning supported by local community groups—the "El" train being constructed east of Cottage Grove Avenue was demolished.

Segregation, poverty, and hostility gave rise to a vivid gang culture, with violent turf warfare between the Blackstone Rangers and the East Side Disciples. At the same time, the

University of Chicago was aggressively "defending" and rebuild-ing Hyde Park via a massive urban renewal regime and found demonizing utility in the specter of danger to the south. But the community was also organizing. With assistance from the legendary Saul Alinsky and the Industrial Areas Foundation, The Woodlawn Organization (TWO) was formed in 1960 to resist encroachment by the university, which had originally seen its territorial perquisites extending to a "natural" boundary at Sixty-Seventh Street, although as it planned its redevelopment, it realized that its ambitions substantially exceeded its economic and organizational grasp.

Under the dynamic leadership of the Reverend Arthur Brazier, TWO not only took a vanguard role in the neighborhood but became an articulate national voice for community empower-ment and civil rights. As TWO garnered power and recognition as an equal player, the tensions between the university and Woodlawn were gradually attenuated, and the university pledged a hands-off policy below Sixty-First Street while main-taining the south campus strip between Sixtieth and Sixty-First as a buffer, parts of which it eventually leased to the community. Trust improved and a spirit of cooperation—even alliance—began to replace an earlier paternalism.

In its first ten years, TWO followed an arc from the opposi-tional to the operational with results that can only be described as mixed. Involvement in educational reform, the Federal anti-poverty and Model Cities programs, and other government and self-organized initiatives got off to good starts but wound up cruelly thwarted by the power of the Daley machine and by institutional territoriality and inflexibility. In his seminal—and sympathetic—*Black Power/White Control* (1973), John Hall Fish argues that TWO showed remarkable resilience in the face of dashed hopes and played a key role not simply in consciousness building and local control but in keeping the idea of community alive, forestalling a fate far worse than eventually overtook it. Notwithstanding this canniness and courage, Woodlawn lost almost half its population between 1967 and 1971, in what the *Chicago Daily News* called "the blitz of Woodlawn." Thousands of fires were set, abandonment accelerated, and the progressive urgency of the Johnson era was replaced by the corruptions of Nixon and the eternal Daley. The result was massive disinvestment and abandonment, which produced the Detroit-like landscape still predominant: gapped blocks, a commercial street without shops, and swaths of empty lots.

But things are changing slowly for the better: Woodlawn is rife with capacity. TWO continues to operate as a service organization and has played a substantial role in housing renovation and the delivery of social assistance. The university has resumed development of its south campus, a certain amount of market-rate housing has gone up, apartments are being renewed, a particularly derelict housing project—an early success for TWO—is being replaced by a much better version, and the hostility between town and gown has abated substantially. Indeed, this is a moment that presents a real opportunity to repair this rift to the mutual benefit of the neighborhood *and* the university: the oppositional stance ultimately benefits neither, and the addition of the Obama library to the mix offers a striking opportunity to leverage great synergies, to effect a coherent program of spatialized mutual aid, and to foster change all can believe—and share—in.

For this to happen, though, the library must be conceived in a way that previous libraries have not been. First, it must become the first presidential center to be truly *urban*. Predecessors have been part of campuses, isolated in park-like settings, or otherwise not woven into the fabric of town. With the exception of the Clinton library, which prompted substantial riverfront gentrification in Little Rock, none has catalyzed the transformation of a community in a way that such a powerful institution might. The Obama Center has the opportunity to be a genuinely local player and to contribute to the authentic improvement of everyday life for the neighborhoods that surround it. This will require a physical and social architecture that is supportive, not aggressive or standoffish. It offers the chance to build a truly model environment.

To achieve this, the library must also expand its scope beyond archive and museum to become a truly living place, to embrace forms of activism that are directed not only at global issues—peace in the Middle East or malaria in Africa—but also at the needs of the place which gives it a home. This begins, of course, with establishing a framework of cooperation and empowerment to channel community desires and a structure that will allow it to be an instrument for leveraging local assets, which must surely include the world-renowned and prosperous university on its doorstep, an institution with which both Barack and Michelle Obama have had a long association. The tools that the president can bring to the situation consist in assuring that Woodlawn authentically benefits, that this is not an occasion for exclusionary gentrification, that the mix of people and uses in Woodlawn is embraced and enhanced with sensitivity, and that there be protection, inclusion, and opportunity for those at the bottom of the income and skills distribution.

What *programs* might such a mix consist in? The core function of the presidential library—the scholarly archive—is the symbolic center of the project, despite having relatively low rates of use. It should occupy the most consequential site, and I urge the blocks of Sixty-Third Street between Ellis and Woodlawn. This would allow the building to act as a fulcrum for the revival of Woodlawn's main street. The creative inclusion of ground-floor commercial and community space can be an interesting challenge for the architect who eventually designs the building. Surely, there will be a museum, and here another possibility offers itself: a direct relationship with the existing DuSable Museum in Washington Park, the country's oldest museum of African American history. Aligning the Obama museum with the DuSable would give it a particular inflection, celebrating a more collective achievement, and lifting it from the generic content that has come to characterize too many presidential museums.

But, to truly rejuvenate the neighborhood, the Obama Center should generate and support a range of additional activities. David Axelrod already directs the University of Chicago's Institute of Politics (and Rahm Emanuel is mayor!), and the university has a graduate school of public affairs. But Chicago has no high school of public affairs nor a school of community organization. These could cluster around the library, which would also, presumably, house whatever facilities Obama's larger philanthropic endeavors might require as well as an incubator and home for a range of local organizations. A mid-Woodlawn campus including these facilities, the university's existing charter school, and links to other neighborhood schools, would kick-start the rebirth of Sixty-Third Street and foster the insinuation of its energy throughout Woodlawn. An addition to the complex might be Woodlawn Tech, a center focused on training neighborhood residents for the kinds of biomedical, computational, and other technical jobs available at the university and in that burgeoning economic sector.

Why stop there? The wave of initiative induced by the Obama Center might also lead to the construction of one of the most needed—and contested—facilities on the South Side: a level one trauma center. While this is most logically located in the heart of the university hospital complex, the Obama Center might embrace a corollary facility deeper in Woodlawn: a center for nutrition and preventive medicine, to help tackle health issues at the front end, something the first lady has been strongly committed to. Logically, this should be accompanied by a series of sites for physical training and recreation and a system for sharing already-extensive resources between the university and its surrounding communities. Finally, the huge reserve of space that Woodlawn offers presents an opportunity for a large-scale and systematic introduction of urban agriculture and community gardens, uses that have begun to flourish throughout Chicago.

While one might expect these facilities to be coordinated by the Obama Center, the larger scale of planning must be harmonized by using these energetic interventions to direct broader objectives still. The current construction of Sixty-Third Street as a low-density residential corridor is a mistake, and the Center should catalyze more ambitious, collaborative, and sensible planning. Most crucial of all, the reestablishment of residential density throughout the neighborhood should be planning's highest objective. Morphologically, the cues are to be taken from existing conditions, from the low-rise default, adding a careful blend of single and attached houses and of multiple dwellings. To facilitate the building of the Obama Center, to fill out blocks that are gapped, and to create a continuous green space, it might be useful to move a relatively small number of houses to sites very nearby. Of course, no resident should be displaced from the neighborhood by any of this activity.

A challenge for the ex-president will be to return to his organizer's career, enlarged by the skills and powers of governing he has so abundantly acquired over the past two decades. The thrilling task will be to assist Woodlawn to become a model mix of classes, races, histories, and desires that can serve as an example to cities everywhere. This will mean that the deployment of subsidy (including the fruits of the anticipated chartable tsunami that such presidential plans attract)—in public housing, Section 8 housing, university housing, mortgage-interest-deductible market housing—must cleave to a clear model of fairness and not simply be left to the disinterested vagaries of the market or the municipality and their prejudices. Clearly, this process is dynamic, but it's crucial to note that the elements of the program described here are not needs from nowhere, but reflections of the objects of struggle—for housing, schools, healthcare, jobs, training, environmental justice, and urban connectivity—that have preoccupied Woodlawn for decades. This beleaguered community can only be rebuilt and reassured by transforming the audacity of hope into concrete acts of fulfillment.

(2013)

38

Critical Measure

Criticism—like architecture—always stands on the shoulders of something called theory, and we all embrace this: no theory, no revolution, of course. But there are so many theories available to us, and, as critics, we sort through them on the basis of both affinity and practicality. Criticism is both enlightened and vexed by the need for conceptual alliances, and if I personally demur at incorporating the arcana of psychoanalytic or philosophical criticism or the up-to-the-minute cybernetic biologism of fashionable fantasies of autopoesis in my own writing, it's not for a lack of underpinnings in realms that can produce a decent account of themselves nor in a special disdain for expository shopping. But what I want to examine here is the augmentation of architectural criticism to exceed a filtered humanities/lit-crit/*Kunstwissenschaft*/analogically based corpus of dogma and tactics and the search for additional informants from the side of my own particular concerns to weigh in judgment. This is not to reject other approaches: criticism needs many modes. But a robust critical field also requires self-criticism and the critique of critique is part of our duty.

I see criticism—and there *is* some utility in separating it from theory—as a service profession. It's not that I think of myself as an architectural barista brewing up steaming cups of truth, but that my perspective is increasingly both quantum and moral and that here criticism must be *practical*. The main issues confronting the planet are distributive—the collusion and apportionment of resources and equity—and architecture always fascinates not just for its capacity to map, but to serve. Again, it isn't that its power to charm—even to move—is negligible, uninteresting, or even less than central, but criticism must situate the nature of its own urgency. Many registers, from the urban to the microtectonic, demand many criticisms and the search for a unified field—even as a metaphor—seems unproductive, particularly given the rapid shifts of taste among both theoretically-minded architects and those who learn their reflexes elsewhere. It is, however, trying to me that so many practitioners of my generation—and of those that follow—have embraced the theoretical as the royal road to a formalism that is then advertised as expressive insubordination (modernism is dead; long live modernism) only to discover—or more often to fail to—that this is precisely the kind of architecture that the voracious global culture machine finds most tasty. While I can be as intoxicated with the power of a torqued ellipse or a morphing facade as the next aesthete, architecture as "pure" form—that is, form that is not answerable to any criterion beyond sensory pleasure—cuts relatively little ice with me. The era of a thousand flowers blossoming hasn't exactly outlived its usefulness but when I gaze upon the ludicrous, gluttonous, size-queen skylines of Qatar or Pudong or Fifty-Seventh Street, I have difficulty suppressing a groan. What victory is won? What is one really to make of those twisted dicks and riven shards and perforated signifiers of nothing in particular beyond the significance of signification?

But there's more: here's what I see. Oligarchy and BTUs. Construction-worker concentration camps filled with South Asian slaves just *hors cadre*. Women not driving. Nobody walking. The Gini coefficient writ huge. Empty $100 million apartments in a city with 50,000 homeless. Too many Starbucks. Slums without end. The greatest minds of my generation diddling themselves on behalf of money and acting as if they have progressive politics. This is truly the architecture of neoliberalism, driven by a market to which it offers not the slightest resistance. Don't get me wrong: if we are to engage in a critique of the distribution of global assets and privilege, access to the beautiful must be numbered among the goods on offer, indeed as indispensable to human survival. But the question that must be asked about architecture and urbanism is precisely whose interests are served and, especially, how particular interests shape relevant ideas of the good. A *political* criticism is urgently needed for a planet that is clearly going to hell in a handbasket, even if I reject the reflexive styles of analysis that have frequently been associated with its standard models. Form is as form does, and we don't want to be victimized by the taste of Comrade Stalin, Anna Wintour, Prince Charles, or *any* other overly empowered arbiter.

This begs many questions. One has to do with exactly what falls under the remit of architecture, and there are cogent arguments on the side of both broad and narrow views. Those of us who also have lives in the academy know well the way in which our faculties have been duking it out over who is to be the discursive Solon of the environment and, in particular just now, the hegemon of the urban. The dopey jostling—by Landscape Urbanism, ecological urbanism, urban design, urban planning, green urbanism, New Urbanism, tactical urbanism, DIY urbanism, informal urbanism, and the rest—to seize and constrain the foundational fantasy of the city is both useless and dispiriting, a distraction from real urgencies. This game of trying to parcelize—rather than distribute—proprietorship of the "environment" is simply meretricious, a way of avoiding the fact that its defense must now pervade *every* design discipline. Our job is not to adjudicate such fly-buggering questions of status but to help save the world. In this sense, begging the question of autonomy is both indispensable and in completely bad faith. The link to *agency* makes all the difference.

The emergence of a broad environmental consciousness has already permanently altered criticism as both a conceptual matter and in the expectations of our publics. In the United States, buildings are now often accoutered with plaques attesting to their LEED (Leadership in Energy and Environmental Design) rating—silver, gold, platinum—which figure comparably (if with a less direct impact on the bottom line) to the stars posted on hotels or restaurants. The meaning in both instances is that someone with nominal critical expertise has "evaluated"—reviewed—the building according to a complicit set of criteria and given it a grade. This is, I believe, authentically criticism, and its nominal objectivity gives it a certain impressive—if often mystifying and phony—purchase. Whatever the actual reliability or usefulness of the score, the idea that buildings should be judged *performatively* is crucial from the standpoint of criticism. We author—and authorize—buildings to act on our behalf.

While I have genuine sympathy for the quantitative—of which more later—the problem with LEED is the fungibility of its criteria. This is evident in the absurdly distorted high marks given to giant office buildings with huge floor plates and non-operable windows and enough embodied energy to power Belgium. These buildings rise in the ratings through some singularly skewing metrics—adjacency to a subway station, for example—that—as with pollution trading regimes—permit fundamentally foul practices to continue, under the cover of the camouflaging aggregation of the score. Like cap and trade, LEED never asks the question of sustainability *for whom*. My point is that a reflexive, *parametric* style of criticism often constitutes a form not of analysis but of evasion, even if the discussion circulates around core values. The risk arises if, as critics, we too readily displace the social with other forms of appreciation and thus cease to truly speak about architecture.

Symptomatically, for decades now, a discourse of procedures has supplanted the question of effects as the focus of architectural discussion, particularly in the schools. It is this tendency, whose origins are triple, that must be reversed. First of these influences is the legacy of functionalism, a language that remains the mother tongue of our modernity and continues to undergird the nature of both the architectural object and act. Buildings exceed the artistic—or the indifferent—by their purposiveness, and this supplement to form is ineradicable, the reason we call it architecture, not sculpture or pastry or dance. While there are plenty of interesting investigations in the turbulence of the expanded sky, the central importance of architecture's utility can only be abandoned at the expense of architecture itself. Which is to say, the fit of form and function will always remain critical, but the actual relationship between generative strategies and outcomes must map the territory for criticism.

The second source of the procedural affect is the legacy of surrealism, which attempted to liberate technique from dogma through its association of the random with freedom and rebellion. Architecture is never *not* political, given both its economic stakes and its commitment to setting social life and agendas. Modernist architecture has bravely—if mainly futilely—held onto the dream of its own subversiveness, its ability to leverage global change; these are its roots. In most ways, this version of the political is simply a rewriting of architecture's historic hubris, the notion that the arrangement of rooms restructures the relationship of souls. While our understanding of this connection has been considerably altered, marked especially by the biopolitical turn (associated, most prominently, with the work of Foucault)—in both the deployment and understanding of spatial power and its focus on the mutability of bodies and the organization of populations in space—precise effects remain fluid and undecidable. However, it's not sufficient for criticism merely to note that things change; our task is to influence the *direction* of change. Are we simply going to allow Genentech to redesign and commodify us? Are we going to give up the struggle for our own privacy and self-control? Are we going to write off architecture as a tool?

Surrealism and its deadpan, in-your-face celebration of the aleatory and the accidental continues to provide a robust, if fraying, critique of idealism and of the dogmatic teleologies that have brought us to our particular end of history. By offering a constant affront to the idea of fixity, surrealist practices are at once engagingly destabilizing and a rebuff to content. This is tricky territory, both protective and dangerous. If meaning is subject to constant deconstruction, we risk destroying the forms of consent that enable architecture and urbanism to become genuinely social practices that advance human needs in measureable ways. This nexus is key: we cannot simply have contempt for benchmarks, for the measurability of—for want of a better word—progress. And let's not mystify the categories, which include breathing, eating, sleeping, gathering, staying healthy, comfortable, even happy.

Finally, the procedural turn has long been an outcome of moves to assimilate the authority of what seem to be comprehensive systems of description and analysis, thought to be more rigorously grounded than any derived from within the architectural field itself. This is certainly true of those who most ardently support the biologism closely identified with the concept of autopoesis. One of the leading exponents of its translation into the social field, Niklas Luhmann, writes that within this condition "the normativity of laws is replaced by the performativity of procedures." While this surely identifies a general historical trajectory of legitimation and a descent of the law from divine authority, it also suggests a kind of self-legitimation *within* the procedural, which is exactly what its architectural exponents seem to have latched onto, as a way of excluding politics from architecture. This is the position of Patrik Schumacher—who builds his own theory largely on Luhmann's—and it offers a vision of architectural outcomes that find their social meaning as avatars of the irresistible wisdom of the neoliberal market.

The problem here lies in this subservience to the will to power and is particularly reified in the difficulty of coming to grips with the nature of the continuity between architecture and urbanism, the apparent change in register begged by that shift in scale and organization. Certainly, we are constrained by the historical—and abiding—idea, per Alberti, that these phenomena are essentially just larger and smaller instances of the same substance and practice. The trouble occurs at the points of attempted convergence, and this territory is the domain of the social and the political. The enormous and persuasive body of work on the city stemming from a generally Marxist perspective—including Lefebvre, Chombart de Lauwe, Williams, Castells, Harvey, Smith, (even Mumford and Jacobs), and so on—has formulated robust conceptual and quantitative tools for tackling the subject. These writers frame the visuality of the city in the context of social relations, as a mapping rather than an instigation. And, the priority of groups over individuals is the key to understanding the social, moving analysis in the *direction* of space rather than—as more purely architectural theory tends to do—taking spatial relations as the primary given.

Surrealist practices actually form a strangely useful bridge between these phenomena. To begin, they stand at the headwaters of the idea of psychogeography (vivid in work as different in mood as the Situationists and Kevin Lynch) and effectively bring the unconscious—hence psychoanalysis—into play as foundational for the understanding of space. While Duchamp and Debord may have been overly fascinated by the potent juju they thought *their* procedures helped excavate, they nonetheless suggested a companionable territory to Marxism's focus on group relations in space for understanding the plastic dimensioning of the terrain of individual subjects. More, their sensitivity to the "irrational" outcomes of random juxtapositions surely opens up a key vein in a general description of the working of the city, both socially and spatially. The *exquisite corpse*—with its combination of regulation and chance—is surely as good a metaphor—and model—as we have for the inventive engine of urbanism.

What it lacks is a mechanism beyond delirium for vetting its outcomes, a deep qualitative or quantitative parametrics of results and effects. Which brings us to a critical and conceptual conversation in which many architects, though few critics, are deeply immersed today. Parametric design is an automated method that seeks to introduce a set of certifying performative criteria on the front end of the process of creation and has spread its claims and operations to every scale, from buildings to cities. The question to be answered is whether this methodology—which surely has demonstrated the capacity to produce beautiful forms, rich with seductive self-referential meanings—can transport its intentions through the process of design in a way that yields outcomes that "live up" to the critical categories that begat them.

It's important to distinguish between parametric design and algorithmic design, terms I am using somewhat interchangeably. Being a relative computational dunce—I dropped out of Nick

Negroponte's class in 1971, stymied by the primitive inscrutabilities of trying to program in Fortran, to await the maturation of the technology and still draw with a pencil—I can only give you my impression of the key differences. Although both locate design at the level within logical structures that generates form, rather than at the level of form itself, parametric design seems to be mainly an accelerant, one which allows the testing of alternative designs by changing inputs quickly, often automatically. Algorithmic design, on the other hand, is authentically recursive and aims to produce successively *better* designs that grow from a series of inborn "selection criteria," the expression of negative and positive desires incorporated in its operations. The relationship between these criteria and their outcomes is subject to "verification" by systems designers—their own form of critical practice—but the connections occupy largely arcane computational realms, and the chain of argument can't really be followed, save by programmers. However, the importance of algorithmic design is that it is explicitly conceived to produce results that the designer could not foresee. And, as a politics, by replacing the idea of an "optimal" design (à la Chris Alexander) with a "stable" one, it seems to have the potential to subvert the received bureaucratic ethos.

Parametricism begs the question of its authority in several important ways. To begin, its discourse—much of it borrowed from the life sciences—seeks to naturalize both its methods and its meaning: a long-standing conversation about artificial intelligence and artificial life is pervasive in parametricism's ambitious self-account. This extends beyond mere metaphor to a nineteenth-century century vitalism that equates architectural creation with the genesis of being itself. Without doubt, the modeling of building as organism, as a self-organizing and self-generating system, seeks to blur the boundary between life forms and forms of living. This is very dodgy territory, and I am not the first to point out the eugenic overtones in much of the discussion of architectural autopoesis and the dangerous ambitiousness of its self-considered reach.

Christine Boyer writes about this with her usual clarity:

While the ... model of autopoetic systems offers new ways of talking about both biological form and urban form and presents new organizational methods to manage populations at risk or the flows of movement into the city and between layers of the city, such management systems, however, strip individual or local details from their context, blend characteristics together in databanks, and statistically manipulate differences into a homogeneous pattern. In architecture, it has led to the study of hallucinatory normality called the "Generic City." But what is the standard of this normality, and what does it mean about individuals or cities that do not live up to this standard? Does it form a new kind of inequality: between those who can afford to develop in "Generic Cities" with all the accoutrements of modernity displayed in their skyscraper towers, shopping malls, and superblocks of housing and those left behind in the backwaters of development?

The broader question raised for architecture is *how* the social is to be embraced, enhanced, and understood, how to hedge against this kind of technological dream that still hungers for a single cybernetic system of organization that produces not simply cities but life itself, how to step back from this overwhelming *tsunami* of post-humanist complexity to elevate human and planetary needs as agents against an irresistible model of emergence? Here, it's useful to recall the formulation of the economist Amartya Sen, who identifies human and social development in a very different way—with *capacity* building. What Sen argues is not simply for specific powers and practices (nor, certainly, for some sweet form of social Darwinism) but for an expanding space in which to acquire them. For politics, this means moving beyond a simple list of rights toward the more fundamental right to *have* rights. This is exactly what Henri Lefebvre argues as "the right to the city"—the idea of an imaginative space from which to envision and move toward a city that's the outcome of desires that may not yet have been conceived. This is a revolutionary formulation and it demands not simply the whimsical change of churning alternatives with completely commutative meanings but a mutually defended advance of human possibilities. We must fight against the convenient embrace of the neoliberal retreat from such broad questions of social welfare—whether expressed theoretically or practically—that springs from the rampant privatization of architecture's chain of being and meaning.

Parametricism's criteria often involve the production of functional outcomes. Although it seems—in much of the work with which I am familiar—less important in practice than the production of new expressive forms, the achievement of novelty, the pursuit of refined vocabularies of shape, and the elision of processes of design and fabrication, I strongly believe that the possibility of creating acute and variegated architectural and urban responses to questions of solar access, ventilation, view, privacy, circulation, and other fundamental—and measureable—parameters of architectural success—particularly in cases of large urban aggregations of structures—is a genuinely important frontier to be pursued full bore. That this might be achieved via the creation of a succession of formal singularities of great structural efficiency is only a bonus in a world of growing scarcity.

Finally, the idea of the closed loop—of a system constantly renewing itself from its own outputs—is resonant for the creation of truly sustainable architectures and urbanisms. I don't have the sense that the leading advocates of architectural parametricism and autopoesis are greatly interested in this particular form of autonomy, but its calculus is critical to the future of construction and is one of the most promising aspects of the computational infusion into architectural practice. The city is important not merely as an outcome but as a critical increment of democratic organization and as the site at which collective resistance to the predations of neoliberalism can be best organized and the autopoetic metaphor best challenged and recast. One cannot simply leap analogically from cellular life to social life: the infinity of a human subject's practical engagements simply doesn't resemble those of a cell.

Without doubt, these technologies have already had a huge epistemological effect—the layered simultaneity of Building Information Modeling (BIM) and Geographic Information

Systems (GIS) have been extensively applied but barely appreciated in their deep transformation of our mode of knowing building. Beyond the consequences for representation and process, it's clear that we are on the cusp of creating architectures and cities with new forms of liveliness and responsiveness. However, these cannot be detached—as the corporatized discussion of so-called "smart cities" so often does—from the real threats to liberty and subjectivity posed by an environment that simply knows too much. Or pretends to.

There is something deeply sinister in the idea of smart cities and buildings—and with the ratcheting up of the idea that information is simply neutral and "free" (so often expressed by the billionaires who control it)—and we are right to suspect any ideology of perfect knowledge that seeks to "optimize" systems far too dynamic, complex, political, and historical for such approaches. However, I remain fascinated by the potential of machine-enabled design to advance environmental transformations because that project is central to the very future of architecture—and the planet—and because the looping patterns of terrestrial respiration and reproduction must increasingly be the model of all of our building practices: earth is mainly a closed system. I know that this might sound, in effect, like a revival of the functionalist agenda and, in a way, it is. But, believing that architecture is always *also* an artistic practice, I reject—as a mode of criticism—the idea that our task is to search for a fundamentally indexical set of relations between the operational aspects of architecture and their form. Indeed, a legitimately operational touchstone is where that fundamentally *surrealist* promise of parametrics and algorithmics gains its appeal: the cat can be skinned in an endless number of ways, *many* of which yield a lovely pelt. This may remind you of those infinite monkeys at infinite typewriters eventually aping Hamlet. But these new design methods are potentially more interesting in their capacity to generate a large number of artifacts that are *not* Hamlet. The task of criticism is to sort out the worthwhile *not*-Hamlets from the mounds of gibberish and to resist the fantasies of optimization and singularity, the oppressive forms of knowledge and practice pretending to perfection.

Which gets us back to the idea of a quantifiable basis for criticism. I've argued that the focus of that activity must be moved from the territory of authenticating procedures to the terrain of desirable effects. But how to articulate these authoritatively? Nobody who has been in an academic design studio in the past couple of decades can have failed to notice that creeping transformation in styles of account offered by students when they present their projects, which surely reflect these larger tendencies in critical language and strategy. As I've already observed, the steady displacement of the discourse of effects by that of procedures works to mute the range of judgments about outcomes, which are simply justified reflexively: this line here represents the connection between Richard Wagner's desk and Otto Wagner's—'nuff said! In part, I think, this neurasthenic silliness is a consequence of the emptying out of the architectural signifier by its asymptotic trajectory in the direction of minimalism and its macho purgation of meaning. This degree zero has also goaded the wild expressionism identified with computational parametricism, and hooray for that outcome. But the stance also seems to be a result of the general displacement of art practices from object to performance. What's striking here is the effective theatricalization of art in which we are invited to embrace the work of Marina Abromović within the same conceptual frame as that of Rembrandt, both being phenomena that seek the same public as well as the shelter and sanction of the museum. Such acts of excess parity threaten the very ground of criticism!

This issue is not simply a displacement of the meaning of an artifact onto the technique that produces it. Rather, it is a conceptual *reweighting* of their relationship that functions in the same way that conceptual art seeks to skew the scales in favor of the quality of the idea that stands at the headwaters of the truncated chain of signifiers that yields the *thing*. Fixation on procedure can often be a form of indirection, a shift of focus away from the performativity of the object to that of the artist. While this may have a certain resonance in other artistic disciplines—and certainly hasn't inhibited our own starchitect cults—it can never be enough in the territory of actual architecture and of the urban, where reception must always be an immanent category as long as other people *live* in it.

My skepticism is quite different from a blanket antipathy to the idea of intention as a critical category. We've all been schooled in the intentional fallacy, the death of the author, and a general dissolution in the probative value of artistic motives, and yet architecture really is *different*. Architectural intent resides in the idea of program, and a program-less building ceases to be architecture, much as a sculpture that arrogates specific characteristics of architectural performance—say shelter from the rain or the management of circulation—becomes, at least partially, architecture. While the notion is now common that this may constitute an "expanded field" for the increasingly irrelevant task of adjudicating disciplinary boundaries (I recently had a glance at the catalog of the School of the Art Institute of Chicago where the degrees have mounted into their hair-splitting dozens, as they have at the New School in New York where the urban has migrated as a sanctifying qualifier to countless indistinguishable programs), mere multiplication does little to interrogate the class of effects that architecture embodies and that form the main locus for its criticism, which—in the social realm—always has a corrective component: advocacy for getting it right. And, many of the effects—thermal behavior, energy efficiency, ease of movement, comfort, mix, and so forth—are both measureable and non-trivial, and can be gotten right in various ways. The more difficult questions concern their intercourse with slipperier categories such as beauty or joy—or justice.

What I am looking for, in other words, is a post-functionalist, quantitative criticism that does not simply live in peace with the unaccountable and expressive but converses and coevolves with them. That is, I am wondering what the measureable elements are to which we can look in architecture that will undergird whatever qualifying supplement elevates a building (and an urbanism or a landscape) into the category of art. While I would preserve something of the timeless formulation that ever isolates —or individuates—the quality of delight and insist that we retain some territory of autonomy (or semi-autonomy in the

Marxian formulation) for the free range of desire and the collusive effects of various taste cultures, I also believe that what
makes architecture singular is that its aesthetics are irreducible
to either *purely* quantitative or qualitative matters, that old
asymptotic conjunction of form and function. Program and
expression are inseparable: buildings have motives. As Gilles
Deleuze puts it: "No one ever walked endogenously." The
chicken did have a reason to cross the road! That is not to say
that mere goals define architecture—they must be seen in their
constant state of change—but that there is no architecture in the
absence of goals and that these can very often be specified and
measured.

This question is especially germane nowadays to the debate
about the scope of the validations offered by computational parametricism, which do bear a risk of creating a set of standards
with a distinctly theistic, ritualistic, auratic, sublime aroma. This
back-and-forth between codification and ineffability is surely
an extended recapitulation of exactly that discussion of the last
few decades about the authority and utility of the procedural
in both its pre- and post-automated incarnations, not simply
in determining architectural value but as a mode of invention.
This does suggest the same sort of collapse between the formal
and the social that functionalism aspired to. Such displacement
onto methodological approaches (doesn't anyone remember the
whole Design Methods school of the sixties?) represents both a
kind of endgame for functionalism and a certain despair over
architecture's actual utility. (I would, by the way suggest that
Walter Netsch's forgotten "field theory" stands at the headwaters of contemporary post-functionalist, formalist approaches
to automated design.) Proponents of parametricism move this
along by their supersession of the modernist idea of space by
the notion of field, a seeming excision of the body, spines suc-
cumbing to splines. While the procedural mood has been, as
suggested, strongly influenced by contemporary minimal, ges-
tural, and purely performative art "practices" that *foreground*
the body as site, the connection to technique remains abstract.
There's an emotional automation in which the surrealist legacy
again figures strongly, especially its conceit that it had discovered

techniques that could directly—and mechanically—access the teeming font of the unconscious. Are computers now meant to dream for us as well as to draw?

I've argued that computational parametricism—and its digital scripting—is, inter alia, a means to rationalize surrealist procedures. That is, effectively, what makes it different from the immemorial techniques of architecture in general, which are, invariably, nothing if not parametric. Indeed, the most theoretically informed parametric practice on the planet is that of the New Urbanists, whose coding is amazingly disciplined, comprehensive, and successful at producing variations of their own homely traditionalist desires. Whether we design with a pencil or a program, no architecture can exist—or wait long—without recognition of constraints, generally starting with gravity and the injunction of every post-Neanderthal parent to "stand up straight, stupid!" In this sense, parametric computation offers a difference of degree rather than of kind. What it produces is still mainly a shape vocabulary and grammar of unusual sophistication, generated at very high speed. At the end of the day, though, the output still needs to be vetted for cybernetic idiocy and submitted to various tests of taste and practicality—including the purging of any accidentally literal or undesired representations, the kind of incidental teratology that comes from anything constituted of skin and bones.

The argument has been made for some time that formal outcomes are pre-inscribed in the parameters of the algorithmic animating programs themselves, that Rhino and Grasshopper are the real brains—and taste—of the operation. This begs a question about the anterior judgment of the procedural, given that the inputs into parametric design guarantee a determinate range of formal outcomes: there's a reason that those CAD monkeys designing in Maya often produce work with deep affinity, and the frequent complaint that you can't actually tell one project apart from another represents more of a failure of connoisseurship than fact. Languages do generate their own characteristic prosodies: there's also a reason that Japanese, its every syllable ending in an open vowel, is not congenial to long-form poetry. Programming languages are surely even more acute examples: they are not the product of eons of evolution and the nuanced accumulation of influence and affect but are the short-term creation of a small circle of inventors whose goals are shaped by a vision of outcomes. CATIA—employed since the seventies in aerospace, marine, and automotive design—was a solution to the problem of *representing* compound curvature, not its source. Indeed, the automation of Zaha Hadid's project has clearly entailed both benefit and compromise. While much of the work could not be built without the computer, there is a risk of loss in translation: it isn't simply a matter of Zaha in, Zaha out. There's a whole field of amateur connoisseurship these days dedicated to discerning the authentic product of the master's hand from the studio simulacrum.

In that sense, the necessity for critical metrics becomes even more acute. If the formal properties of architecture are prevented from any particularly rogue expression by constraining algorithms, then effects become especially important. This begins to refocus the idea of intention, away from its dismissal as fallacy or irrelevance. Tools always mediate intentions (which is what gives rise to the fallacy), but by seeking to inseminate architecture with a certain predictability of functional effect—shading, proximity of the men's room, straight runs for electrical chases, minimum use of reinforcing rods, whatever—parametricism again effectively recapitulates the functionalist argument by insinuating formalism into the lexicon of pure effects, by collapsing the range of choices about building form into a single generative complex. Not that there's anything wrong with that! What's tendentious is the claim more than the practice, the assimilation of procedural authority to outcomes. I certainly believe that, in architecture, the ends generally justify any means, as long as it doesn't involve killing puppies or overexploiting interns. What makes me anxious are more extravagant and repressive claims.

For example, Patrik Schmacher declared in his "Parametricist Manifesto" of 2008 that the "shared concepts" of those working toward the new "parametric paradigm" are "crystallizing into a solid new hegemonic paradigm for architecture." Schumacher elaborates this at great—even amazing—length in his two volume treatise, *The Autopoesis of Architecture* (2011), a work that is admirable in its game efforts to assimilate *everything* but which founders on the same risk that haunts any totalizing system: its heroic lack of skepticism. Hegemonic paradigms are among the most conspicuous of revolver-reaching stimuli and we need, therefore, to react swiftly to them. I may not have made clear that while I do not consider procedures—all of which function via the articulation and valorization of parameters—to be authoritative outside the question of their effects, I don't dismiss any procedure in the absence of the evidence of its outcome: whatever bus gets you to nirvana is fine with me. And, I don't deny the necessity of establishing a supple set of feedback loops between methods and results.

But it's right to be wary of totalities, and parametricism seems to be a new name for what used to be called total design—another high point in a very long history of architectural overreach—albeit with a different inflection and methodology. Both seek a totalizing grasp, and architectural autopoesis argues for a troublingly closed idea of infinity, unable to distinguish a cell from a person. This is true both in the sense that they proclaim the all-encompassing character of a unified field in its self-avowed capacity to eventually produce anything and in the even more all-encompassing claim to be able to take account of anything. This is dangerous. By an explicit arrogation of the social and the political into its methodological armamentarium and by its insistence that it is, as procedure, fundamentally scientific, a can of worms is cracked open. The idea that architecture defends its territory in a fragmenting and allegedly nonhierarchical social field does have a certain hermetic chops, but the move from relative to complete autonomy continues to trouble, smacking of neoliberalism's own special end of history. Again, let me make my position clear. I find that many students and practitioners working via parametric scripting have produced images of truly original and mesmerizing beauty. Beyond that, I am unaware of any outcomes of this methodology that have had dramatically measureable effects on economics, environmental performance, homelessness, real user control, or any other nonvisual characteristic of architecture that *cannot presently be achieved more easily by other means.*

The idea of self-containment suggested by the concept of autopoesis, whether incarnated in Varela and Maturana or in Luhmann, is, however, not entirely ... self-contained. While it is surely a great conceptual convenience when arguing for the autonomy of architectural practice—a kind of idealist partition against contamination—by framing architecture as a system of communication, it invents it as a *reciprocal*, the singularity (or succession of singularities) at the nexus of a variety of intra- and interdisciplinary relations and influences. This might usefully open architecture to the social, but it also means that shifts in these relationships cause the migration of the architectural in relationship to other points within the larger field of disciplines. Today's architecture is not necessarily tomorrow's, and the conceit of self-production—the idea that the system constantly changes in relationship to conditions the system considers *relevant*, is critical. Given that we don't respond to everything but only to certain stimuli, the question is how we determine what *is* relevant. These criteria cannot be completely elastic.

Autonomous or not, parametric design still obliges the designer to choose between alternatives generated by the computational results of the motivating scripting as well as to choose and weight the parameters entered. If anything, this reinforces the reserves of artistry—even informality—that the technique might be capable of, even as it undercuts the domineering mystique offered by its exponents and their troubling claims of universalism. Your parameter, after all, can be my nightmare and a logical—and it seems neglected—area of research for this cadre is precisely the sourcing of parameters and the relationship between such expert systems and the world of the amateurs who will ultimately be the beneficiaries or victims of this work. Once the field is expanded—as it must be—to embrace architecture's "users," claims of disciplinary autonomy become tenuous unless such unwashed feedback is excluded.

And so we get back again to the task of criticism and its measurements. It's a platitude that critics of architecture often arrive on the scene too late, giving their useless thumbs-up or -down to some zillion-dollar pile on which their opinions will have not the slightest impact. I don't mean to trivialize either the function or the concept of criticism, but—just like architecture—it must also be judged by its effects. While our pronouncements may have useful consequences for the general conditions of culture, for the city, for the refinement of the terms of discussion, it is precisely our mission to help vet the instigation of the social and formal parameters of building. In looking at explicitly parametric practice, we should be keen to observe the way in which the parameters of production are inhibited by the parameters of inhabitation, to assess the consequences of their weighting and interaction, to assure that the graphics are not more seductive than the objects, indeed that the avowed parameters actually *inhere* in the objects.

Ironically, the conversation about computation-driven architecture I've encountered actually devotes quite a lot of attention to the idea of effects. But the notion behind the parlance seems quite different from the one I am trying to offer. For the Maya generation, the meaning is congruent with the idea of "special effects," Hollywood lingo. That is, the effects that are being sought are sensory, artistic, or representational, rather than social, political, or functional. This isn't to say that an aesthetic effect has no potential to yield social or environmental consequences, but rather that these consequences are almost invariably indirect, second-order effects. And, I surely wouldn't gainsay that a flamboyant return to form was a critical style of rebellion against ossified modernism and the life-deadening systems of conformity and control that had come to find it so congenial.

But this opens up a familiar interpretive gap, and I'm not yet satisfied with the way in which the current generation—indeed the several generations of postmodern practices of which this is surely one—have sought to bridge it. While the idea that the right riposte to a dreary, universalized, mechanized architecture was broad-based artistic insubordination, the spirit of anything goes, and an exaltation of the individuality of the object made sense at the time, the rapid co-optation of these formal experiments by the Man in his various incarnations is striking. Why is it that the most exuberant formal experimentation all seems to take place under the auspices of various despotisms, from the Persian Gulf to the boomtowns of China to capitals of the Central Asian -stans? That this is an advertisement for the truly marginal effects of formal experiment as such is both painful and indisputable. It is an irony—but not a coincidence—that wild architecture is so easily tolerated, one that should give us pause when thinking about the potency of form qua form. If our agendas our so easily co-opted we certainly bear at least some of the responsibility for their wimpiness.

But, if it's social effects we're looking for as a foundation for criticism, where—beyond raw distributive equity—do we locate them? Surely not in some deracinated form of utilitarianism, in a purely statistical conceit. While I have much sympathy for the position that our obligation as citizens is to assure that there be a fundamental fairness in the allocation of goods, it is not exactly—at least not exclusively—where our duties as architects lie. Sure, there is something measureable gained if we can design the means to make housing accessible and affordable via technical innovations, but there can be a fine line between affirming the logics of distributive inequity and assaulting it. We want everyone housed, but not in the segregated minimum-security prisons of *Existenzminimum* blocks. We want to participate in a project of raised, not diminished, expectations. This means that it is not completely productive to have a criticism that is *entirely* rooted in material expectations, however important it is that material parameters be observed.

The way forward is to focus our critical gaze on situations where the stakes are real. To cite one possible critical direction, the less pervasive—but potentially more liberating and germane—fascination with "informality," which has seen a recent return to the scrutiny of professional interest, actually seeks to come to grips with the major portion of the urban condition—if only by identifying the place where more than half of city dwellers eke out their lives. And yet this too rarely figures in the critical canon, perhaps because it so directly gainsays the question of architecture's discursive autonomy. By parceling off this territory with walls of either infatuation (generally freighted with an excess of the formal) or disdain (why *look* at the slums), we distort our field. But it's worth thinking for a moment about the implications of the informal for our own styles of formal analysis. Although the subject is conceptually fraught, and many of its best students now go so far as to reject the category as simply too slippery, it's too important—too seminal—to ignore its key qualities.

The most central of these is the element that has long made informality so conceptually attractive to those seeking to explore the relationship of architecture's modes of production and the nature of the freedom and self-actualization enjoyed by those who use and inhabit it: its real romance and promise is "user" control. But this immediately raises the question: control of what? Much as the favelas and squatter settlements of Latin America and Asia are alluring for their intoxicating, complex visuality—the image of prismatic squalor spilling down the hills of Rio—so the ideal of participation needs to be taken with a grain of salt. My own school days were filled with the ennobling rhetoric—and the real work on the ground—of John Turner as well as with the ultimately indeterminate speculations of John Habraken and his highly parametric "support structures." The idea behind these and other experiments was to translate the supposed autonomy—the right to build houses of garbage and to have sewage run down the middle of the street—"enjoyed" by third world slum dwellers into a more rationalized form of flexibility and control to suit the trials of expanding and shrinking households in developed economies. The best architects among us—including many invested in parametric techniques—are again working to bring more malleability to our environments, but the question is what is lost in translation. And this, as usual, is politics.

The task of criticism, then, is not simply to acknowledge the political but to struggle to infuse the practice of architecture with the means for understanding and incorporating progressive social values, including ever-expanding rights of comfort and desire. One of the fascinations of architectural criticism is that much of its work must bridge the qualitative and the quantitative, and we should not demote the idea of net-zero energy or mass affordability to a status inferior or ancillary to dancing forms and fascinating finishes. Criticism must play a role both in advocating for the most expansive ideas of artistic self-expression and human possibility and in making ardent arguments through which to expand, refine, and acquire real outcomes for real people; it must be tireless propaganda for the good, the just, the fair.

(2014)

39

Two Hundred Fifty Things an Architect Should Know

1. The feel of cool marble under bare feet.
2. How to live in a small room with five strangers for six months.
3. With the same strangers in a lifeboat for one week.
4. The modulus of rupture.
5. The distance a shout carries in the city.
6. The distance of a whisper.
7. Everything possible about Hatshepsut's temple (try not to see it as "modernist" *avant la lettre*).
8. The number of people with rent subsidies in New York City.
9. In your town (include the rich).
10. The flowering season for azaleas.
11. The insulating properties of glass.
12. The history of its production and use.
13. And of its meaning.
14. How to lay bricks.
15. What Victor Hugo really meant by "this will kill that."
16. The rate at which the seas are rising.
17. Building information modeling (BIM).
18. How to unclog a Rapidograph.
19. The Gini coefficient.

20. A comfortable tread-to-riser ratio for a six-year-old.
21. In a wheelchair.
22. The energy embodied in aluminum.
23. How to turn a corner.
24. How to design a corner.
25. How to sit in a corner.
26. How Antoni Gaudí modeled the Sagrada Família and calculated its structure.
27. The proportioning system for the Villa Rotonda.
28. The rate at which that carpet you specified off-gasses.
29. The relevant sections of the Code of Hammurabi.
30. The migratory patterns of warblers and other seasonal travelers.
31. The basics of mud construction.
32. The direction of prevailing winds.
33. Hydrology is destiny.
34. Jane Jacobs in and out.
35. Something about Feng Shui.
36. Something about Vastu Shilpa.
37. Elementary ergonomics.
38. The color wheel.
39. What the client wants.
40. What the client thinks it wants.
41. What the client needs.
42. What the client can afford.
43. What the planet can afford.
44. The theoretical bases for modernity and a great deal about its factions and inflections.
45. What post-Fordism means for the mode of production of building.
46. Another language.
47. What the brick really wants.
48. The difference between Winchester Cathedral and a bicycle shed.
49. What went wrong in Fatehpur Sikri.
50. What went wrong in Pruitt-Igoe.
51. What went wrong with the Tacoma Narrows Bridge.
52. Where the CCTV cameras are.

53. Why Mies really left Germany.
54. How people lived in Catal Huyuk.
55. The structural properties of tufa.
56. How to calculate the dimensions of brise-soleil.
57. The kilowatt costs of photovoltaic cells.
58. Vitruvius.
59. Walter Benjamin.
60. Marshall Berman.
61. The secrets of the success of Robert Moses.
62. How the dome on the Duomo in Florence was built.
63. The reciprocal influences of Chinese and Japanese building.
64. The cycle of the Ise Shrine.
65. Entasis.
66. The history of Soweto.
67. What it's like to walk down Las Ramblas.
68. Backup.
69. The proper proportions of a gin martini.
70. Shear and moment.
71. Shakespeare, et cetera
72. How the crow flies.
73. The difference between a ghetto and a neighborhood.
74. How the pyramids were built.
75. Why.
76. The pleasures of the suburbs.
77. The horrors.
78. The quality of light passing through ice.
79. The meaninglessness of borders.
80. The reasons for their tenacity.
81. The creativity of the ecotone.
82. The need for freaks.
83. Accidents must happen.
84. It is possible to begin designing anywhere.
85. The smell of concrete after rain.
86. The angle of the sun at the equinox.
87. How to ride a bicycle.
88. The depth of the aquifer beneath you.
89. The slope of a handicapped ramp.
90. The wages of construction workers.

91. Perspective by hand.
92. Sentence structure.
93. The pleasure of a spritz at sunset at a table by the Grand Canal.
94. The thrill of the ride.
95. Where materials come from.
96. How to get lost.
97. The pattern of artificial light at night, seen from space.
98. What human differences are defensible in practice.
99. Creation is a patient search.
100. The debate between Otto Wagner and Camillo Sitte.
101. The reasons for the split between architecture and engineering.
102. Many ideas about what constitutes utopia.
103. The social and formal organization of the villages of the Dogon.
104. Brutalism, Bowellism and the Baroque.
105. How to *dérive*.
106. Woodshop safety.
107. A great deal about the Gothic.
108. The architectural impact of colonialism on the cities of North Africa.
109. A distaste for imperialism.
110. The history of Beijing.
111. Dutch domestic architecture in the seventeenth century.
112. Aristotle's *Politics*.
113. His Poetics.
114. The basics of wattle and daub.
115. The origins of the balloon frame.
116. The rate at which copper acquires its patina.
117. The levels of particulates in the air of Tianjin.
118. The capacity of white pine trees to sequester carbon.
119. Where else to sink it.
120. The fire code.
121. The seismic code.
122. The health code.
123. The Romantics, throughout the arts and philosophy.
124. How to listen closely.

125. That there is a big danger in working in a single medium: the logjam you don't even know you're stuck in will be broken by a shift in representation.
126. The exquisite corpse.
127. Scissors, stone, paper.
128. Good Bordeaux.
129. Good beer.
130. How to escape a maze.
131. QWRTY.
132. Fear.
133. Finding your way around Prague, Fez, Shanghai, Johannesburg, Kyoto, Rio, Mexico City, Solo, Benares, Bangkok, Leningrad, Isfahan.
134. The proper way to behave with interns.
135. Maya, Revit, CATIA, whatever.
136. The history of big machines, including those that can fly.
137. How to calculate ecological footprints.
138. Three good lunch spots within walking distance.
139. The value of human life.
140. Who pays.
141. Who profits.
142. The Venturi effect.
143. How people pee.
144. What to refuse to do, even for the money.
145. The fine print in the contract.
146. A smattering of naval architecture.
147. The idea of too far.
148. The idea of too close.
149. Burial practices in a wide range of cultures.
150. The density needed to support a pharmacy.
151. The density needed to support a subway.
152. The effect of the design of your city on food miles for fresh produce.
153. Lewis Mumford and Patrick Geddes.
154. Capability Brown, André Le Nôtre, Frederick Law Olmsted, Muso Soseki, Ji Cheng, and Roberto Burle Marx.
155. Constructivism, in and out.
156. Sinan.

157. Squatter settlements via visits and conversations with residents.
158. The history and techniques of architectural representation across cultures.
159. Several other artistic media.
160. A bit of chemistry and physics.
161. Geodesics.
162. Geodetics.
163. Geomorphology.
164. Geography.
165. The law of the Andes.
166. Cappadocia firsthand.
167. The importance of the Amazon.
168. How to patch leaks.
169. What makes you happy.
170. The components of a comfortable environment for sleep.
171. The view from the Acropolis.
172. The way to Santa Fe.
173. The Seven Wonders of the Ancient World.
174. Where to eat in Brooklyn.
175. Half as much as a London cabbie.
176. The Nolli Plan.
177. The Cerdà Plan.
178. The Haussmann Plan.
179. Slope analysis.
180. Darkroom procedures and Photoshop.
181. Dawn breaking after a bender.
182. Styles of genealogy and taxonomy.
183. Betty Friedan.
184. Guy Debord.
185. Ant Farm.
186. Archigram.
187. Club Med.
188. Crepuscule in Dharamshala.
189. Solid geometry.
190. Strengths of materials (if only intuitively).
191. Halong Bay.
192. What's been accomplished in Medellín.

193. In Rio.
194. In Calcutta.
195. In Curitiba.
196. In Mumbai.
197. Who practices? (It is your duty to secure this space for all who want to.)
198. Why you think architecture does any good.
199. The depreciation cycle.
200. What rusts.
201. Good model-making techniques in wood and cardboard.
202. How to play a musical instrument.
203. Which way the wind blows.
204. The acoustical properties of trees and shrubs.
205. How to guard a house from floods.
206. The connection between the Suprematists and Zaha.
207. The connection between Oscar Niemeyer and Zaha.
208. Where north (or south) is.
209. How to give directions, efficiently and courteously.
210. Stadtluft macht frei.
211. Underneath the pavement the beach.
212. Underneath the beach the pavement.
213. The germ theory of disease.
214. The importance of vitamin D.
215. How close is too close.
216. The capacity of a bioswale to recharge the aquifer.
217. The draught of ferries.
218. Bicycle safety and etiquette.
219. The difference between gabions and riprap.
220. The acoustic performance of Boston's Symphony Hall.
221. How to open the window.
222. The diameter of the earth.
223. The number of gallons of water used in a shower.
224. The distance at which you can recognize faces.
225. How and when to bribe public officials (for the greater good).
226. Concrete finishes.
227. Brick bonds.
228. *The Housing Question* by Friedrich Engels.

229. The prismatic charms of Greek island towns.
230. The energy potential of the wind.
231. The cooling potential of the wind, including the use of chimneys and the stack effect.
232. Paestum.
233. Straw-bale building technology.
234. Rachel Carson.
235. Freud.
236. The excellence of Michel de Klerk.
237. Of Alvar Aalto.
238. Of Lina Bo Bardi.
239. The non-pharmacological components of a good club.
240. Mesa Verde.
241. Chichen Itza.
242. Your neighbors.
243. The dimensions and proper orientation of sports fields.
244. The remediation capacity of wetlands.
245. The capacity of wetlands to attenuate storm surges.
246. How to cut a truly elegant section.
247. The depths of desire.
248. The heights of folly.
249. Low tide.
250. The Golden and other ratios.

(2014)

40

Bull in China's Shop

I was in Beijing during January 2013's extreme toxic event, hacking in the murk, forced into bed, gasping for air, chugging antibiotics and herbal elixirs. Although meteorology and land-form colluded in intensifying this nightmare, nobody—even the party—could mistake that those particles were being disgorged from the smokestacks of local factories and power plants and by the exponential rise of cars clotting the Fourth Ring Road. This was an anthropogenic nightmare, a symptom of the planetary disaster of climate change and a by-product of the headlong development that has both lifted hundreds of millions from poverty and fouled their new nests.

China has something of a history of anthropogenic night-mares, engendered by headlong transformations. The Japanese invasion, the civil war, the Great Leap Forward, and the Cultural Revolution spread death and distortion on an industrial scale. Modern China fascinates for the intensity of its becoming, for its role as a secondhand hothouse for modernity and for the weirdly intense but emblematically hybrid character of where it's arrived. To think about China is to be immersed in the "how Chinese is it" debate, a long-standing turbulence emblematized by such formulations as "socialism with Chinese characteris-tics" or the more recent "one country two systems." Clearly, the genetic engineering of these hybridizations has produced quite a fair share of freaks.

For an urbanist, China is by far the most overwhelming game in town. In the space of a few decades, the country has gone from predominantly rural to—in the middle of last year—majority urban and is accelerating toward the levels of the "developed" world at a lightning clip: the Chinese government has announced its intention to move 250 million more people from the country to the city in the next ten years. China is building the equivalent of the entire housing stock of the United States every decade, and the vast movement of people from farms to town is the biggest mass migration in history. Pick your statistic: the amount of cement poured and the number of cranes in use approaches half the planetary total. Net greenhouse emissions lead the world. More cars are on the road than in any other country. The "illegal" population of China's cities is as great as all the people in America. Like the Peloponnesian war for Thucydides, the subject is irresistible because it is the biggest thing that's ever happened, simply overwhelming.

But coming to terms with the subject is tough. At once a miracle and a disaster, the urbanization of China and the ubiquitous infusion of "Western" forms and mores surely amounts to another Cultural Revolution with impacts at least as broad and distorting as the first, if less savagely lethal. And, like that weird collusion of canniness and hysteria, it begs the question of the alien gaze, and a critical industry has arisen (both within China and without) that seeks to explain or rationalize this "modernization" while evading freighted, colonizing categories. For example, China is awash with—choose your nuance—appropriations, simulacra, copies, fakes, or "sinicizations." Streets are lined with shops selling knock-offs of running shoes, fashions, and electronics for which most of the originals are also produced in China. Armani becomes Armany, co-opted via the canny simplicity of an orthographic shift.

Across the country, the architectural landscape abounds with Disneyesque pastiche, ersatz White Houses, Versailles, Eiffel Towers, Venetian Canals, and Chrysler Buildings, not to mention more preening "starchitecture" than the Persian Gulf. Perhaps most legendary among those with a tooth for such spectacle are the nine new towns that surround Shanghai, each of which houses 200,000 people and is meant to be a "complete" version of a Dutch, German, Italian, or other European city. Best known is "Thames Town" with its red pillar postboxes and telephone booths, its pubs, bobby-style security personnel, and especially its preternaturally reproduced little chapel—modeled exactingly on Christ Church in Clifton Down, Bristol (and scene of countless photos of brides in white and grooms in cutaways)—and a fish and chips shop culled from composite examples in Lyme Regis. Some days, cruising the mall-besieged downtowns, it looks like the entire national aesthetic was bought from the nether regions of basic cable: call now and we'll double the offer!

This is not entirely without precedent: China is a distorting mirror for ourselves. As with other penetrations by colonial power, domination by acculturation was part of the stock in trade, and the specific forms of resistance and interaction resonate to this day. Historically, China, with some success, attempted to confine the foreigners there to commerce and their exploitation to a series of coastal locations, although invidious tendrils crept inland—often born on plumes of opium smoke—and along the Yangtze. The so-called concessions took on an unusual morphology in which the transoceanic predators were clustered together in a series of proto-Disneylands, effectively colonial theme parks in which the Germans, French, Japanese, Americans, et al., each occupied an autonomous piece of territory within a cluster of adjacent enclaves, marked by their characteristic national architecture, dress, cuisine, and other civic and cultural institutions. These originally excluded Chinese (and dogs!), but as the likes of Jardine Matheson and other big operators morphed from drug dealing to real estate exploitation, the natives with the cash to secure property began to be included.

My own first encounter with urban China twenty or so years ago began at an architecture school in Shanghai, where I discovered not simply the concessionary architecture and urbanism of that city but also the rapidly vanishing remnants of the prerevolutionary and traditional texture, the Soviet-inflected planning and building of Mao's era, and—perhaps most fascinating—a particular architectural hybrid, the so-called "lilong." This type—which proliferated from the late nineteenth century until the Second World War—is a combination of a typical western row house with certain characteristics of traditional Chinese domestic architecture, including, in many instances, an inflected version of the courtyard. The complexes were built in every conceivable style—from oriental(ist) to Tudor-esque to moderne—and this expressive richness and flexibility is part of their appeal. For me, though, what most fascinated was their communal quality, the fact that they were built as enclaves adjoining major streets but with inner networks that excluded cars and defined the physical substrate for the development of neighborhood relations. More, many of these places were not exclusively residential but included a variety of shops, workshops, and other commercial facilities. In their conceit of autonomy, they resonate both with the Mao-era "production units" in which workers were housed around their factories and the hugely popular gated-communities of today, communities based on very different intentions.

These places have tremendous relevance for the style of building that is now predominant in China, which seems stuck in a stage of development that might well be skipped as well as having a more general relevance for thinking about the structure of neighborhoods globally. Not simply are the lilongs and the more generic hutongs (aggregations of courtyard houses linked by narrow lanes, largely wiped out in Beijing although their remnants are currently the object of recuperation through gilt-edged gentrification) models of mixed use; they're rich with potential for un-alienating density. In general, Chinese urbanism is badly in thrall of the great postwar paradigms of "towers in the park," and its evil companions, the highway and the automobile suburb. This, in part, may be due to the fact that cities were held in such contempt by Mao with the result that urban consciousness and practice were severely retarded—effectively picking up from where they left off in 1949 when Deng remade the economy in the 80's—with superblocks, cars, hyper-functionalist zoning, and an overly regimented mentality, now overlaid with the ornamental icing of too-long repressed gluttony. Partially liberated from a forced homogeneity of thought and expression, irony and vulgarity dance hand in hand: Ai Weiwei is the witty, pissed-off, flip side of Thames Town.

China has come a very long way from the days of the Little Red Books and the smashing of the icons of both local and worldly traditions, and the numbers of people raised from poverty in the space of a few decades is truly stunning. And yet, the radicalism of the current metamorphosis is no less thoroughgoing in its effect on hearts and minds and its wanton will to recast the very nature of desire. Full disclosure: most of the work of my own architectural practice these days is in China, and the experience has been at once thrilling and appalling. The convergence of authoritarian administration, haphazard taste cultures, cheap labor, piles of cash, and a civil society that oscillates between the Wild West, imperial refinement, curiosity, cruelty, corruption, canniness, and crazy consumption is a rich stew indeed in which to find oneself. While the bargains being struck by our little studio are something less than Faustian, we still swim in contradictions. One tries to make fine distinctions, but it isn't clear where the ethical balance is fixed when trying to adjudicate the difference in working for Larry Silverstein in New York or some devoluted branch of the party in Xi'an or Wuhan.

The question for practice is where to push, to gain purchase, to seek leverage. A point of entry is not just the vastness of the enterprise and the creation of such a prolixity of opportunity that allows many works of imaginative will to simply fill in handy gaps, but, more crucially, the fact that China talks a lot of good talk about environmental action and that, for all the coal-fired electric generation, jammed highways, and toxic soils, there are also bikeways, breathtaking mileage of new subways and rail lines, and actual new cities (being built in the dozens) attempting to come to grips with the metastatic megacities that dominate actually existing Chinese urban growth. While there has been much media focus on China's so-called ghost cities, these are mainly monuments to bad timing, corruption, and the mislocations of everyday planning ineptitude—not just reflections of overcapacity, casino capitalism, or simple weirdness.

And so, we attempt to design beautiful buildings, to ratchet up their levels of sustainability, to make them safe and welcoming, to perform due diligence. Most exciting is the opportunity to design cities and urban districts from scratch, a dream opportunity presented to us nowhere else and a project that—for all its risks—is indispensable for a planet that is urbanizing at the rate of a million people *a week*. The conundrum is how to avoid proffering simply a more supple colonialism, to avoid historic delegitimations of difference, to find genuine and relevant forms of the local, while avoiding the fool's errand of pretending that the Chinese economy is not fully caught up in the protocols of global neoliberalism. Here the challenge is to demystify actual meanings. While I'm no physical determinist, I do believe that cities that reinforce the opportunities for neighborliness, that promote gathering and encounter at multiple scales, that recognize the needs of a variety of publics, and that—in their form and operation—respect and mend the earth are, in fact, bridges that arc in the direction of justice. More, I believe that a world of difference is reinforced by the avid and legible recognition of the local specifics of bio-climate through the conservation of living cultures, that the capitalism with a human face that seeks to sell the same old shit directly *to you* is opposed by artistic singularity, and that this is an increasingly vital supplement to sound urban practice, battling the exclusion, fraud, and homogeneity that so dominate cities today.

It's clear that we are in the throes of a "great convergence" in the form of the world's cities. Emerging from a history in which the value of the urban—denigrated by Mao as degenerate, parasitic forms feeding on the virtuous countryside—has fluctuated from contempt to reverie, the cities of China are groping to find their form, driven by both massive growth and contesting models—including all the standard-issue global prototypes, from gated suburban communities, to Corbusian forests of isolated towers, to the Manhattan-on-acid of one downtown after another, to that amazingly ubiquitous zoological collection of starchitecture and its myriad knockoffs. But China, by virtue of scale, ambition, and the ambit of its conceptual resources, is surely where the rubber hits the road and a place to ask about the limits of the power of space to create authentic place.

The designer's hubris is that architecture and planning drive the organization of public and private life. What's mainly true is, of course, the opposite; however, cities and buildings are not just voluminous records of order and desire but have the capacity to conduce happiness, convenience, comfort, *and* their variously deformed flip sides. That said, it seems particularly interesting that the field of design is so free in China, that there are so few curbs on formal expression in architecture. To be sure, there are familiar debates about modernism and tradition, about motifs that trouble (a skyscraper in Shanghai was modified because a huge circular aperture was judged too Japanese, resulting in an outcome with an uncanny resemblance to a bottle opener), and, increasingly, about the preservation of historic fabrics. But, in a place where resistance to the system can be heavily penalized, there seems to be special liberty for architecture and the visual arts, a canny acknowledgement of the actual limits—and utility—of architectural expression

There is always a little cult in culture—I am thinking of those Warhol portraits of Chairman Mao—and it seems clear that the era of "one country, two systems" initiated by Deng required the energetic confusion of propaganda and advertising, and that the subject population had been trained to be adept at acting on the messages with which it has been so long and systematically bombarded: to get rich is glorious (as consumption displaces production as the measure of virtue)! If China seems to be a hypertrophic mirror of ourselves, it's because it is. While the mash-up between capital and control is surely more attenuated in China, its capacity to produce excess is commensurately large, and so is the destructiveness of the creativity: in the environmental and human ravages of the Wild West economy, in the endless under-the-table chicanery, and in the sheer scale of it all.

On the other hand, there is no mistaking the miracle. Hundreds of millions have been lifted out of poverty. A gigantic civilian infrastructure has been installed. Health, literacy, mobility, and other palpable and legitimate aspects of human development have been dramatically improved. And, the people have shown remarkable tenacity in evading state strictures on communication and expression. What has struck me with the greatest force is the blazing speed with which they are approaching so many of the qualities of our daily life, including compulsive getting and spending, atomization of families, too much motion, and the quality of contestation between public and private spheres. And herein lies the rub: convergence at our level of consumption is impossible. The earth has a limited bearing capacity, and if we all consumed at American rates, the planet could only support a third of us.

The Chinese are certainly aware both of the problem and of the rhetoric of anxious displacement directed at them by many in the developed world. Although their per capita output of greenhouse gases is far smaller than that of the United States, their aggregate contribution—the majority coming from cities—is larger. Western observers often evince a classically Orientalist assumption that China must bear a special burden because of the stereotype of Asiatic license, irresponsibility, and tolerance for squalor that is implicit in much criticism. The irony is that China—like the rest of us—cannot avoid acting, but the timing of the history of planetary degradation is inopportune as we are now all too conscious that the styles of effluence of the Industrial Revolution have become intolerable, just as China and other developing economies are passing through theirs. Finally, their only choice is to lead the world in the implementation of sustainable practices, to assume the high ground.

One of the most popular TV shows in China is *Supergirl*, an American Idol–type competition in which the winner is determined by the texted votes of the viewing audience: democracy with American characteristics. One certainly wonders what perturbations in the system the experience of such elections elicits. Aspiration has a brand and a sponsor, and, at the end of history, the line between Coke and the Party is blurry. As a visitor in China, there's a constant tension between wanting to offer good service and advice to good people and a reluctance to play the wise colonial, with something superior on offer. This often results in a familiar cautionary rhetoric: don't fuck up the way we did; slow down with those highways and suburbs; get back to your bike-riding days; stop burning all that coal. Whatever the cred of the source, it's good advice.

(2014)

41

Civilian Objects

Was the bombing of Gaza a crime? Bombing cities kills civilians and destroys—in the language of the 1977 Geneva Accords— "civilian objects" (hospitals, mosques, museums, and so forth) and the treaty seeks not simply to protect both but to *criminalize* such attacks, should they be *excessive*. This is but the latest codification of the debate over *jus in bello*—the "just" conduct of war—a question still staged in terms proposed by Augustine, Aquinas, and Grotius, that argues for categories of innocence— women and children, prisoners, the wounded, the elderly, and their benign architectures—constitutive of the civilian. These arguments sit in the context of the idea that wars—however just—involve doing evil things: the immemorial question is over the limits of how much bad can ethically be done, the threshold of *too much* violence. This begs the great conundrum of "proportionality," with its supporting cast of lesser evils: legal norms, fair play, and collateral damage, including the deaths of civilians and demolition of their objects. The 1977 accord was intended, inter alia, to settle the question of competing styles of bombing that arose in the Second World War, to adjudicate and refine the categorical difference between "area" and "precision" (or "surgical") attacks. The former, with advocates like Bomber Harris, Curtis LeMay, (and later Edward Teller, Herman Kahn, and the whole ghoulish Cold War doctrine of mutually assured destruction), is frankly committed to indiscriminate slaughter, to breaking enemy morale via mass annihilation, while the latter claims to attack only military targets, including industrial or transportation facilities that support the fighting.

But the categories are fuzzy and proportionality particularly fluid, a dismal science of converting the value of an eye into the currency of teeth. In his *Least of All Possible Evils* (2011), Eyal Weizman, the most indispensable contemporary analyst of the forensics of the collateral (and the editor of *Forensis* [2014], a landmark in this expanding field) writes that "the principle of proportionality provides no scale, no formulas, and no numerical thresholds." Given this incalculability, the boundaries tend to be discussed in terms of specific events, most emblematically Dresden and Hiroshima, victor's targets in a war almost universally thought just. Was the firebombing of Dresden criminal? For those to whom this remains a question, the answer hinges on the "legitimacy" of the target and on the countervailing extent and value of the collateral damage: the 40,000 incinerated civilians. Worth shortening the war by a day? A week?

The ethics of the Dresden deliberation lie somewhere between an idea of collective guilt (women gave birth to Hitler *Jugend*, all Germans were "willing executioners," and so on) and the idea that the military objective was sufficiently important to sanction the sacrifice of a *certain number* of innocents who were mingled with military objectives, a periphery complicated by the location of military production and assets in the midst of the city. The same arguments were rolled out to justify the A-Bomb attacks on Hiroshima and Nagasaki, both allegedly "military and industrial" sites whose destruction would spare Americans a bloody invasion (not to mention spook the Soviets). The question of Dresden, in particular, has been unpacked by "revisionist" historians, like Frederick Taylor, who have disproved the claims of economic innocence by demonstrating that the city's factories, big and small, had been converted from camera, porcelain, and cigarette manufacture to producing bullets, fuses, torpedoes, and bombsights; that the city had a particularly virulent pro-Nazi history; that the rail yards were critical to the Nazi war effort; that there weren't *that* many refugees. Of course, all such claims ratchet up the permissible disproportion to accord with some idea of retributive justice. The A-bomb—with its capacity to annihilate the entire planet—is proportionality's reductio ad absurdum.

Architecture is consequential because it allows us to speak about the unspeakable indirectly, mangled buildings standing in for mangled bodies. And, the aesthetic side of judgment—the natural home of the familiar architectural discourse—has plenty of usable ready-made categories, an easy retreat from the more difficult moralities of violence against flesh. During the Second World War, as Bomber Harris grew more and more deeply obsessed with area bombing and its grail of the perfect firestorm, he realized that the picturesque medieval centers of German cities, warrens of half-timbered houses, were precisely the tinder needed to set off the conflagration devoutly wished. History became the best source of ignition and was reimagined as an adjunct to the technology of fire, not the home of a civilian population nor an artistic treasure, merely kindling for breaking morale and, perhaps, spreading fire to industrial installations on the far edges of town. And, this was seasoned with the idea that the Germans were universally criminal, that there were, in effect, no civilians at all.

This reinvention of an "authentic," criminal Dresden—a city laced with nefarious manufacture and *bad* people, and that could be ethically bombed—has an eerie resemblance to exculpatory descriptions of Gaza as laced with rocket-making workshops and launchpads so densely interwoven into the fabric of everyday life that the entire environment was cross-contaminated by Nazi-like Hamas values. Netanyahu, in his gross, disingenuous blame-shifting, tries to reckon every death as the simple consequence of malfeasance on the part of Hamas. And so we proceed directly to the numbers game. The claim that hundreds of civilians were killed because *someone else* placed weapons or holed up nearby (in schools, hospitals, apartment houses, shops, on the beach) is simply self-exoneration for murder. We regret every civilian casualty. We called to warn them. But it's their fault.

Weizman describes an extraordinary 2002 meeting in Israel at which Daniel Reisner, head of the "International Law Department" of the Israel Defense Forces (IDF), and a group of colleagues worked out a consensus *mathematica moralia* to determine precisely how many innocents—in one particular scenario—might legitimately be killed to excise a single "militant." Astonishingly, the number arrived at was 3.14—*pi!*—a constant of innocent sacrifice. UN figures cite 2,104 Palestinian deaths in Operation Protective Edge, of whom 1,462 were civilian. By this calculation, the slaughter in Gaza produced a ratio of 3.27— very close to that legitimating margin of non-criminality. The IDF, of course, claims a higher proportion of terrorists, seeking to bank less collateral. This is madness. Weizman writes, "State violence in this model takes part in a necro-economy in which various types of destructive measure are weighed in a utilitarian fashion, not only in the damage they produce, but to the harm they purportedly prevent and even in relation to the more brutal measures they may help to restrain."

Architecture figures in forensic analysis as witness for both the prosecution and the defense. In the case of Dresden, whether or not the city was a genuine military target, there's a supplementary charge in the prosecution's case: the fact that the city was remarkable *architecturally*. Jörg Friedrich's seminal *The Fire*, a German historian's account of the bombing campaign published in German in 2002, is in large part an inventory of architectural and civic treasures lost, an argument that area bombing was "culturecide" aimed at wiping out the memories embodied in these civilian objects, whether books or buildings. These act partially as accessible surrogates for innocent death—perhaps even more innocent than people for their uncompromised beauty, for the pan-Europan belovedness of this "Florence on the Elbe"— and for the embedded suggestion that the neither the Gothic nor the Baroque ever supported Hitler. And, there's an implicit backstory that includes the so-called "Baedeker" campaigns— Coventry for Cologne—touted by both sides as cultural tit for tat, the Morgenthau Plan to reduce Germany to a state of rural impotence (used by Goebbels to whip up fear of an allied final solution to the German problem), and the US decision to spare

Kyoto from nuclear annihilation precisely because of its artistic importance.

Thus, architecture is used to both value *and* devalue targets, and to establish the cultural credentials of various sides in the struggle. Aesthetic outrage is expressed when ISIS or the Taliban destroys some historic tomb, mosque, or statuary, or when Iraqis—in the aftermath of the US invasion—loot their own national museum. I felt guilt at my shock at the destruction of the great Citadel of Aleppo, at grieving for a piece of beloved material culture, ravaged even as babies were dying: where was my own sense of proportionality? Here, the blame is shared because the rebel fighters barricaded themselves there and were attacked by Assad's troops, but this lack of clear-cut guilt for the atrocity (against civilization, something Arabs possessed *in the past* but of which they are failed custodians today) allows a diffusion of responsibility that confirms the narratives of confusion purveyed by the media (and stoked by current efforts by the administration to sort out good and bad insurgents)—suggesting that barbarism is a general cultural feature in the region—and sanctions our own *mission civilisatrice,* our crusade.

Ironically, the problem—or the advantage from the bomber's perspective—for Gaza is that it is almost exclusively described as a place of *no* cultural value. This is a doubly inflected claim. For those in sympathy with the terrible plight of the Strip's residents, the argument from squalor and imprisonment only exacerbates the horror of the assault from the air: how can things get worse? For those manning the drones, tanks, and F-16's, the homogeneity of disadvantage both equalizes the value of the territory—universalizing the target set—and supports the corollary argument that Hamas invariably hides behind civilians precisely because of the absence of a legible infrastructure that would bring it into the open, into a public space that is exactly what Gaza *lacks.*

A particular architectural wrinkle in the coverage of the assault has been the attention given to the destruction of three "high-rise" buildings by Israeli bombs. The media have been fascinated by this but unsure how to internalize it to their ambivalent discourse. At one level, a high-rise elides with a "high-value" target and effectively acculturates Gazans as social climbers (in much the same way that calorie-counting Israeli propagandists attempted to ridicule claims of starvation by distributing a menu from a "fancy" restaurant frequented by the NGO/journalist set in Gaza City). On the other, the demolition of tall buildings by aircraft cannot but evoke New York's own high-rise losses to "Islamic terrorists" and the insistent conflation of al-Qaeda, Hamas, Hezbollah, ISIS, Boko Haram, the Taliban, and so on with Muslims in general, which invents them as malign actors dedicated to the destruction of Western civilization and its hallmarks and landmarks. The destruction was of an inappropriate cultural aspiration, tat for tower, a display of power, or just a particularly photogenic catastrophe.

The aura of artistic outrage is thus used to augment the victimhood of those killed in Dresden or Paderborn and acts by suggesting that their personhood was made ampler by the creativity of their cultures. For Germans, the recurrent question is how such a "civilized" people could go so bad. But the converse is equally true. The destruction of the shrines and urban textures of Japan somehow doesn't rise to the level of Dresden, because the Japanese were demonized throughout the war as lesser humans. In his thorough account of the ethics of area bombing, *Among the Dead Cities* (2006), A. C. Grayling proposes four elements of the racist attitude toward the Japanese that enabled our virtually indiscriminate destruction of their cities: the "perfidy" of Pearl Harbor, their cruelty to prisoners of war, their ferocity as fighters, and the "weird oriental fanaticism" of kamikaze attacks. This almost precisely parallels our construction of the generalized Islamic other, with 9/11 substituting for Pearl Harbor, the ISIS beheadings and slaughter of captives standing in for the Bataan Death March, the insane battles in Syria (not to mention the mine-clearing-human charges by child soldiers during the Iran-Iraq war) burnishing a reputation for fanatical assault and contempt for life, and the daily suicide bombings around the region—and the world—matching the self-annihilating death cult of the emperor-worshipping (read:

Mohammed in the current context) Japanese pilots. What solution for such people but to degrade them and then destroy them. Bring on the burning hooches and free-fire zones of Vietnam. Back to Iraq.

And so we bomb and bomb. Gaza is a *bare city*, a culturally degraded substitute for Tokyo or Hamburg. Because Hamas is fertilized by the anger of a population under siege, all are assumed to be complicit in the rockets, the Charter, the executions, and the rest of the nefarious encyclopedia of terror. The place itself is miserable, without an identifiable piece of architecture deserving conservation. It is, as a piece of the built environment, valueless, providing no more than shelter and a minimal set of provisions for everyday life but lacking any supplement of *art*. The bomber's calculus here meets the preservationist's: there was no building on the strip that was indispensable, worth protecting on its own merits, not a piece of architecture in sight. The inference is carried over to the people who lived in these mediocre places, people lacking the capacity of aspiration. Incapable of building a civilized environment, they were marked for disposability.

In the aftermath of the war I received an e-mail from a friend, a version of something I'd seen a few times before. It was a list of Nobel Prize winners of which seven were Muslim and 129 were Jewish and also included a riff on the hypocrisy of anti-Semitic mullahs who nevertheless avail themselves of medical discoveries made by Jews. The coupling of pride with contempt lies at the core of the idea of "proportionality." The *disproportion* of the Nobel Prize list, of the exchange of 1,000 Palestinian prisoners for Sergeant Shalit, or of the slaughter of 1,400 Gazan civilians against the deaths of six in Israel establishes a moral calculus that weighs their "bare life" against our rich one, establishing a right to kill. This is simply an argument—one that should be particularly familiar to Jews—that can have nothing but a sinister outcome, a calculus of collateral culpability. We made the desert bloom, produced a world-class software industry, and won Nobel Prizes: what the fuck did you do?

(2014)

42

Clear Light

Le Corbusier memorably described architecture as "the masterly, correct, and magnificent play of masses brought together in light." Like no other, Lauretta Vinciarelli was a metaphysician of luminosity, an avatar of light, shining. In her remarkable work, light becomes palpable, not simply an element that reveals form but a material force. Whether in a sharp and clarifying ray, slanting across a calibrating space, or the power that renders form discernable, particular, and precise, her work radiates the force of revelation.

Growing from a singular technique—the meticulous layering of washes with such patient exactitude that the materiality and opacity of paint bearing on paper captures, *as mass*, the incredible being of lightness—the architecture she invents and represents can truly be said to have been *built*, accumulated from laminations of color and imagination, weighted and measureable. Hers is an architecture at once pure and uncanny, a distilled spatial singularity. To describe the forms as simple is both correct and misleading. Lauretta's life's project was the evocation of nuance, the subtleties that attended the infinity of interaction arising from a lexicon of shade and shadow, of spectral color, of reflection and refraction, of surfaces and voids set vibrating by the energy of the sun.

While her visionary work is always representational, her depictions are distilled and "purely" of building, only occasionally extending to an austere landscape beyond. It is not that images of people or other objects are extraneous to the work (although their exclusion assures the viewer is never voyeur) but that architecture itself takes on the task of subjectivity, both as the presumptive setting for the kinds of perceptual engagement it celebrates and as a home for the most rarefied, most deeply architectural, experience. The work is profoundly tectonic, filled with the heaviness and density of construction, elemental in its capture of the Platonic repertoire of the builder: trabeation and arches, apertures and walls, tension and compression.

The paintings, too, always moving toward abstraction, retain the presence of the body through a lucid and insistent sense of scale. The situation of windows, the patterning of surfaces underfoot, the distant sight of mountains and prairies, the sense of hierarchy in the sizing of members, the risers on stairs—all collude in a prosody of dimension that establishes an idea about the intimacy of architecture, about the utter and inescapable relevance of our own presence in these places, while shimmering with hushed reflections of the ineffable. But even her earliest work strains to exceed the presence of the conventionally tectonic as the means and measure of space.

I've recently come to know the work of Nasreen Mohamedi, another great artist gone too soon, and have been struck with its sorority with Lauretta's. Mohamedi's work was described by one critic as "Malevich crossed with Agnes Martin," but comparisons are never really apposite: who can truly trace the anxieties of influence, the miracles of simultaneous invention. To this twinning might be added Sol LeWitt, even John Hejduk in his early days when he wielded his pencil like a knife, bearing down and building up with a 9H lead. What's remarkable about Mohamedi's work is that it stands outside of category, not architectural strictly speaking but—like the work of Vinciarelli—a kind of representational abstraction, deeply spatial. Although the drawings appear rarified and minimal, they are actually rich with figuration. Mohamedi was a faithful and attuned diarist and observer, and the inspiration of threads aligned on the loom, of rills on the beach, of waves rolling cross seas, of the embedded construction of perspective revealed—stripped bare of the architecture that its alignments explained—is incredibly rich.

Mohamedi and Vinciarelli were preoccupied with infinity, with making the inconceivable visible. The idea of the vanishing point captures the birth of the universe, its acceleration beyond the field of view, conceptualized but elusive in its visibility, ultimately comprehensible only as time. Rhythms of day and night, the transformative regularity of the movement of the sun recorded precisely in every painting, add architecture's fourth dimension and stand in for us in another way. Despite their seeming quietude, their deeply meditative character, these places are filled with time and motion pared to its most essential: timeless expressions of time, a still excess of time that shatters time. The work is uncanny for being both calm and incredibly alive, so rich in subtlety and suggestion that each view yields fresh emotion, fresh perception, fresh reverence for the ways that architecture finds its meaning as philosophy and experience.

Both Vinciarelli and Mohamedi followed a trajectory toward the light, understood both in terms of a paring away—of density receding with distance—and of luminosity. However, while Mohamedi worked to bleach her optics to a construct of pure line, Vinciarelli's movement was toward an increasing saturation of color. Here the affinities are very much with Albers and Rothko, and her conversation with them included both the interaction of color and the exacting specifics of tonality, and the idea of the capturing frame, the most fundamental idea of the architectonic: enclosure. Vinciarelli's primary research— particularly in her powerful and mysterious later work—was precisely into architecture's central paradox, that it is a system for the capture and transfiguration of the void, the stage management of nothingness.

In the trajectory of Vinciarelli's development as an artist, there is an obvious, almost ritual, movement—one she shares with Lebbeus Woods, our most brilliant space explorer, paramount master of architecture in continuity with its own image—toward what might be called purification. As her work developed, it became more and more distilled, denser, eventually leaving the representation of building behind in favor of a more magical attempt to capture space like lightning in a jar. Again, the idea of abstraction must be invoked with care, but it is clear that she was after essences. This agenda wasn't simply artistic or philosophical. It's surely critical that both Woods and Vinciarelli began to deepen their research in the seventies, when architecture was under radical interrogation from many of directions. For Vinciarelli, the search started in an interrogation of type, an epistemological construct that descends through the history of architectural theory but reached a certain pinnacle early in the nineteenth century in the work of Quatremère de Quincy, Laugier, and Viollet-le-Duc. Questions of the meaning of type for architecture were especially lively in the Italy of Vinciarelli's academic formation.

In terms of its intellectual sociology, the relevance of type was surely aligned with a widespread feeling that modernist architecture had—in its mainstream incarnations as near-ubiquitous global formal default—become deracinated, up against a dead end, deprived of its own originary sources of meaning in both social purpose and in reaction to the stultifying ornamentalism and privilege of a world remade by the Janus of oppression and liberation embodied in industrial culture, colonialism, and their eventual apotheosis in global war. The movement of the "long" nineteenth century that produced modernity was recapitulated in accelerated form after the Second World War with the ante raised in both the social and physical technology of annihilation. The Baroque styles of consumption that ensued came to be reviled as a return of the squalidly lavish ostentation associated with Victorianism in the fullness of its colonial reach. What had once symbolized the idea of universal hope came to stand for universal alienation.

The reinvention of architecture to which Vinciarelli was so dedicated involved its re-naturing via an assay of its primary constituents. The idea of type might be said to embody a pre-Darwinian notion of origins, an idealist construction that gave special privilege to the authority of points of departure as constituents of form. In the "rationalist" aroma of that period of Italian architectural thought, there was an obvious attempt to find, in effect, a premodern source for architectural renewal and to scrape away extraneous meanings. To be sure, this recycled many of the terms of modernity's own self-invention but diverged in its conscientious efforts to re-historicize architecture, to repair the epistemological break.

For Vinciarelli—deeply immersed in architectural and cultural history—the idea of type took her in several important directions. First, to the idea of architecture's elements, the raw tectonics of anti-gravity, the traditionalized reduction of form, and the creative play of light and space. This investigation quickly converged with parallel investigations in the art world of more purely figural forms of minimalism, and Vinciarelli is a largely unacknowledged source for much the expansion of art's field into the terrains of architecture and environment. But, crucially, Vinciarelli also conducted a long, fruitful, and highly disciplined research—via her remarkable teaching—into a more applied idea of type in her dedication to the problem of replicable forms of housing, particularly that most topological type: carpet housing. In all of her work, she never lost sight of manifold obligations of the architect to shelter, to illuminate, to organize lines of sight, to act in compact with place, and to offer all of this with complete generosity. Such are the politics of light.

(2015)

43

The Architect
as Worker

A ubiquitous German big box is Bauhaus. On first seeing one, I was buoyed by the thought of a repressed's return, modernism's Jerusalem diffused on the landscape of the Jerry everyday. That this turned out to be the Teutonic equivalent of Home Depot didn't exactly sink my reverie. The stores, crammed with pressure-treated plywood, plumbing fittings galore, and hand drills up the wazoo, represented an idea of empowerment, the means by which the priesthood of architecture might be circumvented by citizens with *access to tools*. Bauhaus is no less than a festival marketplace for the consumption of the means of production.

Pier Vittorio Aureli describes the factory as the materialized degree-zero of the Marxian conception of labor, the outcome of a particular historical moment in the development of capitalism. Marx was our primal modernist and—in thrall—architects of the Bauhaus and matching stripes, who rejected the effete perquisites of *haute bourgeois* practice, have long had labor—rather *laborer*—envy. As an outgrowth of an egalitarian, mainly socialist tradition that revered the worker as ideal, that architecture found both form and purpose in response to the imagined requirements of this model subject. Industrial building systems, the domino frame, the minimalized (that is, equalized) housing unit, the celebration of the sites of production—from the Dnieper dam to Ford's Rouge factory to the grain elevators of Buffalo— were where modernism sought to site its project and where its aesthetic of aesthetic denial took shape. There's a reason that the Bauhaus in Dessau took the form of a factory, and why, in standard histories, its photo invariably follows Fagus.

But there's a divide in design's conception of labor—with Marx's proletarian on one side and William Morris's yeoman on the other—that forecasts our own ongoing split in systems of meaning in architecture, a hoary, factory-versus-craft fork between historicism and "new" urbanism; the divergent modernisms now incarnate especially in the anxiety and prospect of both parametric ("automated") and ecological ("save the earth") design. This serial bifurcation tends to fix the location of architecture's own work either on the side of symbolization or remediation and thereby founds its complex politics. Thus, any analysis of the nature of *human* architectural labor (and related questions of compensation, working conditions, and so on) must take into account the differing conceptual and ethical impetus behind it, the ongoing imbrications of the cultural meanings of handicraft (with it imputations of individuality, self-fulfillment, and communal service) and the production line (with its attendant alienation, exploitation, and stoking of the mass-consumption engine). The expectation that architectural activity on behalf of squatters or typhoon survivors will be part of the same ethico-fiscal calculus as that of building condos on Fifty-Seventh Street only points up that there is a morally valenced class system within architecture that cannot easily be collapsed, much as the doctors at Médecins Sans Frontières cannot be *simply* identified with the Park Avenue plastic surgeon doing nose jobs. These are category confusions that underpin ideas both of redress and entitlement, and greatly influence how and who we organize: I don't think of David Childs as a brother in struggle, but many of Skidmore, Owings & Merrill's employees sure are. That some of us think of our "practice" as more closely allied to art or politics or social work than to computer science or real estate development clearly begs the issue of one profession, two systems. *Many* systems.

This ethically grounded doubling is represented in a variety of "professional" circumstances. A tiny subset of those surgeons—all signatories to the Hippocratic Oath—spend time in Africa fixing cleft palates for the poor. Indeed, even Rand Paul periodically goes to Nicaragua to do cataract surgery for those without other access to care. Lawyers take cases pro bono as part of their understanding of the civic nature of their calling and the state sanction that allows them to pursue it. Architects sign on to a code of professional conduct rich with encouragement to be of service. Much of this depends on what might be called the economics of the tithe—charity—as its enabling (if voluntary) authority. In this broader context of inequality—the fact that an underpaid junior architect in New York is immeasurably better-off than a rag picker in Cairo (if with a similar discrepancy with her boss)—there is a certain parochialism to the fight for a (better) living wage. This is not an argument against the struggle but a call to recognize the unevenness both within and without the discipline, and to deal with it.

But further confusion arises, induced by the artistic character of architectural practice. How to parse this? There's a liminal blur generated by the "relative autonomy" of the artistic side of architecture, which does radically distinguish it from the professions with which it is grouped and distorts any attempt to claim it completely for one side or the other. For architecture, questions of politics are partially distributive and partially representational. This is not the dualism of C. P. Snow's two cultures of humanism and technology but the site of an inborn contradiction that animates the *nature* of architecture and suggests that it's a mistake to see the "architect" as a unitary subject. Given that the most fundamental predicate for any politics is *organization*, what can be done about an activity that is susceptible to so many different modes of self-production and of the production of its outcome in something like building? It's urgent to establish a set of useful differences between the work and the workplace.

In the latter case, a struggle comparable to our current battles for fair pay and treatment was the fight of medical interns and residents to curtail their insane hours. Their success was in part due to union affiliation, and in part to several high-profile cases (the death of Libby Zion, whose father was a writer for the *New York Times*, most prominently) in which patients died as a clear outcome of mistakes by overtired and overtaxed doctors in training. Many in the academic medical profession were appalled that there would be objections to this boot camp crucible, the incredibly stressful demands held integral to the formation of the medical personality and to the development of the reflexes under pressure that would, in theory, stand doctors in good stead in future crises. The adversity of an architect's professional apprenticeship shares this same idea of ennobling degradation, but it's a question of the reasons (and the rhetoric) for enduring it. There seems very little cause to suggest that laboring under squalid and exploitative conditions in an architectural office has any positive impact, save on the employer's bottom line and in creating the expectation in the young architect that s/he will one day be in a position to pass it on.

What employers often exploit, ironically, are two characteristics of architectural education that seem, on the whole, to be worthwhile. The first is the charrette and its hyper-focus, which both tests individual capacity for performance and discipline and prepares one for the natural difficulties of scheduling and production—not to mention boom and bust—that are endemic to architectural practice. Whether better management could smooth the output curves is neither here nor there if the circumstances of compensation are fair (take a week off, earn overtime, aid the poor, and so on), and the inborn enthusiasm for the job on the part of participants is present and motivating. The other piece of the educational experience, also native to the charrette, is the tradition of mutual aid, the second-year who helps the third-year in the final hours of thesis preparation. This too is precious but may also conduce a form of false consciousness.

The measure of exploitation is inequality. While I am as shocked, shocked, as the next sansculotte by the thought of the engorged Norman Foster piloting his own jet to the jobsite in some despotic Shangri-la while lesser staff are relegated to the middle seat in coach, this version of the architectural Gini coefficient is typical of the widening gap between CEO salaries and those of average employees in the corporate world more generally. And, as with other corporate functionaries, architects are challenged not just by an endemic culture of greed but by the same offshoring that has decimated so many American industries, which increasingly ship both physical and "immaterial" production to sites of low-wage expertise—to computer coders in India or to architectural renderers in China. These big offices and these strategies are logical sites for insurgency but cannot simply be collapsed into a single architectural field, denying the many social and economic models that comprise its complex ecology.

Not to go all Trotskyite, but we can only solve the challenges of our own privileged predicament through contemplation of our increasingly globalized economy, by making common cause with brothers and sisters who underpin our own efforts. Just as the media focused on the dreadful conditions in the electronics factories of Shenzhen, with their toxicities, cruel schedules, and suicides, so there's been a sudden interest in the condition of exploited labor constructing starchitect projects in the Gulf. One of the problems with exclusively professional organization is that it can perpetuate the very ideas of stratification and exclusion it seeks to overturn, and further reify an undercurrent of privilege. Which suggests that the prospects of revolution in one profession, while appealingly efficient, also amount to a betrayal of those non-professionals lower down the chain of implementation. Or of the non-professionals who are responsible for constructing 98 percent of the built environment. The point is not to de-professionalize in the sense of surrendering expertise but to practice in a conscious way, one that acknowledges that we do not build alone. One big union?

One of the paradoxes of architectural practice is, in fact, the social compression that has become typical of American offices. Where once the output of drawings was largely the product of draftsmen—who learned their skills in trade schools or apprenticeships—now every bathroom tile is drawn by an Ivy League architectural graduate with aspirations to be a star. This narrowed cadre of producers models the big office on the small (witness also the way in which many mega-firms are organized in individual studios, each with its own "master"). As a practical matter, how are we to distinguish this camouflaged corporatism from more authentic, less hierarchical forms of organization? One approach is to look at thresholds of relative expense, of earnings, of the size and density of the "production unit," and at the level of empowerment, intimacy, control, and authority down the ranks. There are many sites where old-fashioned forms of trade unionism are called for.

For this, we happily have a history to look to: during the period from the end of the First World War to the end of the Second, there were a number of successful attempts to unionize architectural workers in the United States. The first serious effort was the International Federation of Draftmen's Unions. This originated as the Society of Marine Draftsmen in 1913—a company union—at the Norfolk Naval Shipyard, but an insurgency established its independence and, in 1918, the American Federation of Labor (AFL) (until 1937, the only national labor federation) granted it a charter. Far more important, though, was a successor, the Federation of Architects, Engineers, Chemists, and Technicians (FAECT), born of the great depression.* According to Robert Heifetz, "By 1932, architects had one-seventh of the work they had had in 1928, and six of every seven draftsmen, specification writers, and construction superintendents had lost their jobs." By 1929, a militant wing of the earlier union had emerged in New York—the Union of Technical Men—which was soon expelled from the AFL for "excessive radicalism." FAECT began in 1933, following publication—by the American Institute of Architects—of suggested minimum wage standards for draftsman (fifty cents an hour!) to be promulgated as part of the National Industrial Recovery Act. This was not only

---

* I owe virtually everything I know about FAECT to Anthony Schuman's article, "Professionalization and the Social Goals of Architects, 1930–1980: The History of the Federation of Architects, Engineers, Chemists, and Technicians (FAECT)," in *The Design Professions and the Built Environment*, Paul L. Nox, ed. (Kent, UK: Croom Helm, 1988); and to Robert Heifetz's "The Role of Professional and Technical Workers in Progressive Transformation," *Monthly Review*, December 2000, which draws heavily on the work of Schuman. My summary borrows shamelessly from both, and they have my gratitude.

pathetically low but the rates were devised without consultation with membership and the pushback was immediate. By 1934, FAECT had over 6,500 members in fifteen locals and declared itself "the progressive vanguard of the technical professions." In 1937, it became part of the Congress of Industrial Organizations (CIO), formed that year under the leadership the immortal John L. Lewis.

During the Second World War, FAECT strongly advocated for an increased role for labor in industrial decision making and made clear that it expected such a cooperative model should also be central to peacetime production. Management thought otherwise, and the union was viciously red-baited: the revolting Representative Martin Dies—of House Un-American Activities Committee fame—described the union as "under the complete control of the communist party." It didn't help that FAECT members were involved in atomic research, including Robert Oppenheimer (and his brother) and Julius Rosenberg, and, in 1943, the War Department called for FAECT to be banned from the Berkeley (now Lawrence) Radiation Lab. Heifetz quotes no less a figure than General Leslie Groves, head of the Manhattan Project, who wrote in a memo, "Activities of the FAECT Local No. 25 have already seriously compromised the security of the Berkeley work ... It is essential that action be taken to remove the influence of FAECT from the Radiation Laboratory."

In the postwar Red Scare, FAECT continued to be tarred as a tool of the Kremlin and, to stay alive, it merged, in 1946, with the leftish Union of Office and Professional Workers of America, which was itself purged from the CIO—then drifting protectively right—in 1948. During its brief heyday, such important architectural figures as Simon Breines, Percival Goodman, James Marston Fitch, Vito Battista (representing the union's own right wing), Morris Zeitlin, and Tom Creighton, the editor of *Progressive Architecture*, were members of FAECT, which also ran its own school to help members prepare for licensing exams and to top up their knowledge of current technology. The school conducted two design studios, one along beaux arts lines, the other modernist and, at its height, enrolled 600 students. In the end, what was most consequential about FAECT was its consistently progressive orientation, its structural efforts to build bridges between professional and technical workers of all stripes (its membership was never more than 15 percent architects), its efforts in culture and education, and its allegiance to the idea of a broad labor movement, empowered by wide solidarity and the fight for social justice.

FAECT offers an object lesson in both forgetfulness and possibility. Recalling this struggle—and it is not the only instance of architects organizing outside institutional professional structures—is critical to our possibilities today, especially in the context of the increasing dominance of corporate offices. We must disabuse ourselves of the notion that, as "professionals," we stand apart from the fundamentals of the contest of labor in general, while at the same time recognizing our own heterogeneity. Because so many who theorize this question are also involved in academic "practice," our approach is greatly informed by struggles in our beleaguered universities where we see the rapid emergence a new mode of production: the pressures to be "entrepreneurial" in seeking funding for design studios, the appalling salaries and lack of benefits offered to piece-working adjuncts, the speedup in workload, and the general decline in importance of full-time faculty—the creation of a two-tiered class system. These workers are our natural allies: the professoriate offers a far closer parallel to the situation—and pay scales—of architectural labor than do most lawyers or doctors.

Our academic pickle is underwritten by a special historical conceit in professional education: the idea that teaching is a supplementary responsibility of practitioners, a remnant of the earlier system of apprenticeship, the white man's noblesse oblige. This has morphed into a rhetoric of involuntary altruism that is deployed as an unspoken pressure to sacrifice, disguised as civic duty and a route to initiation into our priesthood, an *opportunity*. Indeed, rates of compensation for visiting professors are sometimes inversely proportional to the "prestige" of the institution and the job represented as either resume-building fodder or a chance for insider trading in the recruitment of talented students. However, the majority of practicing architects (as opposed to the majority of publishing architects), while not part of this academic-architectural complex, still suffer from (or exploit) the expectations and habits it creates. The press of students and recent graduates seeking internships in high-gloss offices is enormous, creating a buyer's market of such magnitude that it has produced a class of willing slaves, ready to work for nothing for their own resume-burnishing brush with celebrity. Again, this is not exclusive to our profession, and perhaps even greater numbers queue up for a chance to lick Anna Wintour's Louboutins than do chez Zaha Hadid. The cult of celebrity is an incitement to *not* organize, and that's why its critique is so important.

Speaking of Hadid, her inopportune remarks about working conditions in Qatar beg questions not simply of responsibility, liability, and the vertical organization of the building process, but of the architect's role in the *design* of the process of construction, often very difficult to influence. We are, at the moment, seeing a resurgence of interest in modular building and in factory fabrication of various components (including very large ones) that were previously put together on-site. While this has a fine old modernist flavor and certain attractions—especially when it's foregrounded as a solution to housing cost or scarcity—it's also an obvious ploy to dodge higher-cost union labor by exploiting lower wages typical of factory work, even when unionized. A current case in point is the construction of the Atlantic Yards project in Brooklyn, touted for the bargain costs of its production-line modules but now arrested by quarrels between builder and developer over questions of the quality of its components. Is it for architects to have an opinion about the comparative merits of producing housing for less and paying workers more? You bet it is. One argument for a big tent organization—for unionization in league with others—is precisely to foreground such issues of solidarity and cause.

Questions of our relationship to labor—material or immaterial—define who we are, just as the nature of patronage or the content of program require us to make hard choices. These decisions must have results that are more than ornamental. In my day, the fashionably attired MIT architecture student expressed solidarity and defiance by wearing bib-overalls and carrying a big measuring tape and a claw hammer, the better to instantly reconstruct our congenial slum of a studio—we too were squatters! Not that such cultural manifestations of resistance were useless: we also wore our costumes and long hair in the streets and were well aware of the corruption of our aspirations by racist urban renewal and the burning villages in Vietnam. Many of us refused to work for what we understood to be "the man," which surely bolstered our self-regard as subjects and had legible effects on the ground. But refusing architecture was a dead end and too-often resulted in abstention rather than real resistance. The beast just rumbled on.

Time to turn this around, and the model of the union (interestingly, FAECT, recognizing problems with traditional union organization for architects, always identified itself as a "federation," as "an economic organization functioning in much the same manner as a labor union") is both bracing and material. Unions have always, at their best, had a double agenda. The first is the workplace, the assurance of fair wages and rules, of a safe and humane environment, and of access to jobs by all who are qualified. Second, though, is a broader objective, the idea that these conditions should characterize society as a whole, and this impetus has led to the labor movement's role in the vanguard of struggles for peace, civil and human rights, and an ethical internationalism. Our own organization should likewise embrace both. A focus on the immaterial qualities of intellectual labor—or on our vaunted "professionalism"—is to miss the point. It's the solidarity that we need and the forms of subjugation—the Taylorism and the terror, the power of the 1 percent, the grotesque environmental injustices—that remain our constant foe.

Our fight is to assure equity and justice both in architecture's effects and in the mode of its production. Let's organize together!

(2015)

44

Travels with Zaha

One of the best weeks I've ever had was spent traveling in Brazil with Zaha Hadid, twenty-nine years ago. We began at a big conference in São Paolo, speaking to an earphoned audience via simultaneous translation into half a dozen languages. Unfortunately, the organizer was short of funds, and the translators began to walk off the job—resulting in babel and bedlam. Four of us—me, Zaha, my wife, and a traumatized friend, just dumped by her partner—beat a retreat to the Copacabana Palace hotel in Rio and headed for the beach across the street.

It was a topless beach in the most body-conscious country on earth, and I relaxed into connoisseur mode. Zaha immediately began giggling at my gaze and suggested I take a better look at the beefy legs and bulging bikini bottoms of the gorgeous creatures I was pretending not to be staring at. It was the *transgender* topless beach! Perfect! Zaha loved formal transformations of all sorts—delighted in the play of parameters, the style-drive, and the *freedom*—and had a rich architectural vocabulary to describe various body parts.

A couple of days later, in Brasilia, we had a friendly audience with Oscar Niemeyer, one of Zaha's most revered influences (too many overemphasize the Russian constructivist and miss the tropical sultriness). Skirting the language barrier, Niemeyer had an assistant bring in a big manila pad, which was set up on an easel. He began by drawing the curving roof of the yacht club in Belo Horizonte—unmistakable in a single line—and continued to sketch the history of his work. As he finished each sheet, he tore it off and threw it on the floor. Our eyes flitted between the discarded drawings and each other as the treasures accumulated. At the end of the meeting we left slowly, empty-handed, glancing back, tortured. No one had the nerve to speak up or make a grab. Later, chatting with one of Niemeyer's ex-wives, we told the story and she said we were crazy, that he'd have been delighted if we'd helped ourselves. Zaha and I retold this story for decades.

We left Brasilia on a Friday afternoon. There's no terminus on earth more crowded than that airport at the end of the week as thousands flee the city's longueurs for lively Rio. We were stuck in a long check-in queue and Zaha was not travelling light. When we finally reached the counter and her numerous bags were on the scale, the agent declared that the flight was too crowded to load them all. A slow burn: Zaha pushed back, ratcheting up the insults by degree and peppering them with her legendary salty language. The agent was unyielding, and the line behind us pressed. Suddenly, Zaha emitted a blood-curdling shriek. The vast terminal fell completely silent. The agent, face drained of blood and wide-eyed in terror, grabbed the bags and sent them on their way.

Zaha was a brilliant traveling companion: she would not be denied. Restaurants that had closed reopened to cook for us. Prices fell for everything from knickknacks to precious stones under the irresistible force of her bargaining (I once witnessed this on a shopping trip to the couture floor of Bergdorf Goodman in New York). But what a friend: on our Carioca idyll, these interventions—despite the drama—always included the rest of us. We all ate well, got the first cab, received excellent service everywhere, and were warmed by her generous radiance. When my wife admired a vivid chartreuse wrap of Zaha's, she immediately gave it to her.

I've never known anyone who combined such artistic intensity with a love of lollygagging like Zaha. To be sure, she kept her own time and—when I was forced to play the organizing "guy" role during our travels—the bus waiting, Zaha still in her room, my wife tapping her foot, our friend wandering fully dressed into the sea—she could be exasperating. But then she'd arrive, full of light and zest, ready to get going. There would be gales of laughter, oceans of gossip, acute observations, urgent detours, deep appreciation, and the greatest tenderness. What a trip.

(2016)

45

Pinkwashing Zion Square

When the Freedom of Information Act became law, many of my comrades from the struggles of the sixties sent away for their files. For a number there was a terrible outcome: the files were empty. How terrible to think yourself a dangerous enemy of the state only to discover you'd been completely beneath its notice!

Slightly similar feelings arose when I received a note from the director of media affairs at the Israeli Consulate General wondering if I would be interested in covering a just-announced architectural competition for the redesign of Jerusalem's Zion Square, a Mandate-era public space in West Jerusalem that has, since the 1930s, been a commercial center (the eponymous Zion was a cinema) and the go-to site for a wide variety of demonstrations, including mass rallies by both Right and Left. The competition is intended both to refresh the site and to rebrand and repurpose it "from Protest Square to Tolerance Square." As the press release elaborates this false—even invidious—antithesis, "Zion Square which drew demonstrations and protests will become a square of tolerance and mutual respect." Apparently my old pieces denouncing the fraudulent "Museum of Tolerance" (currently under construction on the site of a historic Arab cemetery not far away), originally to have been designed by Frank Gehry (who wisely backed out), hadn't made it to my dossier! Perhaps I have no dossier! Let one be opened and let my protest against this grotesque undertaking be the first page!

This isn't the first time there's been effort to reconsider the square. In 2006, the Jerusalem Foundation proposed to rebuild it and to rename it Rapoport Plaza, "in honor," according to the Jerusalem Post, "of the Waco, Texas tycoon who pledged $2-million for urban improvements," including a colossal corten sculpture by Ron Arad. Although this scheme disappeared quickly, the funkiness and formal incoherence of the time-altered place has been an enduring source of dismay to *fastidious* planners, concerned with its failures as streetscape. The design brief for the new effort at transformation is couched in anodyne architectural language, calling for an "innovative, creative, and sustainable" solution to create a "beating heart of the city" that will become the "focal point for of the city's cultural activity," supporting a "heterogeneous" "target [*sic*] audience" of "residents, tourists, and visitors" while attentive "to the needs of a diverse population, including children, seniors, and those with disabilities."

Concealed behind these "universal" categories is the more salient fact that this transformation will further ratify and reify steps already taken to shut down the square as a political space. In 2012, after the opening of Jerusalem's light rail, the municipality signed a contract with CityPass, the system operator, that "prohibits the train being stopped by a roadblock." This smooth-sailing clause has been both motivated and enabled by, among other things, the government's ongoing denial of any permits for demonstrations by *anyone* in Zion Square, through which the tram passes. In formulation and practice, tolerance is here equated with prohibition and silence, with restrictions on speech rather than its encouragement. The competition organizers attempt to divert attention from this effective intolerance by a vaguely formulated dedication of the project "in memory of the 16-year-old stabbed during last year's Gay Pride parade in Jerusalem."

As a further marker of the particular species of exclusionary tolerance hovering over the affair, the adjudicating jury is made up entirely of Jewish Israelis, including the Likudnik mayor of Jerusalem, three highly placed municipal officials (two current, one former), four architects, and the mother of Shira Banki, the girl murdered by an unrepentant settlement-dwelling *Haredi* homophobe, who killed her shortly after his release from a ten-year prison term for having stabbed five people at the 2005 Pride march (he knifed another six in 2015). What a sad exploitation of grief to serve such a cravenly elastic idea of tolerance. But the self-congratulatory propaganda that seeks to use one form of ostensible liberality to mask a far more endemic repression is, alas, an old story. For many years, Israeli officialdom has been working hard to celebrate its welcoming attitude toward gay tourists. According to a much-cited op-ed by Sarah Schulman in the *New York Times* in 2011, the government launched "Brand Israel" in 2004, a marketing campaign aimed at men aged eighteen to twenty-four (posters galore of buff boys on the beach), which was expanded a few years later in a $90 million ad blitz to brand Tel Aviv as "an international gay vacation destination."

The strategy has been widely described as "pinkwashing," for the calculating effort to universalize gay "solidarity" in order to obscure Israel's attitude toward more intolerable forms of identity. As Jasbir Puar and Maya Mikdashi wrote in the e-zine *Jadaliyya* in 2012, pinkwashing functions to help the Israeli state "to gloss over the ongoing settler colonialism of historic Palestine by redirecting international attention towards a comparison between the supposedly stellar record of gay rights in Israel and the supposedly dismal state of life for LGBTQ Palestinians in the Occupied Palestine." The ploy is even more fundamentally invidious: Mikdashi argued in an earlier piece that this focus on gay rights—or women's rights—serves to displace attention from the larger question of *political* rights and calls out the canny, if racist, Israeli self-promotion as advertising "a safe haven for Palestinian queers from 'their culture.'"

Conspicuously absent in the publicity announcing the architectural competition is any acknowledgement of an earlier attack in Zion Square, the attempted lynching (a word widely used in the Israeli media) of four Palestinian teenagers by a Jewish mob in 2012, which resulted in the near-death of seventeen-year-old Jamal Julani. The incident was itself marked by its own particular version of "tolerance": as a headline in *Haaretz* put it, "Hundreds Watched Attempt to Lynch Palestinians in Jerusalem, Did Not Interfere." That the organizers of this competition have chosen, in effect, to so narrowly *celebrate* a particular form of intolerance with the commemorative dignity of a refreshed architecture only demonstrates—like the opposition it offers between "protests" and "mutual respect"—that intolerance will not be protested here.

There's a fine essay by Herbert Marcuse—written in 1965 as part of the volume *A Critique of Pure Tolerance*—on the subject of "repressive tolerance," in which he describes how the idea of tolerance acquires a particular valence depending on the circumstances of its promotion. Marcuse elucidates the conundrum of the ideal of tolerance in an environment of violence and "total administration" in which the exercise of nominal democratic liberties (voting, demonstrations, letters to the editor) serve to *reinforce* the ability of the system to pursue its own bad ends. In effect, tolerance—the enlargement "of the range and content of freedom," something most desired as an ultimate good—is made the instrument by which all it strives for is ignored: "tolerance" becomes a fig leaf for intolerance. Such unquestioning is used to make dissent meaningless, purging truth-seeking by offering effective equality to *any* value at all under the guise of an impartiality that reinforces the status quo.

The Jerusalem government—through this competition—seeks to create an advertisement for its own warped idea of tolerance rather than to enable the thing itself. As Marcuse put it, "When tolerance mainly serves the protection and preservation of a repressive society, when it serves to neutralize opposition and to render men immune against other and better forms of life, then tolerance has been perverted."

No designer of conscience should participate in this awful sham, which only insults the memory of the victims—and the heroes—of Zion Square.

(2016)

Burden of Gilt

When it opened in 2010, the second-floor lounge at the Trump SoHo condo-hotel—the "Library"—was decorated with a lavish collection of books bespeaking the seriously stylish. Cocktail tables groaned with weighty monographs devoted to leading architects and designers. On the shelves, though, was something more rare: a complete run of *Playboy,* bound in luxe leather. If Donald Trump has a master in matters of taste, it's surely his fellow teetotaler and sex fan, Hugh Hefner, the pajama-clad, Pepsi-swilling (covertly bourbon-spiked, some allege) progenitor of the lifestyle that so intoxicated boys of the Donald's generation. Did creased editions of the magazine reside under the Donald's military school mattress as they did under those of every lad of conventional boomer proclivities? Even more important: Were the most distressed pages the centerfold or J. Paul Getty's 1961 column, "How I Made My First Billion?"

Trump's politics are, like Hefner's "Playboy philosophy," an impossible combination of liberalism, hedonism, blovia-tion, and misogyny. These two men have made world-class contributions to the objectification of women, whether via centerfolds, Miss Universe, Miss USA, Miss Teen USA pageants, sleazy remarks, or the slimy prurience of their lecherous gazes. My daughter is *hot*! Melania's a *ten*! But Trump does more: he objectifies—brands—everyone. Professional wrestling does for bulked-up guys what beauty pageants do for bosomy gals. And what could possibly be more objectifying than his ownership of jocks, whether Herschel Walker and Doug Flutie (who played for Trump's New Jersey Generals of the short-lived United States Football League), or Trump's erstwhile supporter, the rapist, ear-biting brute, Mike Tyson?

Is it simply an inadvertent influence of the countercultural '60s that his logo is tonsorial and the persona political? Like Hitler's moustache, the helmet of hair is his metonym. I don't make this comparison lightly. While *The Art of the Deal* (1987) is no *Mein Kampf*, the media fixation, the facility for propaganda, the grandiosity, have uncanny parallels. As Hitler (who also wanted to make his beleaguered country great again) put it, "The correct use of propaganda is a true art." The Donald is even more succinct: "I have always gotten much more publicity than anybody else."

Because Trump's main field of play is real estate—hence, architecture—the coincidence of his rise and architecture's own theoretical and practical fascinations with branding is telling. For several decades, the intercourse of modern architecture and mass media, and its own status as a form of media, has been lively, and Playboy's role has been much marked. The magazine was, from the first, thick with articles and images of modernist building and interiors, featuring no end of Eames, Bertoia, Knoll, Wright, Mies, Bucky, Lautner, Safdie, Ant Farm, and many more. Paul (formerly Beatriz) Preciado points out in the marvelous *Pornotopia* (2011) that "in the late 1950's and '60's, only one other article ... managed to match the popularity of the Playmate nudes: the foldout of the second feature on the Playboy penthouse published in 1959." Bachelor pad pictorials were a staple throughout the 1960s, including such gems as an "Airy Eyrie" in Malibu, "A Baronial Bi-level for a Busy Bachelor," "Exotica in Exurbia," and "A New Haven Haven."

Preciado—expanding on Barbara Ehrenreich, Bill Osgerby, and Beatriz Colomina—describes Hefner's fascination with architectural space both as an enlargement of his claims on hip modernity and as leverage for the co-optation of the domestic for his ideal subject: the heterosexual bachelor playboy. In wresting domesticity (and its designer swag) from suburban imprisonment (Hefner as a misogynistic inversion of Betty Friedan!), it was crucial that *Playboy* be dissociated from both the stereotypical "woman's magazine" such as *Better Homes and Gardens* and from any taint of the gay. As Arnold Gingrich, first editor of *Playboy's* obvious model, *Esquire,* recounted, it was crucial to include elements "substantial enough to deodorize the lavender whiff coming from the mere presence of fashion pages." Per Ehrenreich, "The breasts and bottoms were necessary not just to sell the magazine, but to protect it." Cheesecake (and those *serious* articles) guaranteed that *Playboy* was giving it to you straight, and it sited women in an architectural environment as objects of desire who also unfailingly knew their place. How like the way in which buffoon Trump (who claims it was he who actually broke the glass ceiling!) deploys the distaff at his events, that inevitable chorus line of beautiful white women—his wife and daughter front and center—to both insulate himself from appearing a chauvinist bachelor and to assert his timeless attraction for—and ability to breed—hotties.

Like Hefner and Trump, Hitler also worked hard to situate himself in the context of "female" space. In her fascinating book, *Hitler at Home* (2015), Despina Stratigakos recounts the assiduous rebranding of the Führer, from violent agitator to pacific country squire, after his assumption of the chancellorship in 1933. A main medium for this was depicting Hitler in situations of domesticity, especially at his Alpine aerie, the Berghof. Meticulously decorated by Gerdy Troost (whose dialectical relationship to Leni Riefenstahl—the one focused on signifiers of individuality, the other of the mass—is a rife story still incompletely told), the sobriety and elegance of the structure, and relationship to those mythic mountains—viewed through a movie-screen sized picture window—served as a corroborating background for an elevated, feelingful Hitler.

This calculated indoor/outdoor contrast marks all three specimens. Hitler, increasingly confined to a series of bunkers (a word staffers apparently used to describe the Playboy offices), was formed by his doss house life in Vienna, his failure to get "in" to the Academy of Fine Arts, and his years sheltering in the trenches of World War I. Reactively, he sought to order exterior space with grandiose urban schemes, perhaps most dramatically in the Nuremberg rallies, where every subject was situated with unyielding precision. Hefner was more completely interior still, never leaving his bedroom, even travelling in it in his customized DC-9 with its flying boudoir. Hef's Los Angeles estate was indoors out, a high-walled Neverland he could traverse in robe and slippers. The germ- and insect-phobic Donald is likewise no outdoorsman: his preferred open-air setting is the golf course, nature in its most tortured, subordinated, and disciplined state.

All three worked overtime to establish and defend their brands through both media and retail goods. Disseminated through such best-selling books as *The Hitler Nobody Knows* (1932) as well as through a rash of souvenir objects, from postcards to dollhouses, the fascist marketing project spiraled out of hand, and Joseph Goebbels grew concerned about the proliferation of "tasteless" Nazi-themed merchandise, leading to the passage, in 1933, of the "Law for the Protection of National Symbols." As Stratigakos explains, the law was meant to counter such excesses as "Storm-trooper gingerbread, wine bottles and ashtrays ornamented with swastikas, women's brooches with 'Heil Hitler' in imitation diamonds, and alarm clocks that played the Nazi anthem, 'The Flag on High.'" No patch on the Donald, who once filed a lawsuit against two brothers named Jules and Eddie Trump for using their own names for *their* real estate company, The Trump Group, and managed to have their trademark revoked.

Hitler, Hefner, and Trump—the *real* rat pack—share a logo fetish—the big T, the bunny, and the swastika are among the most ubiquitous signifiers of the age—and a powerful fascination with building and design. Hefner in the Playboy Mansion, Hitler in the Berghof, and the Donald in his Trump Tower triplex are obsessed with self-corroboration by decorative context and the dramatic possibilities of the public marketing of a "private" lifestyle. Playboy's masculinization of interiority is nowhere more clearly stated than in Hefner's editorial in the maiden issue of the magazine: "We don't mind telling you in advance—we plan on spending most of our time inside. We like our apartment. We enjoy mixing cocktails and an hors d'oeuvre or two, putting a little mood music on the phonograph, and inviting in a female acquaintance for a quiet discussion on Picasso, Nietzsche, jazz, sex."

The Donald likewise inhabits interiors in lieu of an interior life and shows them off with hyperbolic self-celebration. The tour of the penthouse with its fifty-three rooms, African-blue onyx lavatory, ivory friezes, and chandelier "from a castle in Austria" always seems to culminate in a view of Central Park and the skyline outside the glass walls, Donald's own Alps. Excess is irresistible. Trump himself recalls an early meeting with the architect Der Scutt at his first Manhattan apartment in which Scutt opined that there was simply *too much furniture* and proceeded to move half of it into the hall. However, while Trump's architectural taste is not exactly refined, it does have a certain middle-of-the-road precision and an eye for branded talent and pedigree. His "portfolio" adumbrates grandiosity without actual risk-taking: the architecture is far more Ralph Lauren than John Galliano, product not provocation. Indeed, like his father before him (who had Morris Lapidus do a few lively lobbies in his otherwise generic apartment houses in Brooklyn), the Donald has fundamentally conservative taste, and his buildings break no artistic ground but are accessorized like crazy with shiny signifiers of the sumptuous.

The architects he employs are, if never avant-garde, often from the upper commercial echelon. Adrian Smith—designer of the actual world's tallest building, the Burj Khalifa in Dubai—authored Trump's tower in Chicago. That beloved old Nazi, Philip Johnson, did the new skin at Columbus Circle; at age eighty-six (Freudians take note: same age as Trump's dad Fred), he was invited to tart up Trump's Taj, and, at ninety-three, to add his brand to Riverside South. Der Scutt (who weirdly changed his name from Don to the German definite article, perhaps as homage to *the* Donald, although Donald himself, not yet birther-in-chief, was claiming at the time that the family moniker was Swedish), the designer of Trump Tower, once worked for Philip Johnson who also loved all things German. Gilt by association!

Trump's breakthrough into the big time was the Grand Hyatt Hotel, designed by Scutt in 1974, an admitted feat of financial legerdemain and, in its transformation from brick opacity to mirror-clad reflectivity, an apposite symbol of the meister's narcissism, repeated in the global acreage of pure *shininess* that so embodies *Trumpsterstil*. There is a method here that joins the self-celebration of an office suite lined with hundreds of magazine cover pictures of its occupant with a mirror's ability to enlarge, dazzle, and deceive. In a 1997 profile in the *New Yorker*, the Donald articulated his aesthetic succinctly: "I have glitzy casinos because people expect it ... Glitz works in Atlantic City ... And in my residential buildings I sometimes use flash, which is a level below glitz." This capacity to make distinctions that are always hyberbolic is surely at the core of the man's charm as well as the obvious register of a certain, er, anxiety that Trump is now working through at our expense.

Strikingly, although the small-handed Trump has been involved with some very tall buildings, including the fairly high, fifty-eight-story Trump Tower (a repeated Trumpian sleight-of-hand is to skip a few floors in the numbering system so that the top-most floor can appear to be higher than it actually is: Trump tower starts on ten, the Grand Hyatt, a twenty-six-story building, became thirty-four by beginning guest rooms on fourteen, as did the Taj), he has had to settle, in the end, for having his name on multiple runners-up, including such second-tier superlatives as the Empire State Building (as part-owner), the tallest residential tower in Canada, the tallest *occupied* residential building in the world (a title that will lapse in about ten minutes), the formerly tallest residential tower in New York, and the tallest building in New Rochelle.

Trump's one actual go at the *world's* tallest building was the Television City project of 1985 on the huge West Side railyards site, which featured a proposal for a 150-story, 1,910-foot (with spire) shaft as part of a complex that also included seven dwarfed skyscrapers, each higher than the Trump Tower and designed by Helmut Jahn in his manliest neo-ICBM style. Community and critical pushback was immediate, and Trump soon dumped Jahn for Alexander Cooper—the planner for "traditionalist"

Battery Park City—an amiable architect whom Gwenda Blair aptly described as the "anti-Jahn."

This quick recognition of the limits of his power to manipulate a complex situation led, by turns, to a series of somewhat more "urbane" proposals (adding streets and smaller buildings to the mix, chopping down towers, plazas). Finally, when strong community opposition serendipitously coincided with Trump's own parlous financial position, an entirely new approach emerged in the form of Riverside South, designed by Alan Ritchie and Costas Kondylis and branded by Philip Johnson. This was a dumbed-down take on a scheme independently commissioned by a consortium of civic groups from architect Paul Willen— proposed *in opposition* to Trump's initial grandiosities—and many of these were abashed when Trump himself seized the initiative and became the new plan's leading exponent.

The now-completed outcome is simultaneously a monument to both heightened sensitivity and diminished expectations. The key public benefits in the community scheme were to have been the relocation of the elevated West Side Highway to ground level at the inboard edge of the site and the creation of a major park in the liberated space. Not only have neither of these materialized, but the executed project is architecturally bleak, a monochrome reach of vaguely variegated apartment houses that reproduce the cookie-cutter ethos of his father's buildings but with bigger rooms, better finishes, and higher prices. And each, of course, is emblazoned with a giant "Trump" above its entrance.

As architectural patron, Trump does better with acquired imprimatur, and a number of his holdings—or brandings—have been purchases of distinguished historic properties, such as the Barbizon, the Plaza (now sold), 40 Wall Street, and, of course, Mar-a-Lago, which offer old money cachet to new money tenants. (Writing about Trump Tower in *The Art of The Deal*, the Donald declares, "The one market we didn't go after was old-money New Yorkers, who generally want to live in older buildings anyway.") His eclectic collection also includes glitzy renovations of well-located dogs (the transformation of the hideous Gulf and Western building into the differently hideous Trump International Hotel and Tower and the sow's ear to silk purse of the Grand Hyatt) as well as construction of new structures, including the eponymous Tower and the contemporaneous Trump Plaza, not to mention his participation in a plethora projects around the city and, indeed, the planet under the sign of "the world's only global luxury real estate super-brand."

But it isn't the architecture that makes the man dangerous. Trump and Hefner, his virtual twin, are apostles of "models of masculine consumption" which Bill Osgerby argues "elaborated a form of sexual politics that was, to a large part, reactionary and exploitative … the masculine consumer is better seen as part of wider developments in the fabric of American capitalism that saw the rise of a new middle-class faction whose habitus and value system was oriented around an ethos of youthful hedonism and leisure-oriented consumption." Like Hefner (Hitler, Kraft durch Freude notwithstanding, gets a pass here!), Trump is a man whose fortunes derive precisely from hedonism and leisure-oriented consumption (are these the jobs he plans to bring back to America?), and both rose as vulgarian embodiments of their playboy "philosophies," as preening objects of venal desire (I am trying to imagine Trump dilating on the will to power to Miss Teen USA over Diet Cokes).

They also derive from his mastery of the con. As he skipped around his creditors during the bankruptcy of his casinos, the bankers put Trump on a personal budget: $450,000 a month, affirming the success of his fuck-you/gimme-gimme attitude toward the system. Trump's career, like that of his father's before him, has been built on playing us for suckers, enjoying house odds, and collecting every available "legal" advantage—from greasing political palms, to screwing his shareholders via bankruptcy protection, to an array of tax subsidies, zoning bonuses, and other forms of public largesse. The billionaire tribune of the working class is a welfare queen.

An ironic staple of current cocktail dish: Was it like this in Berlin in 1932? *That fool will never become chancellor.* The bombast, the racism, the moustache: impossible. Of course, the comparison goes too far, doesn't it? Demonizing Muslims is very different than demonizing Jews. And the plan is to keep them out, not throw them out, right? It's the 11 million *Mexicans* we actually want to deport, and they're all criminals. And we're going to build great things, walls as wide as a country and as long as the autobahn. That sound we hear is the glass ceiling shattering, not *Kritallnacht*.

Isn't it?

(2016)

Architecture against Trump

We are dismayed at the temperate, agreeable, indeed feckless, statement that the director of the American Institute of Architects has issued on behalf of—although clearly without any consultation with—its membership on the election of Donald Trump. While his words appear anodyne and reflect the judicious position and celebration of America's history of peaceful transitions of power articulated by both President Obama and Hillary Clinton, they are an embarrassment to those of us who feel that the Trump presidency represents a clear and present danger to many values that are fundamental to both our nation and our profession.

Architects and other designers working in the built environment have special insight into both the mentality and the behavior of Donald Trump, who has gained his fortune as a builder, developer, and brander of architecture. While the work that bears his name is of decidedly mixed formal quality, the circumstances surrounding both its social and physical construction are troublesome to say the least. Trump's well-documented history of racial discrimination, tenant harassment, stiffing creditors (including architects), evasive bankruptcies, predilection

This chapter is from a letter to the executive director of the American Institute of Architects immediately following Trump's election.

for projects of low social value—such as casinos—and his calculated evasion of the taxes that might support our common realm are of a piece with his larger nativist, sexist, and racist political project. We do not welcome Donald Trump to the White House, and will revile and oppose him until he can conclusively demonstrate that the hideous pronouncements and proposals of his campaign have demonstrably been set aside and in favor of positions and actions that genuinely seek to serve our national cause and purpose—to build a better America rooted in the principles of justice, equity, and human dignity.

Given our commitment to the physical environment, we must evaluate President-elect Trump's actions in the areas outlined below. These will reveal not only his true character and mettle but ours as well, both as a basis for shaping our ability to countenance his government and also to set standards for our resistance to the mentality of the highest bidder and lowest ethical common denominator.

1. Decent affordable housing for all citizens as a matter of right. Trump's presidency is in some ways an aftereffect of the great recession brought on—in large part—by the kind of predatory financial practices of which he is himself an emblem. The mountain of mortgage debt and its "securitization" via high-risk financial junk collapsed, robbing millions of their homes and savings. We bailed out the banks but not the people. We now need robust means—including dramatic subsidy—to create genuine residential security for all Americans.

2. The earth's environment is inarguably in a dire state and this imperils us all. The stunning and unsupportable ignorance that Trump and the cabal of climate change deniers are likely to foist on us is alone grounds for radical measures to resist and impeach a Trump presidency. We face an emergency, and unless truly radical steps are taken to move us toward a post-carbon economy, to conserve energy, to use our precious planetary resources with the great care and most considered stewardship they demand, we will rise up against any government bent on leading us down the path to global suicide.

3. Of course, we strongly support investment in our national physical infrastructure. This means jobs, an economic shot in the arm, increased competitiveness, and much else. But such an investment begs the question: "in what?" When Barack Obama took over the reins of government and applied himself to the task of digging us out of the hole Republican greed had put us in, the phrase "shovel-ready" became part of our vocabulary. Unfortunately, too much of what was ready to go was based on systems and standards that were already obsolete. We certainly need to repair lots of roadways and bridges and, especially, to fix crumbling sewer and water systems. But is the best we can do? We also need to think about the infrastructures of the future, those that will reduce our reliance on the automobile and fight sprawl and other increasingly unsustainable urban forms. How much of that half trillion Trump proposes to spend will go to public transit? How much to reconfiguring our imperiled coastlines? How much to assuring that our insane production and disposal of waste enters a circular system of conservation and reuse? And how much will be invested in fair wages, good work, and environmentally just material extraction, production, and use? All of this is the ethical purview of the architect. Has Trump given ten minutes thought to a future that doesn't conform to the worst practices of today? How much of his infrastructural investment will be spent on insane border fortifications, prisons for illegal "aliens," and runways for fleets of atomic bombers?

4. In order to secure a sustainable future, we need enormous investment in research and education. This will not simply be to invent the new technologies to enable a more sustainable future—including that gamut that surrounds building and fabrication—but to create generations of citizens who know the value of living in harmony with the planet's rhythms and resources and who have had the practices of sharing and generosity imbued in them. Can this ultimate avatar of selfishness and hyper-consumption even contemplate what such an education might entail? Can he shift the focus of his allies from demonizing public education and frothing about who goes to what

bathroom in order to help bring up our children with hearts full of respect for the earth and for the science that describes it?

5. Finally, can this tribune of wealth and disdain for the other—for people of color, women, the disabled, Muslims, Hispanics—ever understand that many of us entered the design professions because we so clearly saw the capacity of our practices to influence and structure the way in which the world's resources are distributed and deployed? Trump's newly "presidential" demeanor—his claims that he seeks to "bring us together"—will continue to ring completely false until he dedicates himself to seeking genuine equity not just for Americans but for all of those who struggle to live good lives on our crowded and troubled planet.

We must carry on the struggle for a just and sustainable environment with redoubled strength, opposing the reactionary policies that so gravely threaten our most fundamental values. Trump's agenda—and that of his allies—will only accelerate the privatization and erosion of our public realm in both its social and physical forms and practices. We call upon the American Institute of Architects to stand up for something beyond a place at the table where Trump's cannibal feast will be served! Let us not be complicit in building Trump's wall but band together to take it down!

(2016)

The City after the Autonomobile

Like many New Yorkers, I often use Via, a ride-sharing app which—for five bucks—will transport you between any two points in Manhattan below 125th Street. They've got their algorithms in a row and, in general, the system works very smoothly. But it's clear, when the car pulls up, that something's slightly off. The trip is almost completely automated, and computers organize the pickup, drop-off, journey, and payment: the anomaly is the driver. Watching the route unfold—following the instructions of that bland, robotic, female voice from the GPS—I catch the sad whiff of impending obsolescence. The self-driving car is about to arrive.

The implications are profound, and not just for the employment prospects of the immigrants and "shared economy" operatives who drive the vehicles. Something radical looms, both for the fundamental nature of our mobility and for the form of the cities in which we circulate. Just as earlier technological innovations, like streetcar lines, railways, and horseless carriages, had transformative effects on urban morphology and life (exponential growth, suburbanization, corridorization, and other dramatic physical and social changes), so the advent of the autonomous vehicle—*autonomobiles*—will transform our cities decisively.

In the United States, we've long relied on the radical inefficiency of private cars, or on rail and bus trunk lines that are only economical in conditions of high density, and which often produce the classic "last mile" conundrum getting all the way home from the station. Public transport is not one of America's glories: despite many decades of argument for transit-oriented development and other densification policies, close to 90 percent of daily trips are by car, and our sprawling cities are its natural habitat and spawn.

As the modal mix rapidly transformed in the early twentieth century, much creativity—and loopiness—was devoted to imagining cities reshaped by this technological maelstrom of planes, trains, and automobiles. These visions ranged from the extreme lamination of the vertical metropolis, with its multiple modes stacked in space—subways, cars, elevated trains, pedestrians, auto-gyros, and airplanes shish-kebabbed together by elevators; to the fantasy of the linear city—an endless band of settlement along a rail line; to the "people mover"—a desperately constrained system that attempted to hybridize the car and the railway but which could never rise above the tyranny of its fixed routes or crude technology; to the car-enabled edge city that has so complicated the historically centrifugal relations between urban centers and peripheries. What all have in common is the idea of modal separation, producing systems of isolation in which the least powerful yields to the most: pedestrians give way to bikes, bikes to cars, cars to trolleys, trolleys to trains, and so forth.

Autonomobiles could present a truly new model of on-demand, point-to-point mobility. Indeed, new shared, responsive systems have already had major impacts on urban patterns and habits. I've been working on planning projects for the South Side of Chicago for decades, and the transformations brought about by the arrival of Uber and Lyft in many of its relatively low-density, transit-poor neighborhoods is startling: sparsity becomes practical. My survey is not scientific, but I'm impressed, when using ride-sharing services there, by how many fellow passengers are on simple errands of moderate distance, otherwise impossible without a personal vehicle. This surely suggests capacious possibilities for urban transformation—new mixes of use, local centers, flexible access to available housing, and networks of sociability that are otherwise thwarted by distance, danger, and inclemency.

Autonomobility will have perhaps its greatest formal impact in altering the most critical matrix of public urbanity: the street. In New York, our streets are both troubled and changing. The widespread growth of cycling, an increase in tree cover, and various managerial efforts to ease traffic via modal mixing have resulted in an even more horizontally laminated streetscape that retains and reinforces modal isolation (sidewalk, bike lane, parking lane, bus lane, traffic lane, median, repeat). We haven't had the courage of more radical mixing tactics like the Netherlands's *woonerf*, or shared street, in which all modes coexist in one minimally regulated space. And we haven't even begun to look at what the recapture of the street might look like if it were considered from scratch, with a radically reformed mix in mind—one in which individually owned cars headed for urban extinction.

One immediate effect could be the liberation of well over a third of street area from use as vehicular storage space. If small-scale mobile passenger and logistics "particles" were deployed around the clock and on demand, a radical reduction of the number of actual vehicles in service would occur (an MIT study of Singapore suggests the reduction could be at least two-thirds) and with it the liberation—and lubrication—of an enormous portion of urban streets. A variety of robotic and sensor technologies would also allow the efficient utilization of curb space for the transfer of both goods and people from the street to buildings or sidewalks. Indeed, the defeat of the hydra of storage parking and delivery double-parking would have a cascade of beneficial impacts, from eased mobility to reduced pollution and accident reduction to the most important prospect of all: the capture of this public space for more authentically public uses.

In New York City, the street could become a true public service conduit. Traffic would move at a rational pace and bikes could safely join the mix. Sidewalks would be augmented with new uses, including plantings and bioswales, recreational areas, small public facilities, and—most crucially and transformatively in New York and other cities that don't have service alleys—could become the site of operations for managing our solid waste. Replacing our Alpine heaps of plastic sacks of rubbish, a fascinating new architecture of collection, recycling, redistribution, and remediation might arise, anticipating the day when the very idea of waste is relegated to history's own dustbin. Ultimately, this freeing and reappropriation of the street can be part of a truly localist metabolics in which our air, water, climate, energy, mobility, education, sociability, and nutrition become the central focus of the space we most urgently share.

The horizontal re-lamination of city streets is likely to be accompanied before long by a vertical one as well. Given the imminence of ubiquitous drone movements—as well as the soon-to-appear flying Ubers (the company has already branded its vertical-lift ride-sharing operation "Uber Elevate")—the space above the city is also sure to be reconfigured. Although the physics (and acoustics) of flying cars will seriously limit their point-to-point capacity at first, NASA and others are already deep into the study of the laminar systems and "rules of the road" to allow large numbers of unmanned aircraft systems to operate above and in cities, bringing consumption's necessities from Amazon and Grubhub. A variety of concepts—including sky-lanes, sky-corridors, and sky-tubes—renew that early fantasy of the laminar city that includes flying vehicles, although most seem to be based on the conventional geometry and parameters of deference that rule roads.

Such revolutionary technology can have fundamental impacts on the form of both current and coming cities. To keep it friendly, however, will demand fighting the growing dominance of the "smart city" mind-set and its uncritical accumulations of "big data" to improve efficiency and control, without much deep thinking about noncorporate forms of desire. This must include the defense of many of our traditional gathering places—our squares, plazas, parks, and sidewalks. The reasons for mobility are not merely logistical. We move to live, to experience the other, to engage the pleasures of place, to collaborate, to enjoy happy accidents of encounter, and to enlarge the space of the political, which demands the verifying integrity of the face-to-face. New mobility systems, however, risk undermining urbanity in favor of a distributive entropy that arrives under the false flag of convenience. Mobility may become more flexible, but it might also become far less accessible (Uber Elevate won't be cheap), a privilege rather than a right.

This surge of technology could simply yield three-dimensional traffic jams, and it's urgent that the transition to these new means be finessed with art and determination. Just adding a new class of vehicles will have the same effect as adding more miles of highway: more traffic. For an autonomobile system to truly fulfill its promise demands radical subtraction. Fewer vehicles and less pavement will mark the truly sustainable cities we might have if we're authentically dedicated to sharing them equitably and efficiently.

(2017)

In Memoriam

Anthologies clock time, and looking at these pieces from the past half dozen years chronologically brings sad moments of punctuation. What keeps hope alive for art is the work of talent and generosity, and, as my cohort shuffles toward eternity, its loss becomes an ever more foregrounded marker of the urgency of expression.

No departure has been more grievous than that of Lebbeus Woods, beloved friend, spirit guide, and authentic genius. Not a word to be tossed off lightly but something vivid and recognizable: a talent always already there. Leb was both lodestar and millstone, his unmatchable powers at once a glowing object of aspiration and—unachievable by us mortals—a reason to give up and go back to bed.

Leb taught me many things, not simply from the heights of his confidence and capacity but also from his anxiety and sense of justice. We converged over the years around discussions of the dispositive stimulations and exigencies of "pure" expression, the dancing relativity of architecture's manifold content, and, especially, the urgent location of the social. Leb's early trajectory through fairly conventionally utopian agendas of visualized meaning, established in tension with the always-imperfect match-up of form and organization, forced him onward from the heroics of geometry and its discontents to the more mysterious and incalculable regime of physics, and this nexus sites his resistance both in practice and concept. To draw is always to propose some formula for coherence, but Lebbeus came up hard against both the un-representable (there are some cats—Shrödinger's for one—that simply won't sit still for a portrait) and the irrational.

Lebbeus dwelled long in the fields of warfare—he bravely hunkered down for months in besieged Sarajevo, wrote and designed copiously about the mechanics of destruction, both via bombardment as well as plate-shifting quakes, and other upheavals. These media of mass reordering fascinated him for "automatically" producing architectures of mesmerizing, foreboding, *othered* form: crises for a stable idea of building. Leb strived to reconcile this ubiquitous risk with a free—if not exactly safe—space for the expression of desire and the projects of his "middle period" were preoccupied with an architecture of insinuated liberation that had the power to transform and to heal both cities and souls. This speculation was empowered by a clear-eyed understanding of the simultaneous danger and necessity of totality and he rigorously and critically thought his propositions through to their conclusions, characteristically at once celebratory and cautionary. By unyieldingly situating his architecture in the provisional terrain of the unbuildable, Lebbeus argued with unmatched eloquence that nothing was to be unthinkable.

As his work assumed what was to be its final form, Leb seemed to realize that the fertilizations of eye/hand operations became precise in inverse proportion to their legibility, and he delved deep into expressive, relativity-rich ambiguity. Of course, drawing was a *drive* and couldn't be renounced, but the form-making became increasingly interior, and he found himself more and more impelled to write things down and to found relationships that were not about artist and spectator but more sagacious, interactive, dialectical. He blogged, he taught, he criticized, he befriended and his absolute renunciation of conventional practice was the marker of his unshakeable intellectual integrity and refusal to oppress. On the road to quintessence, one must pare, and greatness resides in knowing where and when to stop. Leb died—with Superstorm Sandy raging outside—at the height of his powers of both art and self-awareness.

Our other great and premature loss of talent during these years was Zaha, likewise a force of nature. I did love her too although the character of her ambition was very different from Leb's. Both were brimmingly confident, but Zaha had fewer outward doubts and another idea of architecture's instrumentality. To call her a formalist is not to diminish her stupendous achievement but simply to situate it. Her immersion in lush totality was not so much a sybarite's (though she was a sensualist for sure) as it was a perfectionist's. For Zaha, art always exceeded the circumstances of its production, and her quest for architectonic sublimity invariably ruled out distraction at what she felt was the margin. The idea that a talent so capacious is unanswerable to "externalities" both propelled and troubled her work, especially as she emerged from the artistic colony to go global and professional.

With Leb, the axis of derision was to call him an illustrator or to pigeonhole his production as science fiction. Zaha was tarred for political indifference, for the work she did in Azerbaijan and the Gulf. This criticism was both just and rankly unfair, begrudging. What big practice today doesn't build for oligarchs and sheikhs, for Kushners and Trumps? And what are the burdens and duties of being the most stupendous architectural talent to emerge from the Islamic world since Sinan? Zaha was assailed from a position of pious expectation that sprang from her being a woman and an Arab, and from the sheer intensity of her talent, which gave monumental rise to envy and the nattering cavils of taste. Zaha's seeming indifference to social and political "externalities" was not cavalier but regal: she always demanded that the world come to her and that she was uncompromising on behalf of her art both ennobled and tarnished her reputation. For me, the exquisite poetry of her Aliyev art center in Baku is astonishing and if this can never negate its mode of production or the despot it celebrates, the building—and the rest of her amazing body of work—has forever expanded architecture's capacity to embody the beautiful.

Acknowledgements

Long ago, when I wrote for the *Village Voice*, I occasionally spotted someone reading one of my columns on the subway. I found this extremely disconcerting and felt compelled to bury my head in whatever I was myself reading, sometimes even getting up to move to the next car. Putting these collections together evokes a similar anxiety, although I can now complete the whole fretful circuit of stimulus and response without relying on some stranger on the IRT. Most of the pieces here are journalism, which means done in a hurry and, to me, it shows: what leaps from the page are inept or absent arguments, points made too many times, the embarrassment of seeing passages recycled from one magazine in another (result of laziness, of not having a really regular gig to continue an argument, of propaganda's dependence on repetition), and especially the shopworn-ness of certain words and phrases. Did I really invoke "the right to the city" that many times? Wasn't it possible to find an argument about housing inequality somewhere but Engels? Why did my inner censor not staunch my reflex to write the words "conduce," "preservation," "anodyne," "informality," "relative autonomy," *"existenzminimum,"* "the man," "neoliberalism," or "Gini Coefficient" in what feels like every third sentence? And what's up with that spastic use of colons when so often a semi would do? Reader, forgive me!

On the up side, that collation *is* a fairly telling biopsy of the tissue of my concerns. The fact that this contracted vocabulary didn't distort every sentence I wrote is testament to work and support of wonderful, charitable, editors. In particular, I'd like to thank John Palatella at *The Nation* for his sympathy, intelligence, friendship, and many kindnesses with his red pencil. At *Architectural Record*, Cliff Pearson has been a paragon of patient reading and wisely spritzed many an overheated claim and phrase. Cathleen McGuigan, editor in chief, has always made me feel welcome: both she and Cliff like their martinis up and dry, confirming their acumen and taste. At Verso, thanks to the eagle-eyed, expert, and professional Sam Smith and, especially, to Leo Hollis, who has been all that I could ask, generous with candor and insight. Having an editor who is himself an extremely astute student and analyst of the city and a gifted, stylish, writer is both intimidating and reassuring. That he has suffered me so gladly marks both the elegance of his discretion and his keen sense of solidarity with a brother urban explorer. Thanks Leo! Let's do another book!

Finally, all my love to Joan, without whom neither this book nor its author would exist.

Chapter Credits

Chapter 1. Lynne Elizabeth and Stephen A. Goldsmith, eds., *What We See: Advancing the Observations of Jane Jacobs*, New York: New Village Press, 2010.

Chapter 2. *Baumeister* B5, May 2011.

Chapter 3. Presentation, Village Alliance, New York, June, 2011.

Chapter 4. Various contributors, *While We Were Sleeping: NYU and the Destruction of New York—A Collection of Pieces in Protest*, New York: McNally Jackson Bookstore, 2012.

Chapter 5. *Spontaneous Interventions,* US Pavilion, Thirteenth International Architecture Exhibition at the Venice Biennale, August 2012.

Chapter 6. Rick Bell, Lance Jay Brown, Lynne Elizabeth, Ron Shiffman, eds., *Beyond Zuccotti Park, Freedom of Assembly and the Occupation of Public Space*, New York: New Village Press, 2012.

Chapter 7. *Architectural Record*, December 2012.

Chapter 8. *Architectural Review*, March 2013.

Chapter 9. *Architectural Review*, June 2013.

Chapter 10. *Nation*, September 2, 2013, thenation.com.

Chapter 11. *Nation*, September 16, 2013, thenation.com.

Chapter 12. *Nation*, December 18, 2013, thenation.com.

Chapter 13. *Nation*, March 10, 2014, thenation.com.

Chapter 14. *Nation*, April 21, 2014, thenation.com.

Chapter 15. *Nation*, June 9, 2014, thenation.com.

Chapter 16. *Nation*, August 18–25, 2014.

Chapter 17. *Metropolis*, September 2014.

Chapter 18. *Architectural Record*, May 16, 2015, architecturalrecord.com.

Chapter 19. *Nation*, June 17, 2015, thenation.com.

Chapter 20. Architectural Review, August 2015.

Chapter 21. *Nation*, December 1, 2015, thenation.com.

Chapter 22. *Nation*, December 21–28, 2015.

Chapter 23. *Nation*, April 25–May 2, 2016.

Chapter 24. *Metropolis*, July 2016.

Chapter 25. *Architect's Newspaper*, October 26, 2016, archpaper.com.

Chapter 26. Max Page and Marla R. Miller, eds., *Bending the Future: Fifty Ideas for the Next Fifty Years of Historic Preservation in the United States*, New Haven: University of Massachusetts Press, 2017.

Chapter 27. Lecture, University of Michigan, October, 2011.

Chapter 28. Lecture, Modern Then and Now Hollin Hills House and Garden Tour, Hollin Hills, VA, 2012.

Chapter 29. Barry Bergdoll and Reinhold Martin, eds., *MoMA: Foreclosed: Rehousing the American Dream*, New York: Museum of Modern Art, 2012.

Chapter 30. Peggy Deamer, ed., *Architecture and Capitalism: 1845 to Present*, New York: Routledge, 2013.

Chapter 31. Ilka Ruby and Andreas Ruby, eds., *The Economy of Sustainable Construction*, 2013.

Chapter 32. *Nation*, May 13, 2013, thenation.com.

Chapter 33. *Nation*, June 10, 2013, thenation.com.

Chapter 34. *Architectural Record*, August 2013.

Chapter 35. Unpublished, September, 2013.

Chapter 36. *Nation*, September 16, 2013, thenation.com.

Chapter 37. *Nation*, October 28, 2013, thenation.com.

Chapter 38. Louise Noelle and Sara Topelson de Grinberg, eds., *Critical Juncture: Joseph Rykwert Royal Gold Metal and CICA Symposium*, Mexico City: Docomo, 2014.

Chapter 39. Neil Spiller and Nic Clear, eds., *Educating Architects:*

How Tomorrow's Practitioners Will Learn Today, London: Thames & Hudson, 2014.

Chapter 40. *Nation*, February 4, 2014, thenation.com.

Chapter 41. *Nation*, November 17, 2014, thenation.com.

Chapter 42. Various contributors, *Clear Light: The Architecture of Lauretta Vinciarelli*, New York: Oscar Riera Ojeda Publishers, 2015.

Chapter 43. Peggy Deamer, ed, The Architect as Worker: Immaterial Labor, the Creative Class, and the Politics of Design, London: Bloomsbury Academic, 2015.

Chapter 44. *Architectural Record*, April 5, 2016, architecturalrecord.com.

Chapter 45. *Architect's Newspaper*, April 6, 2016, archpaper.com.

Chapter 46. *Nation*, August 2016.

Chapter 47. Unpublished, November 2016.

Chapter 48. *Architectural Record*, April 1, 2017, architecturalrecord.com.

Index

1 percent, 5, 113, 151, 315
9/11 (2001), 56, 73, 105, 147, 299
9/11 Memorial, 48, 56, 142
9/11 Museum, 57

abortion clinics, 137, 239
Abromovic, Marina, 266
Abu Dhabi, 27, 36
Abzug, Bella, 154
adAPT NYC, 98
Adelson, Sheldon, 137
ADPSR (Architects/Designers/
    Planners for Social
    Responsibility), 239
affordable housing, 23, 67, 70–71,
    80–86, 88–90, 99, 117, 119,
    120, 152, 161–7, 274, 333
Africa, 93, 252, 280, 308
African Americans, 249, 252
Ai Weiwei, 289
Alexander, Chris, 262
Alinsky, Saul, 250
Allure Group, 159
American Civil Liberties Union,
    137

American Institute of Architects,
    239, 311, 332, 335
Amtrak, 133, 135
Angotti, Tom, 71
anti-Semitism, 300
apartheid, 92, 238
Arabic, 86
Arab Spring, 40
Arad, Michael, 58
Arad, Ron, 320
Architectural Graphic Standards,
    195
Area Median Income (AMI), 89
Arendt, Hannah, 225
Aristotle, 64, 280
Art Institute of Chicago, 267
Art Students League, 121–2
Asia, 274, 275, 292
assemblage, 126–7, 202, 234
Atlantic (magazine), 99
Aureli, Pier Vittorio, 306
Auschwitz, 227, 238
Austria, 222, 327
    Linz, 221
    Vienna, 82, 220, 221, 325–6

Awlaki, Anwar al-, 176
Axelrod, David, 252
Azerbaijan, 343

Baer, Steve, 207
Bain Capital, 195
Banki, Shira, 321
Barnes Collection, 76–7
Baroque, 189, 280, 297, 304
Battista, Vito, 312
Bauhaus, 76, 238, 306, 307
Bayat, Asef, 201
Beaux Arts architecture, 54, 312
Being John Malkovich (film), 140
Belgium, 258
Benjamin, Walter, 177
Bentham, Jeremy, 241–2
Bergdorf Goodman, 317
Berman, Andrew, 166
Berman, Marshall, 62–4, 279
bicycles, 6, 25, 27, 31, 33, 45, 135,
    138, 278, 279, 283, 293, 337
  bike lanes, 6, 32, 139, 289, 338
billionaire's row, 70, 121
Blair, Gwenda, 329
Bloomberg, Michael. See
    Bloomberg administration
Bloomberg administration, 68–73,
    80, 84, 91, 95, 98, 117–19,
    134–5, 138, 151, 158, 159
Blow, Charles, 24, 83
Bluhm, Neil, 126
Bomber Harris, 296
booksellers, 33–4, 45
Boston, 80, 124, 283
Boyer, Christine, 262–3
Bratton, William, 138, 135
Braun, Werner von, 222
Brazil, 7, 62, 63, 197, 201, 316
  Belo Horizonte, 317
  Rio, 201, 202, 209, 275, 281,
    283, 316, 317
  São Paolo, 62, 316
Breines, Simon, 312

Brewer, Gale, 84, 160, 163
Bristol, 287
Brody Bond, Davis, 104
Brown v. Board of Education, 188
Burden, Amanda, 98
Burundi, 123
Bush, George H. W., 242
Bush, George W., 242, 248
business improvement district
    (BID), 26, 31, 32, 94

Calatrava, Santiago, 59–61, 102,
    138, 141–6
California, 243, 244, 247
  Berkeley, 312
  Los Angeles, 10, 201, 326
  San Diego, 80
  San Francisco, 27, 80, 99, 154,
    239, 247
Canada, 328
Capalino, James, 158–9, 160
Cape Advisors, 115
Carnegie, Andrew, 155
Caro, Anthony, 105
Carpenter Center, 125
Carrère and Hastings, 54
Carter, Holland, 126, 128
Carter, Jimmy, 247, 248
Casella, Jean, 243
CATIA, 270, 281
CB2 (community board), 160–63,
    166
Chang, David, 157
Chartres, 140, 146
Chelsea Piers, 157
Chicago, 80, 122, 248–54, 267,
    327, 337
Chicago Daily News (newspaper),
    250
children, 45, 182, 188, 294, 320,
    225
Childs, David, 55, 56, 57, 307
China, 3, 4, 10, 92, 133, 213–14,
    274, 285–93, 310

Beijing, 280, 285, 288
Shanghai, 27, 86, 133, 281, 287, 291
Shenzhen, 310
Wuhan, 289
Xian, 289
Christie, Chris, 133
Chrysler Building, 22
CIA (Central Intelligence Agency), 2, 185
Cirque du Soleil, 158
citizenship, 31, 39, 64
City College of New York (CCNY), 9, 62
City Planning Commission, 71, 85, 160, 161, 164, 165
class struggle, 24, 79–87, 111, 120, 131, 307, 313, 314
climate change, 12, 47, 49, 177, 231, 285, 333
Clinton, Bill, 242, 247, 248, 251
Clinton, Hillary, 332
Clinton Foundation, 155
CNN, 244
Cohen, Preston Scott, 216
Cohen, Yonatan, 215
Cold War, 295
Columbia University, 30, 35, 37, 116
Columbine, 187
Columbus, Christopher, 130
Community Preservation Corporation (CPC), 85
Community Service Society, 90
Con Edison, 46
Cooper, Alexander, 328–9
Cooper Union, 56
Cox, B. Elton, 136
Crain's New York Business (trade newspaper), 115, 159, 163
Creighton, Tom, 312
Cross and Cross, 110
Cuba, 10, 187
CUNY, 98

Cuomo, Andrew, 70, 132, 134
Cuomo, Mario, 154

Dadaab, Kenya, 9
Dakota Apartments, 121–2
Davidson, Justin, 127
de Blasio, Bill. *See* de Blasio administration
de Blasio administration
    housing, 68, 84–6, 88, 90, 114, 117–19
    planning, 71–2, 114, 158–60, 165
    subways, 132
    Times Square, 134–5, 138
    zoning, 68, 80, 114, 118, 151
Debord, Guy, 261, 282
demolition, 6, 75–8, 93, 102, 115, 116
    housing, 81–2, 84, 119, 120, 168–9, 249, 294
    rent regulation, 9, 84, 168–9
Deng Xiaoping, 288, 291
Denver, 80
Department of City Planning (DCP), 45, 71, 116, 138, 161, 164, 165
Department of Housing Preservation and Development, 90
Department of Transportation (DOT), 26, 135
de Soto, Hernando, 206
Detroit, 8, 201, 251
Dies, Martin, 312
Diller, Barry, 156, 164
Diller, Elizabeth (Liz), 73, 75, 76
Diller Scofidio + Renfro (DS+R), 73, 75, 76, 77
Diller's island, 157
Disneyfication, 138, 248
DLR Group, 244
DNAinfo (journal), 159
drones, 177, 298

Drop City, 206, 207
Dubai, 93, 327
Duchamp, Marcel, 261
Dunlap, David, 60
Durst, Douglas, 157–8, 164
Dykers, Craig, 212

Eastern Bloc, 23, 125
East River, 68, 80, 85, 86, 89, 109
Economic Development
    Corporation, 71, 157
Ecuador, 7
Egypt, 201, 218
    Cairo, 200, 308
Ehrenreich, Barbara, 324, 325
Eisenhower, Dwight, 247
Ellsworth, Lynn, 115
Emanuel, Rahm, 252
emissions, 31–2, 33, 50, 134, 286
Empire State Building, 21–2, 57, 70,
    103, 122, 328
Empire State Development (ESD),
    159
Engels, Friedrich, 91, 196, 204,
    206, 283
Enlightenment, 181, 196
Equitable Building, 66
Esquire (magazine), 325
Europe, 27, 35, 133, 140, 144, 196,
    220, 287
Existenzminimum, 96, 99, 196,
    205, 274
Extell, 80, 122, 123

Facebook, 11, 176
FAECT (Federation of Architects,
    Engineers, Chemists, and
    Technicians), 311–13, 315
FAR (floor area ratio), 66–7, 71
fascism, 12, 92, 226, 326
Fatal Attraction (film), 187
FDR. *See* Roosevelt, Franklin
    Delano
Federal Housing Administration

(FHA), 88–9, 190
Federal Reserve. *See* US Federal
    Reserve
FedEx, 161
Fernández- Galiano, Luis, 212, 218
Fish, John Hall, 250
First Amendment, 33, 137, 139
Fitch, James Marston, 312
Flack, Roberta, 186
Flaubert, Gustave, 141
Flutie, Doug, 324
Fogg Museum, 124
Folk Art Museum, 73–8
Ford, Gerald, 248
Ford Foundation, 155
Fordism, 97, 207, 278
Fortran, 262
Foster, Norman, 54, 309
Foucault, Michel, 241–2, 259
Fox (television), 82
France, 112
    Eiffel Tower, 123
    Paris, 26, 34, 35, 66
Freedom of Information Law, 159,
    319
Friedrich, Jörg, 297
Fukushima, 125
functionalism, 3, 23, 76, 126,
    128–9, 143, 205, 258, 265, 268,
    270, 288

Gabbay, Yair, 213
Galliano, John, 327
garden cities, 180, 182, 184
Gardner, Chuck, 139
Gates, Bill, 155
Gay Pride, 20, 320, 321
Geddes, Patrick, 183, 231, 281
Gehry, Frank, 9, 21–4, 319–20
General Motors, 190
Geneva Accords (1977), 294
gentrification, 5, 9, 168, 171
    Chelsea, 128
    Chicago, 252

China, 288
Lower East Side, 128
Meatpacking District, 128
NYU, 27, 37
Tribeca, 115, 150
waterfront, 68, 85
geodesics, 207, 236, 282
Germany, 225, 279, 297, 306
Berlin, 1, 95, 104, 214, 221, 223, 226, 330
Dessau, 307
Dresden, 295–7, 299
Holocaust Memorial, 104
Nuremberg, 222, 326
Getty, J. Paul, 323
Gilbert, Cass, 110
Gingrich, Arnold, 325
GIS (geographic information systems), 264–5
Giuliani, Rudy, 56
Glaeser, Edward, 69
Glen, Alicia, 88, 91
Glick, Deborah, 160
Globes (magazine), 211
Gluck, Peter, 100
Goebbels, Joseph, 297, 326
Goffman, Erving, 241
Goldberg, Arthur, 136
Goldman Sachs, 56
Goodman, Charles, 185
Goodman, Percival, 312
Gosfield, Maurice, 148
Gothic, 21, 22, 123, 141, 143, 280, 297
Governors Island, 116
Grand Central Station, 54, 60, 63, 68, 120, 133, 141, 152
Grayling, A. C., 299
Greece, 64, 112, 284
Athens, 64, 188
Greenbelt, 182–3
green space, 25, 69, 253
Greenwich Village Society for Historic Preservation, 160

Grizzly Adams, 180
Gropius, Walter, 96
Ground Zero, 5, 17, 39, 55–61, 87, 102–7, 140–47, 195
Groves, Leslie, 312
Gruen, Victor, 189
Guantánamo, 243, 244

Haaretz (newspaper), 212, 322
Habraken, John, 208, 209, 275
Hadid, Zaha, 270, 283, 314, 316–18, 343
Hamas, 296, 298, 299–300
Hanadiv, Yad, 211–12, 216, 218
Hancock building, 224
Hardenbergh, Harry, 121
Harkness Tower, 123
Harvard, 9, 30, 125, 213, 214, 216, 230, 248
Harvey, David, 7, 203, 260
Hawthorne, Nathaniel, 76
Heatherwick, Thomas, 164
Hefner, Hugh, 323–6
Heifetz, Robert, 311, 312
Hejduk, John, 302
Herzl, Theodor, 179
Herzog and de Meuron, 109, 111, 150
Hiroshima, 295
Hirst, Damien, 74
Hitler, Adolf, 220–28, 295, 297, 324–6, 330
Berghof, 325, 326
Nuremberg, 222, 326
Holland Tunnel, 31, 94
Hollin Hills, 179–84, 186, 345
Holocaust, 104, 177, 187
Holston, James, 201
homelessness, 89, 117, 256, 271
Honolulu, 248
Hoover, Herbert, 246
Horton, Willie, 242
Houses of Parliament, 21
Howard, Ebenezer, 180, 183

Hudson River, 29, 80, 126, 131, 133, 151, 153, 154, 156, 163
Hudson River Park, 29, 70, 154, 156–61, 164
Hugo, Victor, 10, 177, 277
Huxtable, Ada Louise, 52–4
HyperBina Design Group, 215

India, 10, 170, 197, 201, 310
  Mumbai, 6, 200, 283
Indignados, 40
Industrial Revolution, 95, 292
inequality, 13, 40, 41–2, 82, 117, 206, 208, 263, 308, 309
International Union of Architects (IAUA), 92, 214
Intrepid (ship). *See* USS Intrepid
Intrepid Air and Space Museum, 157
Iraq, 248, 298, 299–300
Irving Trust Company Building, 110
ISIS, 298, 299
Israel, 92, 211–19, 226, 297–300, 319–22
  gay rights, 321
  Jerusalem, 211, 213, 214, 306, 319–22
  Palestine, 36, 92–3, 294–300, 321–2
  Tel Aviv, 321
  Zion Square, 319–22
Israeli Association of United Architects (IAUA), 92
Italy, 209
  Florence, 279
  Genoa, 130
  Naples, 130
  Rome, 112, 145

Jacob, Klaus, 51
Jacobs, Jane, 5–8, 17–20, 28, 37, 54, 69, 118, 202, 260, 278
Jadaliyya (e-zine), 321

Jahn, Helmut, 123, 328–9
Jakarta, 201
Japan, 10, 133, 279, 285, 299–300
Javits, 164
Jefferson, Thomas, 179, 181, 189, 246, 247
Jerusalem, 211, 213, 214, 306, 319–22
Jews, 170, 220, 225, 300, 321, 322, 330
Jim Crow, 186
Jobs, Steve, 175
Johns, Jasper, 109
Johnson, Corey, 160, 166
Johnson, Lyndon B., 247–8, 251
Johnson, Philip, 226, 327, 329
JonBenét, 187
Juan Carlos, King, 27

Kahn, Herman, 294
Kahn, Louis, 76
Kalven, Harry, 136–7
Kapoor, Anish, 112
Karachi, 201
Karmi-Melamede, Ada, 212
Katrina, Hurricane, 47, 49
Kerkorian, Kirk, 137
Kew Gardens, 181
Khalifa, Burj, 122, 327
Khan, Samir, 176
Kiev, 181
Kiley, Dan, 182, 185
Kimbell Art Museum, 124
Kimmelman, Michael, 122, 127–8
Koch brothers, 154, 155
Komissar-Barzacchi, Elinoar, 213, 218
Kondylis, Costas, 329
Koolhaas, Rem, 1
Koons, Jeff, 74, 103
Kracauer, Siegfried, 2, 6
Kraków, 170
Krier, Léon, 220–28
Kunstwissenschaft, 53, 255

Kushner, Jared, 343
Kyoto, 281, 298

La Concha Acústica, 93
Lagos, 6
LaGuardia Airport, 135
Lang House, 110
Lapidus, Morris, 327
Las Vegas, 137–9
Latin America, 203, 275
Lauren, Ralph, 110, 327
Lauwe, Chombart de, 260
Le Corbusier, 17, 21, 125, 236, 290, 301
LEED rating, 257–8
Lefebvre, Henri, 7, 19, 41, 203, 260, 263
LeFrak City, 23
Legos, 97
  Levittown, 97
Lewis, John L., 312
Lewites, Herty, 93
LeWitt, Sol, 122, 302
LGBT, 169, 321
Libeskind, Daniel, 142
Lincoln, Abraham, 246
Lincoln Center, 77
Little Rock, Arkansas, 251
London, 181, 206, 282,
Long Island, 51
Long Island Railroad, 133
Long Island Sound, 50
Loos, Adolf, 220
Looshaus, 220
Lower Manhattan Development Corporation, 157
Lower Manhattan Islamic Center, 58
Lowry, Glenn, 73, 76, 77
Luhmann, Niklas, 260
Lyft, 135, 337
Lyme Regis, 287
Lynch, Kevin, 261,

Mad Men (television series), 52, 187
Maki, Fumihiko, 56
Managua, 93
Mao Zedong, 288
Marcuse, Herbert, 322
Marie Antoinette, 179, 207
Marx, Karl, 63, 180, 198, 230, 260, 261, 268, 306, 307
Marx, Roberto Burle, 281
Marxism, 230, 260, 261, 268, 306
Maryland, 182
Maupassant, Guy de, 123
May, Ernst, 96
Maya, 269, 273, 281
Mayer, Matan, 215
McDonald's, 31, 198
Médecins Sans Frontières, 307
megacities, 19, 289
Meière, Hildreth, 110
Mexico, 242, 281
Meyer, Danny, 126
Michael Sorkin Studio, 4
middle class, 23, 46, 81, 82, 90, 112, 188, 207, 249, 330
Middle East, 252
Mies van der Rohe, Ludwig, 57
Mikdashi, Maya, 321
military industrial complex, 207
Milwaukee Museum of Art, 61
minimalism, 56, 57, 77, 95, 122, 129, 205, 207, 305
MIT (Massachusetts Institute of Technology), 203, 314–15, 338
Mitchell, Don, 202
modernism, 20, 203, 226, 256, 268, 273, 306–7
  China, 291
  FAECT, 312
  Fordism, 97
  Gropius, Walter, 96
  Hollin Hills, 180, 183, 185
  housing, 23, 95, 118, 204, 208
  Huxtable, Ada Louise, 53

Marx, 306
modernist architecture, 76, 107,
    202, 209, 222, 227, 236, 259,
    304
    New Urbanism, 230
    planning, 19
modernity, 74, 180, 185, 186, 196,
    197, 202, 258, 278
    Berman, Marshall, 62, 63
    Brazil, 63
    China, 285
    England, 22
    Hefner, Hugh, 324
    Italy, 304–5
    Pennoyer, Peter, 124
Mohamedi, Nasreen, 302–3
MOMA (Museum of Modern Art),
    73–8
Momofuku, 157
Moneo, Rafael, 212
Moran, Meirav, 211–12
Morgan Library, 124
Morgenthau Plan, 297
Morocco, 87
Morris, William, 180, 223, 307
Moses, Robert, 81, 135, 154,
    202–3, 279
Moynihan, Patrick, 154
MSNBC (television), 2
MTA (Metropolitan Transportation
    Authority), 26, 132–5, 138
Mumford, Lewis, 183, 260, 281
Muschamp, Herb, 149
Museum of Modern Art. See
    MOMA
Muslims, 299–300, 330, 335
Mussolini, Benito, 110, 222
Myerson, Bess, 226

Nagasaki, 295
NASA, 339
National Housing Act (1949), 89
Nazis, 138, 223, 224, 295–6, 326
Negroponte, Nicholas, 262

neoliberalism, 6, 91, 116, 149, 201,
    260, 264, 271, 290
Netanyahu, Benjamin, 92, 296
Netherlands, 338
Netsch, Walter, 268
New Criterion (magazine), 124,
    125, 126
New Deal, 182
New Frankfurt, 96
New Jersey, 51, 54, 61, 133, 135,
    182, 324. See also PATH
    Atlantic City, 328
New Jersey Transit, 135
New Jersey Turnpike, 138
New Orleans, 47–8
New School, 267
New Urbanism, 230, 232, 257,
    269
New York (magazine), 127
New York City, 67, 73, 84, 98,
    108, 149, 153–67, 181, 290,
    308, 327, 336
    Battery Park City, 85, 329
    Bronx, 64, 84, 119
    Grand Concourse, 63
    Parkchester, 112
    Tremont, 64
    Brooklyn, 6, 27, 37, 85, 86, 108,
        109, 119, 135, 177, 282
    Atlantic Yards, 22, 98, 314
    Brooklyn Bridge, 22, 70, 152,
        156
    Dumbo, 85
    East New York, 90, 114
    housing, 144, 152, 156, 201, 327
    waterfront, 68, 80
    Williamsburg/Greenpoint, 71,
        80, 86
    Brooklyn Bridge Park, 70, 152,
        156
    Council on Tall Buildings and
        Urban Habitat, 55
    Manhattan, 5, 22, 33, 46, 47, 48,
        56–7, 58, 63, 66

Central Park, 70, 108, 120, 121, 152, 156, 181, 182, 196, 327

Chelsea, 128, 163

Columbus Circle, 327

Custom House, 54

Garment District, 169

Greenwich Village, 5, 18, 25–34, 79, 157, 160–61, 163, 166–7

Ground Zero, 5, 17, 39, 55–61, 87, 102–7, 140–47, 195

High Line, 70, 77, 128, 156, 158, 230, 232

Hudson Square, 94, 115, 157, 161, 164

Hudson Yards, 164

Lower East Side, 8, 128, 158, 206

Meatpacking District, 124, 128, 131

Midtown, 56, 67, 78, 150

Pier 40, 28, 31, 157, 158, 159, 162, 163, 164, 166

skyline, 21–3, 55, 56, 67, 110, 115, 127, 128, 131, 153, 163, 327

St. Vincent's hospital, 28–9

Times Square, 67, 134, 135–8

Tribeca, 5, 109, 113–16, 120, 149–50, 157, 163

Washington Square 36, 37

West Side Highway, 70, 153, 329

West Side Urban Renewal Area, 81

World Financial Center, 107

World Trade Center, 105

Zuccotti Park, 5, 39, 40, 194, 344

Queens, 48, 51, 68

Staten Island, 48

Transit Authority, 45

unions, 311, 312

Williamsburg Bridge, 86

New York City Department of City Planning (DCP), 116

New York City Housing Authority (NYCHA), 23, 81, 84, 89, 92, 99, 112, 118, 119, 152

New York City Landmarks Preservation Commission, 113, 115, 166

New York Daily News (newspaper), 98

New Yorker (magazine), 128, 183, 218, 328

New York Harbor, 116

New York Public Library, 74

New York Review of Books (journal), 80, 130, 218

New York State, 133, 156

 Albany, 90, 160

 Auburn, 241

 Hyde Park, 246, 249, 250

 New Rochelle, 328

New York Times (newspaper), 10, 17, 24, 47, 52, 60, 83, 108, 116, 126, 127, 144, 240, 309, 321

Nicaragua, 93, 308

Niemeyer, Oscar, 63, 283, 316–17

Nietzsche, Friedrich, 327

NIMBYism, 10

Nixon, Richard, 247, 248, 251

Nordenson, Guy, 144

Nordstrom Tower, 122

North Korea, 20, 92

Nouvel, Jean, 123

Novogratz, Michael, 158

NSA, 11, 12, 56

nuclear power, 226, 239, 298

nuclear weapons, 187, 296, 298

Nuremberg tribunals, 225

NYU (New York University), 27–9, 35–8, 47, 69, 99, 158

Obama, Barack, 126, 246, 248, 251–3, 332, 334

Obama, Michelle, 252

Occupy movement, 5, 39–42, 194–5, 206

Oculus, 141–6
Oklahoma City, 104
Olmsted, Frederick Law, 181, 182, 183, 230, 281
One57, 123
One World Trade Center, 55–61, 122
Open Society Foundation, 30
Oppenheimer, Robert, 312
Orfield, Myron, 188–9
Ortega, Daniel, 93
Orwell, George, 2, 6, 12
Osgerby, Bill, 324, 330
Otterness, Tom, 133

Palestine, 92–3, 294–300, 321–2
    Gaza, 294–300
    West Bank, 36
Pardo, Yaniv, 211–12
Paris, 26, 34, 35, 66
Paris Commune, 40
park space, 6, 70, 85, 86, 182
PATH, 56, 59, 60, 61, 102, 138, 141, 144. See also Calatrava, Santiago
Paul, Rand, 308
Paxton, Joseph, 180–81
Pearl Harbor, 299
Pei, I. M., 17, 53
Pelli, César, 74
Pennoyer, Peter, 124–5, 127
Penn Station, 54, 60, 133, 141, 142
Perlman, Janice, 201
Persian Gulf, 274, 287, 310, 343
Philadelphia, 76, 241
Photoshop, 177, 282
Piano, Renzo, 124–5, 126, 130, 131
Picasso, Pablo, 327
pinkwashing, 319–22
Planning Commission (New York City), 71, 85, 160, 161, 164, 165
PlaNYC 2030, 71, 72
Plato, 64, 125, 181, 185, 302
Playboy (magazine), 323–6

Plaza de la Fe, 93
Plaza Hotel, 121, 329
Politico (journal), 159
Pollack, Jackson, 109
poor door, 79–87, 111
POPS (privately owned public spaces), 156
Port Authority Bus Terminal, 141
Portland-sur-Hudson, 157
Portzamparc, Christian de, 123
Prada, 1, 149
Preciado, Paul, 324
prisons, 13, 30, 125, 239–45, 274, 294, 298, 300, 321, 325, 334
    panopticon, 22, 241–2
    supermax prisons, 92, 239–40, 244
Pritzker Prize, 3
privatization, 5, 137, 245, 164, 335
Producers, The (film), 223
Progressive Architecture (magazine), 312
Puar, Jasbir, 321
public-private partnership, 6, 39, 67, 82, 151, 155, 164
public space, 6, 9, 25, 33, 60, 135–6, 162, 165, 166
    Arendt, Hannah, 225
    Gaza, 298
    Jerusalem, 319
    Occupy, 206
    POPS, 156
Pugin, A. W., 21–2

Qatar, 93, 256, 314
Quinn, Christine, 81

racism, 10, 125, 188, 242, 299, 315, 321, 330, 333
Ratner, Bruce, 22–4, 98
Reagan, Ronald. See Reagan administration
Reagan administration, 106, 242

Reagan library, 247, 248
Red Scare, 312
refugees, 3, 4, 41, 207, 296
Reisner, Daniel, 297
Rembrandt, 266
rent control. *See* rent regulation
rent regulation, 6, 9, 27, 81–4,
  90–91, 111–12, 113, 168, 169,
  171
rent stabilization. *See* rent
  regulation
RIBA (Royal Institute of British
  Architects), 92, 93
Rice, Condoleeza, 105
Ridgeway, James, 243
Riefenstahl, Leni, 325
Ritchie, Alan, 329
Rivington House AIDS nursing
  home, 158, 159
RMS Titanic (ship), 130, 131, 163
Rockefeller, Nelson A., 125, 154,
  155
Rockefeller drug laws, 244
Romero, George, 187
Romney, Mitt, 175
Roosevelt, Franklin Delano, 110,
  222, 246, 247
Rosenberg, Julius, 312
Rothko, Mark, 109, 303
Rothman, David, 241
Rothschild family, 211, 213, 218
Rotterdam, 86
Rousseau, Jean-Jacques, 180
Rowland, Ingrid, 130
Roy, Ananya, 197, 200, 201
Rudolph, Paul, 76, 111, 150

Sadik-Khan, Janette, 135
Saegert, Susan, 98
Safdie, Moshe, 97, 150, 324
Saltz, Jerry, 127
Sandinista Renewal Movement
  (MRS), 93
Sanders, Bernie, 144, 155

Sandy, Hurricane, 46–8, 49–51, 59,
  118, 131, 342–3
San Francisco, 27, 80, 99, 154, 239,
  247
Sarajevo, 342
Scarpa, Carlo, 76
Schulman, Sarah, 321
Schumacher, Patrik, 260, 270
Schütte-Lihotzky, Margarete, 96
Schwabsky, Barry, 128, 129
Schwartz, Fred, 107
Schwartz, Gaby, 213
Schwartz, Samuel, 134
Scientific American (magazine), 240
Scutt, Der, 327, 328
Seattle, 154
Second World War. *See* World War
  II
Section 8 vouchering program, 81,
  90, 254
Segal, Rafi, 211–19
Sen, Amartya, 263
Sereny, Gitta, 222
Sergeant Bilko (television), 148
Serra, Richard, 143
Seven World Trade Center, 56, 103
Sexton, John, 38
Shalev, Sharon, 241, 244–5
Sharon, Arad, 212
SHoP, 85–6, 122
Shorris, Anthony, 159
Shortt, Sara, 99
sidewalks, 18, 26, 27, 32, 43–5,
  62, 77, 126, 137, 138, 184, 186,
  338–9
Silvers, Phil, 148
Silverstein, Larry, 102, 109, 289
Simbel, Abu
Simpson, Tom and June, 247
Situationists, 261
Skidmore, Owings & Merrill, 238,
  307
Slate Property Group, 159
slavery, 188

SLCE (Schuman, Lichtenstein, Claman, and Efron), 149
slums, 13, 19, 188, 201, 208, 256, 274, 275
Small, Glen, 93
Smith, Adrian, 122, 327
Smith, Roberta, 126, 128
Snøhetta, 104, 218
Snow, C. P., 308
socialism, 2, 3, 7, 82, 190, 198, 185, 306
Society for Ethical Culture, 73, 75, 78
Socrates, 63, 187, 190, 192
solitary confinement, 239–43
Solitary Watch, 240
South Africa, 93
    Johannesburg, 238
    Soweto, 279
South Village Historic District, 166, 167
Soviet Union, 97, 288, 295, 312
Speer, Albert, 140, 220–28
Sperry, Raphael, 239
squatter settlements, 186, 201, 203, 205–7, 209, 275, 282, 307
Stalin, Joseph, 2, 222, 257
Standard Oil, 190
starchitecture, 2, 17, 24, 108, 121, 123, 154, 148, 218, 266, 287, 290, 310
Statue of Liberty, 141
Steel, Robert, 159
Stein, Clarence, 183
Steinway Hall, 122–3
Stern, Bob, 108, 110
Stern, Robert, 223
Stevenson, Adlai, 186
Stewart, Martha, 157
St. John's Terminal Building, 158, 159, 162
Stonewall Inn, 169
Stratigakos, Despina, 325, 326
Stuyvesant Town, 23, 89, 112

subsidies, 6, 189, 190
    to developers, 80, 108, 114, 117, 152
    rent subsidies, 82, 277
    tax subsidies, 330
suburbs, 35, 97, 179–84, 185–93, 208, 279, 288, 293
    garden suburbs, 183
    inequality, 5, 23, 89
    urban suburbs, 19
subways, 10, 51, 62, 65, 85, 151, 154, 281, 289, 337
    flooding of, 47
    Shanghai, 133
    stations, 5, 26, 68, 132, 133, 138, 141, 258
Sullivan, Louis, 236
supermax prisons, 92, 239–44
Supreme Court. See US Supreme Court
surrealism, 259, 261, 265, 268–9
surveillance, 5, 11, 39, 77, 107, 175, 242
sustainability, 3, 12, 91, 189, 193, 205, 210, 229, 231, 258, 290
Syria, 92, 299
    Aleppo, 9, 298

Tahrir Square, 134
Taliban, 94, 298, 299
Taniguchi, Yoshio, 74
taxation, 69, 80, 90, 108, 121, 152, 155, 193, 330
Taxi and Limousine Commission, 135
Taylor, Diana, 157
Taylor, Frederick, 295. See also Taylorism
Taylorism, 96, 315
Tcholakian, Danielle, 159
Terreform, 4
Texas, 247, 248, 320
Thames Town, 287, 289
Thoreau, Henry David, 180

Titanic (ship). *See* RMS Titanic
Toll Brothers Northside Piers, 80
torture, 239, 240, 243, 317, 326
totalitarianism, 2, 3, 7, 226–7
Triangle Shirtwaist fire, 169
Tribeca Tower, 149
Troost, Gerdy, 325
Trump, Donald, 1–2, 4, 9–12, 80,
    144, 152, 155–6, 323–31, 332–5
Trump, Jules and Eddie, 326
Trump, Melania, 323
Trump Tower, 156, 326–9
Tsien, Billie, 73, 76
Turkle, Sherry, 134
Turner, John, 203, 209, 210, 275
Twitter, 1, 134, 175, 176
TWO (The Woodlawn
    Organization), 250–51
Tyson, Mike, 324

Uber, 135, 337, 229, 340
ULURP (Uniform Land Use Review
    Process), 160, 161
Unabomber, 180
unions, 23, 97, 136, 154, 310, 311,
    315
United Nations, 240, 297
Universal Declaration of Human
    Rights, 113–14
University of Chicago, 249–50,
    252
University of Texas at Austin, 247
UPS, 161, 164
urbanism, 88, 152, 203, 232, 257,
    259–61, 264, 267, 287, 307
    China, 3–4, 288
    green urbanism, 191, 229
    Jacobs, Jane, 8, 19
    landscape urbanism, 230–31
    Moses, Robert, 202
    neoliberalism, 91
    Occupy, 39, 40
    suburbs, 190, 191
Urist, Jacoba, 99

US civil rights movement, 52, 136,
    250
US Congress, 246
US Federal Reserve, 71
US military, 41, 107, 151, 207, 244,
    295–7
USS Intrepid (ship), 128, 129
US Supreme Court, 136, 169, 211,
    240, 249

Valencia, 59
Vanke, China, 159
Vaux, Calvert, 181
veterans, 112, 188
Via (app), 336
Vietnam War, 52, 300, 315
Vietnam War Memorial, 103–5
VillageCare, 159
Vinciarelli, Lauretta, 301–5
Viñoly, Rafael, 84, 122
Virginia, 185

Wachsmann, Conrad, 97
Wacquant, Loïc, 242
Wagner, Otto, 224, 225, 266, 280
Wagner, Richard, 221, 225, 266
Walentas, David and Jed, 85
Walker, Herschel, 324
Walker, Ralph, 110
Wall Street, 39–42, 110, 194–5, 329
Wall Street Journal (newspaper),
    124, 159
Wambua, Mathew, 98
Wanda, Dalian, 159
Wang, Bing, 214–17
Warhol, Andy, 291
Warnecke, John Carl, 109, 149
wars, 12, 48, 89, 104, 285, 286,
    294–300
Washington, George, 247
Washington, DC, 56, 246, 247
    Holocaust Museum, 104
Washington Monument, 57
Watergate scandal, 153

Weisbrod, Carl, 116, 159, 164
Weizman, Eyal, 213, 214, 295,
    297
Wells, Pete, 126
Westbrook Partners, 163
Westfield Corporation, 147
Westway, 49, 153, 154
White Horse Tavern, 18
Whitney Museum of American Art,
    124, 125–6, 128–31
Wikipedia, 176
Willen, Paul, 329
Williams, Tod, 73, 76
Wils, Madelyn, 157, 159
Wines, James, 229–37
Wintour, Anna, 257, 314
Woods, Lebbeus, 233, 303–4, 341
Woolworth Building, 22, 109, 147
working class, 9, 48, 68, 82, 204,
    330
Works Progress Administration,
    110
World Financial Center, 107

World Trade Center, 105
World War I, 311, 326
World War II, 69, 104, 221, 288,
    294–300, 304, 311, 326
Wright, Frank Lloyd, 76, 123
Wynn, Steve, 137

Yale University, 36, 123
Yemen, 176, 177

Zandberg, Esther, 219
Zeitlin, Morris, 312
Zion, Libby, 309
Zionist architects, 213
zoning,
    contextual zoning, 70, 117, 161
    down-zoning, 68
    inclusionary zoning, 67, 80, 84,
        90, 112, 156, 161
    rezoning, 68, 69, 157
    up-zoning, 67, 68, 117
    zoning code, 66
Zuckerberg, Mark, 11